D0938924

REMEMBERED PRISONERS

★ OF A ★

FORGOTTEN WAR

AN ORAL HISTORY OF
KOREAN WAR POWs

LEWIS H. CARLSON

ST. MARTIN'S PRESS ✄ NEW YORK

www.stmartins.com

Library of Congress Cataloging-in-Publication Data

Carlson, Lewis H.
    Remembered prisoners of a forgotten war : an oral history of Korean War
POWs / Lewis H. Carlson.—1st ed.
      p. cm.
    Includes bibliographical references.
    ISBN 0-312-28684-8
    1. Korean War, 1950–1953—Prisoners and prisons. 2. Prisoners of war—United
States. 3. Prisoners of War—Korea (North) I. Title.

DS921 .C37 2002
951.904'27—dc21

                                  2001048878

First Edition: April 2002

10 9 8 7 6 5 4 3 2 1

This book is dedicated to Studs Terkel, whose oral histories so well illuminate the experiences of those Americans never found in history books, and to all former Korean War prisoners, that no one will again challenge their collective integrity and courage.

CONTENTS

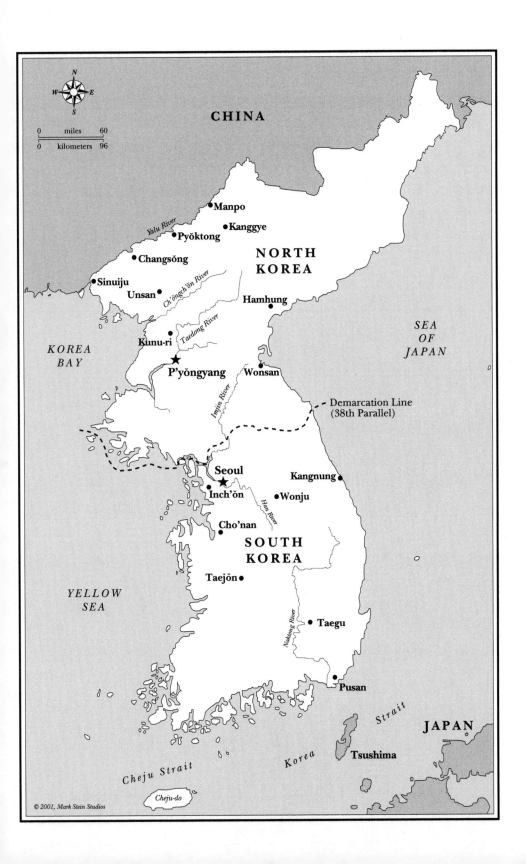

N
W   E
S

| 0 | miles | 60 |
| 0 | kilometers | 96 |

CHINA

● Manpo
● Kanggye
● Pyŏktong
● Changsŏng
● Sinuiju
Unsan ●

Yalu River

NORTH KOREA

Ch'ŏngch'ŏn River

Taedong River

Hamhung ●

Kunu-ri ●

★ P'yŏngyang   Wonsan ●

Imjin River

KOREA BAY

SEA OF JAPAN

Demarcation Line (38th Parallel)

Seoul ● ★
Inch'ŏn ●
Kangnung ●
● Wonju

Han River

Cho'nan ●

SOUTH KOREA

Taejŏn ●

YELLOW SEA

Naktong River

● Taegu

● Pusan

Strait

JAPAN

Korea

Tsushima

Cheju Strait

Cheju-do

© 2001, Mark Stein Studios

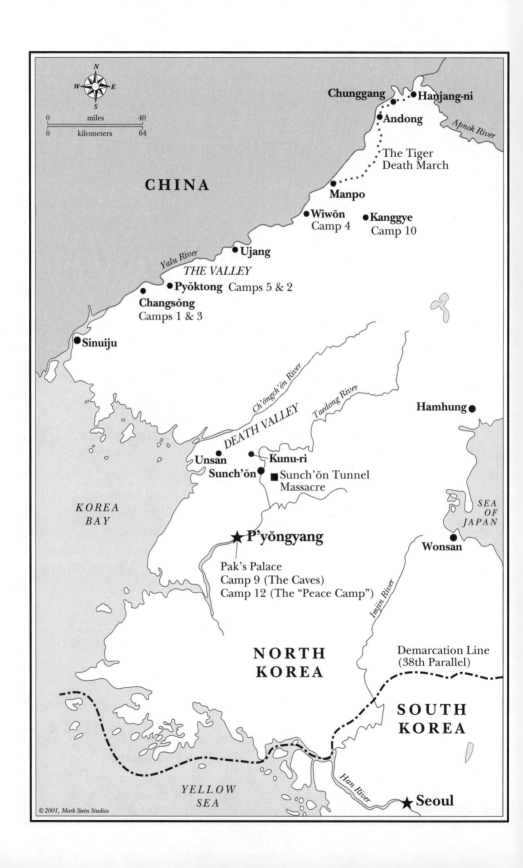

CHINA

THE VALLEY

DEATH VALLEY

Chunggang • •Hanjang-ni
•Andong
The Tiger
Death March
•Manpo
•Wiwŏn   •Kanggye
Camp 4   Camp 10

•Ujang
•Pyŏktong Camps 5 & 2
•Changsŏng
Camps 1 & 3

•Sinuiju

Hamhung•

Unsan•   •Kunu-ri
Sunch'ŏn• ■Sunch'ŏn Tunnel
           Massacre

KOREA
BAY

SEA
OF
JAPAN

★P'yŏngyang

Wonsan•

Pak's Palace
Camp 9 (The Caves)
Camp 12 (The "Peace Camp")

NORTH
KOREA

Demarcation Line
(38th Parallel)

SOUTH
KOREA

YELLOW
SEA

★Seoul

Yalu River

Ch'ŏngch'ŏn River

Taedong River

Apnok River

Imjin River

Han River

N
W   E
S

0   miles   40
0   kilometers   64

© 2001, Mark Stein Studios

ACKNOWLEDGMENTS

There are so many people to thank, but none more important than the former POWs themselves. Without them there is no story, and a significant segment of American history would have remained distorted. For most of these men talking about such painful memories was a wrenching experience. Nevertheless, they wanted their stories told, at the very least to establish some measure of redemption. Among the more than fifty former prisoners I interviewed, I especially want to thank "Shorty" Estabrook and Jim Crombie, both of whom not only told their stories but also provided additional information, photographs, and the kind of encouragement I needed to complete what turned out to be a formidable challenge and responsibility. I also want to thank Larry Zellers who, in addition to a lengthy and very enlightening interview, allowed me to quote extensively from his memoir, *In Enemy Hands: A Prisoner in North Korea.* John Kersie helped identify former prisoners, as did Gordon Beem. In addition to sending along helpful publications, Robert MacLean arranged interviews with several of his fellow ex-POWs at the James Haley Veterans Hospital in Tampa, Florida. Jack Browning and Don Poirot provided very helpful personal narratives, as did Richard Bassett, whose 121-page memoir is certainly the most comprehensive history of Camp Five, which held more prisoners than any other camp in North Korea.[1]

Family members of former prisoners also made significant contributions. Mrs. Daisy Lawrence sent a very moving narrative her late brother, Roy Hardage, wrote in 1954. Mrs. June-Marie Lam sent lectures, letters, and several articles in which her late husband, Dr. Gene N. Lam, recounted his medical experiences treating fellow prisoners. I am also grateful to those other wives who so candidly shared what it meant to live with a former POW. Thanks also to Ms. Della Adams, who twice met with me in Memphis to talk candidly about her late father, Clarence Adams, who was one of the twenty-one American prisoners who chose China over repatriation. Dr. Thomas Collins, professor of Anthropology at Memphis State University, helped me contact Ms. Adams and also scoured the Memphis *Commercial Appeal* for old and current articles about Clarence Adams. A special thanks to friend and colleague Bob Doyle for his unflagging support and wise counsel.

Western Michigan University provided a research and travel grant that defrayed part of the expenses for this project. Retired President Diether A. Haenicke of Western Michigan University also provided generous financial and intellectual support, as he has done for so many of his faculty's professional activities.

I also thank former students Michelle Hill, Daren Cowen, and Michelle Brunzie for transcribing many of the interviews, and Western Michigan University research librarian Stefan Sarenius who is always there when I need him.

Once again, I am most grateful to Jane Jordan Browne of Multimedia Product Development, Inc., who introduced this project to Marc Resnick, my editor at St. Martin's Press, who also provided invaluable assistance and counsel.

Finally, I thank my wife for once again putting up with a husband who spends far too many hours in the nether regions of his den gazing darkly at a computer.

PREFACE

The past is not dead; it's not even past.
—William Faulkner

Despite the fact that more than 40 percent of the 7,140 Americans taken prisoner during the Korean War died in captivity, the survivors remain the most maligned victims of all American wars. For more than a half century, the media, general public, and even scholars have classified literally hundreds of these former prisoners as "brainwashed" victims of a heinous enemy or, even worse, as "turncoats" who betrayed their country. In either case, those accused apparently lacked the "right stuff" America expected of her brave sons. The most notorious reinforcement of this condemnation appeared in the well-made but badly distorted 1962 film, *The Manchurian Candidate,* but many lesser films, countless novels and short stories, myriad news accounts, and even scholarly treatises perpetuated this negative image. To be sure, there were those few POWs who were guilty of gross misconduct and even collaboration, and twenty-one prisoners did refuse repatriation. There was also an equally small percentage of prisoners who courageously or imprudently, depending on the particular circumstance, adhered rigidly to the military code of total noncompliance. The vast majority of prisoners, as has been true throughout history, simply tried to survive under the most intolerable of conditions. And their conduct, rather than manifesting personal or societal weaknesses, as their critics charged, was far more likely to reflect the changing conditions of their captivity.

Remembered Prisoners of a Forgotten War combines oral history and historical analysis. It explores how popular culture and scholars portrayed these POWs, but, above all, it features the narratives of those survivors whose stories have remained largely untold. The reading of these memoirs should help Americans understand what these prisoners—indeed, what all POWs—had to endure and will also help dispel many of the myths that have long surrounded these men.

The inspiration for this study grew out of a five-year oral history project I conducted on World War II American and German prisoners of war which led to published books in both Germany and the United States.[1] These books tested the actual experiences of former POWs, as gleaned from their narratives, against the common cultural myths that surround war captivity, especially those that have emerged in popular films and literature.

I asked my subjects to reflect on a series of questions: What did it mean to become a prisoner, especially if one is a product of a culture that stresses independent action and responsibility? What personality types best survived the rigors of internment? What coping methods proved effective and what kinds of behavior jeopardized the individual and collective welfare of the prisoners? What was the official and private reception that awaited repatriated prisoners? And what have been the long-term effects of incarceration?

Such questions, of course, apply to the POW experience in any war, but none of my World War II prisoners faced the public opprobrium and rejection suffered by their Korean War counterparts. Surely, I thought, American boys had not changed so dramatically in five short years. Was the POW behavior America found so abhorrent among Korea POWs also to be found among World War II prisoners, especially if conditions were sufficiently horrifying or hopeless? Clearly some men did act heroically, in the conventional sense, but most of the World War II men I interviewed simply sought the line of least resistance. At best they passively waited out their captivity, but at worst they turned inward, often in the most destructive of ways. All but a few readily admitted they are still suffering nightmares and flashbacks, as well as ongoing psychological and physical problems. If such were the case with former prisoners of the so-called Good War, what must be the prolonged burden suffered by those men incarcerated in Korea?

Getting former prisoners to open up is always a challenge. For years after incarceration many former World War II prisoners were unwilling to talk, and this has been even truer of Korean War POWs. For example, for twenty years one wife had no idea her husband had been a prisoner until she inadvertently opened a letter from the Defense Department. Before attempting to contact subjects either by phone or in person, I always sent a letter of explanation in which I asked them to return an enclosed postcard if they were willing to be interviewed. Approximately half of the World War II men returned the cards, but less than a quarter of the Korean War POWs did. One former Korean prisoner who did respond wrote, "No, no, no! I don't talk to anyone!"

Talking to these men is always an emotional experience. Often they break down in tears when particularly painful memories surface. Sometimes we simply have to stop the interview. One former prisoner, whom I interviewed just before Christmas, complimented me on the timeliness of my arrival. "Over the last couple of years," he announced, "I have attempted suicide during the holidays." Another confessed that during one of his uncontrollable rages he had tried to murder his son. Two men, who had initially fully cooperated, later wrote asking that I destroy the audio-tapes and anything I might have written about them. After I interviewed my first Korean War POW, his wife asked me, "Did you get what you wanted?" I replied that it had indeed been a good interview. She then responded, "Good, because I will have to cope with the nightmares he is sure to experience in his sleep tonight."

No one can work with former prisoners of war without wondering how he would fare as a POW. Serious doubts come immediately to mind. As a person for whom food is very important, would I be able to withstand the ravages of malnutrition? What of the lack of sufficient clothing, which in below zero temperatures left so many men with frostbitten extremities? How would I have handled insect infections, lice, chronic dysentery, and going without bathing for months on end? And, what of the psychological damage that inevitably occurs when losing one's sense of freedom and even time? Happily, such an extreme experience will not afflict most of us; yet, there are lessons for anyone facing unavoidable challenges. What allows all of us to be survivors, to cope with indignities and disappointments that all too often seem insurmountable?

INTRODUCTION

In every war but one that the United States has fought, the conduct of those of its service men who were held in enemy prison camps presented no unforeseen problems to the armed forces and gave rise to no particular concern in the country as a whole. . . . The exception was the Korean War.
            —Eugene Kinkead, author of *In Every War But One*

Men died so that it could not be said that Americans are ready to collaborate with the Communists, but it was said anyway.
            —Albert Biderman, author of *March to Calumny*

In September of 1953, 10,000 citizens of Harlan County, Kentucky, flocked into the small town of Benham to honor one of their own. Jack Flanary was only eighteen when he joined the Army to fight for his country. He served well and achieved the rank of staff sergeant. Unfortunately, he also became a prisoner of war and spent thirty-two months in captivity. Now he was free, and family and friends were ready to welcome him home with a parade, followed by a celebration in the local football stadium. The festivities, however, were barely underway when officials from the Veterans of Foreign Wars and the American Legion interrupted the proceedings to announce "rumors" that Sergeant Flanary had been one of the hated "Progressives" who had been "responsive to Communist indoctrination." Flanary admitted he had done a lot of reading in his Chinese POW camp library, but his explanation that he had done so "to better his vocabulary" had aroused suspicion.[1]

Early in 1952, Capt. Web Sloane appeared to be living proof that Americans taken prisoner during the Korean War had uncharacteristically caved in to their Communist captors. "Brainwashing" was an ugly, new phrase for Americans, but Sloane had clearly collaborated with the enemy. While his starving fellow prisoners wasted away, victims of inhuman conditions and insidious torture, Sloane grew increasingly plump and comfortable. Shocking behavior to be sure, but in reality there never was a Captain Sloane.

Instead, he was a movie actor named Ronald Reagan, and the POW camp was a Hollywood set constructed for a 1954 film entitled *Prisoner of War*. According to the script, Intelligence Officer Sloane had parachuted into the prison camp, then posed as a collaborator to collect evidence on how Communist brutalities affected the behavior of captured Americans. Years later, convinced that the film showed the true spirit of Americans under duress, Reagan insisted that "every torture scene and incident were based on an actual happening." But *Prisoner of War* was not based on fact. Like most POW films, it was a reflection of American popular culture and accumulated prisoner of war myths, some of which dated back to Indian captivity stories and the inevitable "fate worse than death."

In the popular mind, the POW experience has long been reduced to a simple morality play in which courageous American boys suffer terribly at the hands of uncivilized brutes who clearly represent an alien culture. Such portrayals allow neither subtleties nor ambiguities, only images of clean-cut, innocent, freedom-loving American boys caught in the clutches of villainous enemies whose values stand in sharp contrast to everything Americans hold dear. But what if reality does not square with popular expectations? Well, so much the worse for reality.

Many of the myths surrounding American POWs in the Korean War have their roots in popular perceptions of World War II POWs. American and Allied POWs during the Good War always appeared as self-sufficient, independent agents who stood tall, no matter what the odds. Ample evidence of their exemplary behavior can be found in countless novels, biographies, autobiographies, popular histories, and above all, in such films as *Stalag 17, Bridge on the River Kwai, The Great Escape,* and *Von Ryan's Express,* as well as in the popular television series, *Hogan's Heroes.* Whatever the circumstances, these media-generated World War II POWs waged incessant war on their dim-witted captors, escaped when possible, sabotaged and killed when necessary, and always retained their faith in God and the superiority of the American way of life.

In a conventional sense, there were few heroic Korean War POWs, unless one considers simple survival a heroic act. There were no successful escapes from the permanent camps, no acts of sabotage, and no jaunty, irrepressible individuals fooling a befuddled enemy. According to government figures, 7,140 Americans were taken prisoner during the three years of fighting, and 2,701 of them did not survive captivity.[2] Several scholars, however, have pointed out that the official statistics greatly underestimated the numbers of those who died from atrocities committed immediately after capture, from untreated wounds, or during the long, deadly marches northward to the permanent camps. For example, H. H. Wubben estimates that atrocity deaths alone "numbered over a thousand."[3] Historians T. R. Fehrenbach and William L. White argue that the death rate was closer to 58 percent than the official figure of 38 percent.[4] And Dr. Sidney Esensten, who as a prisoner witnessed countless deaths, estimates that 75 percent of those captured between June 1950, when the war began, and September 1951, when conditions improved, died in captivity.[5]

Despite such horrifying statistics, the Korean War POWs had apparently not conducted themselves as had World War II captives who, at least in popular film and literature, never gave in to adversity and always comported themselves with exemplary courage. Accustomed to such role models, Americans wondered why Korean War prisoners appeared so inadequate and disappointing. A U.S. Army study attributed their alleged deficiencies in part to "some failure in the childhood and adolescent training—a new softness."[6] Many critics agreed, blaming castrating mothers for turning their sons into passive Milquetoasts who then became Silly Putty in the hands of their diabolical Chinese captors.

Such critics often cited Philip Wylie, whose *Generations of Vipers* introduced the term "momism" into the American lexicon. Among other things, Wylie accused American mothers of retarding their sons "logical development." "Mom is a jerk," wrote Wylie, a product of "hot flashes, rage, infantilism, weeping, sentimentality, peculiar appetites, and all the ragged reticule of tricks, wooings, wiles, suborned fornications, slobby onanisms, indulgences . . . connivings, cries, malingerings, deceptions, visions, hallucinations, needlings and wheedlings which pop out of every personality in the act of abandoning itself and humanity." She was, concluded Wylie, "a middle-aged puffin with an eye like a hawk that has just seen a rabbit twitch far below . . . [who] raped men, not sexually, unfortunately, but morally, since neuters come hard by morals."[7]

Four years after *Generation of Vipers* first appeared in 1942, psychiatrist Edward Strecker reached many of the same conclusions in a book entitled *Their Mother's Sons.* This idea of "momism" producing less than adequate sons inspired Richard Condon's 1959 novel *The Manchurian Candidate* and the much acclaimed 1962 film of the same name, both featuring the deadly misdeeds of a brainwashed Korean War POW. Of course, those willing to blame overprotective moms for weakening the moral fiber of their Koran War sons conveniently ignored the fact that both Wylie and Strecker initially were writing about young men who served in World War II.[8]

President Eisenhower did not attack motherhood, but he did agree that "the sad record of Americans in Korea" mandated extensive reforms in prisoner behavior. He argued that those entering service no longer possessed a "knowledge of what America is . . . and why they were fighting." In 1955, Eisenhower approved a Code of Conduct, to counter these alleged shortcomings, but which, in reality, reinforced many cherished and romantic myths about military captivity. The new Code began with the statement, "I am an American fighting man, responsible for my actions, and dedicated to the principles which made my country free. I will trust in my God and in the United States of America." The Code then instructed:

> Each member of the armed forces liable to capture shall be provided with specific training and instruction designed to better equip him to counter and withstand all enemy efforts against him, and shall be fully instructed as to the behavior and obligations expected of him during combat or captivity. . . . When questioned, should I become a prisoner of war, I am bound to give only name, rank, service number, and date of birth. I will evade answering further questions to the utmost of my ability. I will make no oral or written statements disloyal to my country and its allies or harmful to their cause.[9]

Among those publicizing the alleged misdeeds of the Korean War POWs, the attacks of journalist Eugene Kinkead and Army psychiatrist Major William E. Mayer achieved the greatest notoriety. In 1957, Kinkead published a long article in the *New Yorker* that, along with his later books, solidified the position of those convinced that a disproportionate number of American prisoners had disgraced themselves during captivity:

> In every war but one that the United States has fought, the conduct of those of its service men who were held in enemy prison camps presented no unforeseen problems to the armed forces and gave rise to no particular concern in the country as a whole. . . . The exception was the Korean War. As everybody knows twenty-one of the Americans captured as members of the United Nations forces decided to remain with the enemy. . . . What was even more shocking . . . was the fact that roughly one out of every three American prisoners in Korea was guilty of some sort of collaboration with the enemy.[10]

Citing official U.S. Army reports, Kinkead described men who after capture "appeared to lose all sense of allegiance not only to their country but to their fellow prisoners."[11] According to Kinkead, chaos appeared everywhere in the ranks, with the men allegedly refusing to obey orders or even to help wounded prisoners. But such behavior was not uncommon among prisoners in other wars. The shock of capture, followed by extreme disorientation and acute hunger, often reduced prisoners to their most basic instincts. They fought with each other, often acted like children, and felt abject pity for themselves. One moment they had been independent agents, in the next they had become objects, forced to perform abhorrent acts to stay alive.

Complaints about the American fighting man certainly did not originate in the Korean War. George Washington complained during the Revolutionary War that many of his soldiers lacked "public spirit." There were also "reluctant warriors" during the War of 1812, who either defected or refused to extend their time in service. In the Civil War many young men bought their way out of service or simply deserted once inducted. During World Wars I and II draft evaders and deserters numbered in the thousands.

One of the Army's own reports concluded that the average World War II soldier "gave little concern to the conflicting values underlying the military struggle"; nor did he "subordinate his personal interests to the furtherance of ideal aims and values."[12] A typical interview with a World War II POW indicates how common selfish behavior was among prisoners concerned only with their survival:

> In a prison camp, the will to survive supersedes a lot of niceties, including the Golden Rule. Do unto others as you would have them do unto you? Bullroar! When it was my turn to reach into the pot with the food, I was not about to give it to somebody else. What was mine, was mine, and you better not touch it.[13]

For those held by the Japanese, conditions were even worse, and so was the behavior. Physician Alfred Weinstein describes a Marine officer's collaboration and his stealing of medicine. Other officers also sought special privileges, and were willing to do anything to attain them. According to Weinstein, "Hard living, disease, and starvation made heroes out of few men. More frequently does it make animals out of men who, in the normal course of living, would go through life with a clean slate."[14] Unlike Korea, however, few blamed such behavior during the so-called Good War on perceived social, moral, and educational decay at home. What had changed, of course, was the advent of the Cold War and the resultant Red

Scare and the pervasive McCarthyism that engulfed the years of the Korean War.

Kinkead also insisted that too many POWs succumbed to a disease called "give-up-itis." But this too was nothing new. In the Civil War soldiers referred to going "around the bend," while World War II prisoners talked of "barbed-wire psychosis" or "the bamboo disease." Simply shutting down one's system was common, even rational, when confronted by untenable or seemingly hopeless conditions, and even the strongest prisoners occasionally did so. In extreme cases the men simply stopped eating and remained in their beds until they died.[15]

Five Korean War physicians, who were themselves POWs, also challenged Kinkead's contention that perfectly healthy American POWs just gave up and died:

> The erroneous impression has been created that prisoners of war who were in good physical health gave up and died; this is not true. Every prisoner of war in Korea who died had suffered from malnutrition, exposure to cold, and continued harassment by the Communists. Contributing causes to the majority of deaths were prolonged cases of respiratory infection and diarrhea. Under such conditions, it is amazing not that there was a high death rate, but that there was a reasonably good rate of survival.[16]

Kinkead, however, rather than attributing the 2,701 official Korean POW deaths to debilitating conditions and brutal treatment, blamed the personal and cultural shortcomings of the victims themselves:

> There was evidence that the high death rate was due primarily not to Communist maltreatment but to the ignorance or the callousness of the prisoners themselves. . . . The prisoners, as far as Army psychiatrists have been able to discover, were not subjected to anything that could properly be called brainwashing. Indeed, the Communist treatment of prisoners, while it came nowhere near fulfilling requirements of the Geneva Convention, rarely involved outright cruelty, being instead a highly novel blend of leniency and pressure.[17]

Kinkead argued that as many as 30 percent of the men were guilty of some sort of collaboration, including sending home Christmas messages in which prisoners assured their loved ones that their treatment was good, and that 13 percent were guilty of serious collaboration such as writing "disloyal tracts . . . or agreeing to spy or organize for the Communists after the war." Kinkead also claimed that in February 1951 the Communists sent small groups of American captives back to their own lines who "had been heavily indoctrinated and had come back prepared, with the aid of propaganda leaflets, to put pressure on our troops to desert."[18]

Kinkead concluded that more stringent training and indoctrination would do much to curtail any future problems. "There can be no compromise with evil," he wrote. "If this means that our troops must withstand emotional pressure and psychological pain, then, for the good of the country, these must be done. If the Communists alter their methods to include physical torture, that, too, must be endured."[19]

Kinkead was not alone in calling for the United States military to emulate the enemy's brutality in order to safeguard the American way of life. Maj. William E. Mayer voiced his criticisms in a lengthy interview in *U.S. News and World Report,* during extensive lecture tours, and through a tape-recorded speech that reached countless armed forces units, ROTC programs, and civic organizations. In fact, one of his taped speeches is still available on the Internet.[20] Like Kinkead, Mayer argued, "The behavior of many Americans in Korean prison camps appears to raise serious questions about American character, and about the education of Americans. . . . The behavior of too many of our soldiers in prison fell far short of the historical American standards of honor, character, loyalty, courage and personal integrity."[21]

Mayer also denied that harsh treatment could in any way explain his conclusion that approximately one third of all American POWs yielded to brainwashing. According to Mayer, this forceful indoctrination did not necessarily turn the men into Communists, but "created a substantial loss of confidence, among prisoners, in the American system, raising doubts and confusion in the prisoners' minds about themselves and their country."[22]

Manifesting his own disdain for the average American soldier, Mayer graphically described the contempt he imagined the captors had for their prisoners:

They obviously believed that the average American soldier was poorly informed to an extreme degree about his own country, his own economic and political system; was even more poorly informed about the politics, economics, and social problems of other countries; was an individual who based his sense of security and often of superiority on transient, materialistic values, and was a man who, if deprived of material sources of support, would prove to be insecure, easily manipulated and controlled, lacking in real loyalties and convictions.[23]

Mayer specifically targeted three defects in the American fighting man: a lack of an internalized system of discipline, which he blamed on domineering mothers; an ignorance of American democracy, for which he condemned progressive and less than patriotic educators; and, finally, something he called "a lack of moral and characterological elements in war," which he attributed to the U.S. Army being too solicitous of its soldiers' welfare.[24]

Ironically, Kinkead and Mayer's insistence that American POWs would have conducted themselves better if American society were less permissive and more authoritarian and if the military had been more dictatorial was precisely what one would expect to find in the totalitarian states that comprised the nation's enemies during the Cold War.

Critics of the American POWs often drew invidious comparisons with the alleged exemplary behavior of other U.N. prisoners, especially the Turks. Again, Eugene Kinkead's comments were typical. He argued that "the Turks produced a spectacular example of mass resistance to psychological pressure, and of other kinds of resistance as well." The reason for their success, wrote Kinkead, was maintaining "discipline and organization" and keeping "their chain of command unbroken." Finally, Kinkead pointed out that not one of the 229 Turks died in captivity.[25]

Many of the American prisoners interviewed for this book confirmed that the Turks conducted themselves well as prisoners,[26] but there were extenuating circumstances. As elite, voluntary, professional soldiers, the Turks should only have been contrasted with a comparable group of Americans, rather than to enlisted men, many of whom were unwilling reservists or draftees. More important was the fact that most Turks were captured after the deadly winter of 1950–51 when the highest percentage of prisoners died. Americans who were fortunate enough to be captured after that first winter also had a very good survival rate. The Turks also did not have to endure the tedious propaganda sessions, simply because the Chinese had few if any "educators" who spoke Turkish. Nevertheless, according to W. W. Wubben, the Chinese did release a photo of "cooperating" Turks carrying Communist banners. One Turk was also a member of the "Peace Committee" in Camp Five, and one initially refused repatriation but changed his mind at the last moment.[27]

One of the more unlikely critics of the American POWs was emerging

feminist Betty Friedan who argued that the passive and unproductive behavior of middle-class housewives, which she so graphically described in
her 1963 bestseller, *The Feminine Mystique,* could first be observed in the
conduct of American POWs in Korea:

> The shocked recognition that this passive non-identity was 'something
> new in history' came, and only came, when it began to show up in
> boys. But the apathetic, dependent, infantile, purposeless being, who
> seems so shockingly nonhuman when remarked as the emerging char-
> acter of the new American man, is strangely reminiscent of the familiar
> 'feminine' personality as defined by the mystique.[28]

Friedan, who based her conclusions on the same segments of the U.S.
Army reports that Kinkead used so extensively, accepted without challenge
that the Korean War prisoners represented a failed generation of American
young men:

> There was certainly something terribly wrong with these young men . . .
> I would call it ego-failure—a collapse of identity. . . . Adolescent growth
> can and should lead to a completely human adulthood, defined as the
> development of a stable sense of self. The Korean prisoners, in this
> sense, were models of a new kind of American, evidently nurtured in
> ways inimical to clarity and growth at the hands of individuals them-
> selves insufficiently characterized to develop the kind of character and
> mind that conceives itself too clearly to consent to its own betrayal.[29]

In the immediate months after repatriation, many mainstream periodicals dealt with the perplexing problem of prisoner behavior. Most were not
as harsh as were the writings of Kinkead and Mayer, but their titles alone
often supported allegations that the Korean War POWs were somehow
different: "Brain-Washed Korean POWs" (*Scholastic,* May 12, 1954), "Cowardice in Korea" (*Time,* November 2, 1953), "GI's Prison-Mates Accuse"
(*Life,* October 11, 1954), "Brainwashing: Time for a Policy" (*Atlantic,* April
1955), "POW Types Who Cave In" (*Science Digest,* December 1955), and
"Why POWs Collaborate" (*Science,* May 11, 1957).

Typical of such articles was "Why POWs Collaborate," which, citing the
same U.S. Army study that most critics used, argued, "The more our men
were abused and mistreated, the less willing they were to collaborate."
Although the article did not define collaboration, it concluded that only
15 percent of the prisoners actually cooperated with their captors, a figure

far less than the 30 percent published by Kinkead and Mayer. It also pointed out that 80 percent of the prisoners withdrew and did nothing, while only 5 percent actively resisted.[30]

There were also numerous articles on the twenty-one Americans who, refusing repatriation, chose China over the United States. These defections were even more difficult to accept than were the charges of general misbehavior leveled at repatriated prisoners. After all, some form of collaboration while incarcerated might be explained, although not excused, by acute hunger, bitter cold, and harsh treatment, but these twenty-one prisoners chose to stay behind while awaiting repatriation in a transition camp controlled by neutral powers.

Typical of the articles castigating the twenty-one was "Korean Puzzle: Americans Who Stay," published in October 1953 in *U.S. News and World Report*. It argued that some of the twenty-one had "ratted" on their comrades, that the majority were from rural southern or small town backgrounds, and that several had suffered unhappy home lives. The article concluded that most had little formal education, that several were career NCOs, but that none was an officer, "probably because of relative maturity, higher degree of education and hence a normally greater ability to analyze Red arguments." Surprisingly, the article included a statement from those planning to refuse repatriation:

Our staying behind does not change the fact that we are Americans. We love our country and our people. Therefore, we love personal freedom. Our greatest concern is to fight for peace and freedom, not only for ourselves but for the American people and people of the world.[31]

Two months later, *U.S. News and World Report,* which published more articles on the alleged shortcomings of the POWs than did any other mainstream periodical, again attempted to explain these defections: "They were lonely, bitter men who felt betrayed by fellow Americans. They were in a mood to swallow the Communist line. . . . They were unable to acquire the self-discipline needed to resist despair in prison camps [and] all of them appeared sullen and shifty-eyed."[32]

In an article entitled "The Sorriest Bunch," *Newsweek* described the defectors as "the sorriest, most shifty-eyed and groveling bunch of chaps" and that "about half the Americans were bound together more by homosexualism than Communism."[33] Other conservative voices also blamed homosexuality, as well as drug addiction, criminality, a lack of religious training, and progressive schooling. The *Chicago Tribune*'s Col. Robert Mc-Cormick contended that most of the defectors had come from the slums of New York where "subversive European ideologies" flourished.

Concluding that such extreme generalizations were scarcely accurate, Harold Lavine, writing in *Commentary* in July 1954, attempted a more in-depth analysis of the twenty-one Americans who remained behind. He discovered that three of the men were African-Americans, but none was Jewish. One came from abroad, and one's parents were foreign-born. The rest were of Anglo-Saxon or Irish stock whose families had been in the United States for generations. A majority were practicing Protestants or Catholics who did come from small towns or rural areas. Eighteen had been career soldiers. Two had attended college, but among the others only three had graduated high school. Three were married. Most, concluded Lavine, were quiet, often passive or easily led, poorly educated, from broken homes, or had lost a parent to death.[34] But certainly such criteria also described hundreds of other POWs who chose not to remain behind.

Countering the many negative articles on the twenty-one and those accused of collaborating, were the heroic stories of individual American prisoners who had apparently successfully resisted their captors. Typical were "Tough Prisoners" (*Time,* September 21, 1953), "GIs Outshine Eggheads in Resisting Reds" (*Saturday Evening Post,* October 31, 1953), "Reactionaries" (*Time,* September 7, 1953), and "Some of Us Didn't Crack" (*Colliers,* January 22, February 5 and 19, 1954).

"Is there any pressure so great that men can be excused for caving in?" asked *U.S. News and World Report* in a February 1954 article. Apparently, not, because "the future security of the United States, conceivably, could hinge on the outcome."[35] Quite naturally, such articles embraced stories of those prisoners, called reactionaries by the Chinese, who did openly resist. *Time* magazine, in a condescending but enthusiastic article, quoted "Buster Brown" White from Alabama City, Alabama, who reported, "If they accused us of somethin', we said we didn't know nuthin' about it. If they tossed us in 'the hole,' we just kept our mouths shut. We just didn't do nuthin' they told us to do." Other prisoners "set fire to a lecture hall, poured ink into Chinese laundry baskets, refused to carry Red banners in demonstrations, and cussed out their guards."[36] In another story, *Time* quoted an American POW who "fixed up" American histories in the prison camp library, "which stated we had mistreated the Indians and Spanish."[37] *Life* magazine reported how the prisoners fooled their propaganda instructor by singing the following lyrics to the tune of *Let the Good Times Roll:*

Hey, you-all!
Don't be no fool
You want to thank Mao Tse-tung
For sending you to school
You want to thank Mao Tse-tung
For all the things he done.
Hey, you-all!
You know I will
I want to thank Mao Tse-tung
For all the guys on the hill.[38]

Above all, it was Gen. William F. Dean's story that seemingly reassured Americans that there had indeed been American POWs who covered themselves with glory.[39] Although he was to receive the Medal of Honor, Dean, who was America's highest ranking prisoner, did not consider himself a hero:

If the story of my Korean experiences is worth telling, the value lies in its oddity, not in anything brilliant or heroic. There were heroes in Korea, but I was not one of them. There were brilliant commanders, but I was a general captured because he took a wrong road.[40]

Dean was not physically tortured, but he was certainly mistreated during his first eighteen months in captivity. He suffered a broken shoulder, various foot problems and infections, dysentery, terrible loneliness, cold, long interrogations, and, initially, poor food, but so too did most other prisoners. He never attempted to escape, although he did attempt to commit suicide. Dean, who often engaged in discussions with his captors, which prisoners were not supposed to do, later admitted that "one of the most difficult problems for a prisoner is that of maintaining his judgment."[41] He was referring to a letter in which he stated he was not being mistreated. In truth, he wanted his loved ones back home to know he was alive, but his captors distorted the letter for propaganda purposes. Significantly, several prisoners of lesser rank would be accused of collaboration for writing similar letters.

Dean had a marvelous memory and was able to recall the smallest details of his captivity. He was not, however, a deep thinker. He made little attempt to learn Korean except the few necessary words needed for survival, and, in one of the most revealing comments in his book, he admitted he was embarrassed when his captors asked him if he had ever discussed with his troops what the war was all about.[42]

He did not, however, demonize his guards, liking some but not others. He did try to teach them English and tried to convince them of the superiority of the American way of life. Except for his extreme isolation, and the accolades he received after the war, Dean's story was not so different from that of most other American POWs.

Publications covering the POW controversy reached millions of readers, but nothing did more to perpetuate images of brainwashing and collaboration than did a single Academy Award–winning Hollywood feature film. Released in 1962, *The Manchurian Candidate* was based on Robert Condon's best-selling novel of the same name. John Frankenheimer directed and Laurence Harvey starred as the brainwashed Sgt. Raymond Shaw, who had been programmed by his Chinese and Russian captors to murder the U.S. President. Angela Lansbury played Shaw's brutal, Communist-controlled mother who had so dominated her weak and ineffectual son that he proved an easy and willing mark for his diabolically clever captors. Maj. Ben Marco, played by Frank Sinatra, had also received "the Communist special treatment," as had the several other brain-dead prisoners shown in the infamous "indoctrination" death scene, during which Shaw garrotes one of his fellow prisoners and shoots another. Before an appreciative audience of Russian and Chinese dignitaries, a proud Dr. Yen Lo, who had been trained at the USSR's Pavlov Institute, explained how he programmed his prisoners to be assassins: "We have trained Americans to kill and then having no memory of having killed. . . . [Shaw's] brain has not only been washed, it has been dry-cleaned."

The Manchurian Candidate was filled, as one critic put it, "with suspense, Cold War intrigue, political satire, sexual inadequacy, and even incest." True enough, but it was the killing spree launched by the thoroughly indoctrinated and helpless Sergeant Shaw that remained indelibly etched in the minds of moviegoers. In fact, its scenes of murder and assassination were so alarming the film was withdrawn from circulation after the political assassinations of the 1960s.[43]

Without question, *The Manchurian Candidate* was an extremely well done but unsettling film. Social historian Greil Marcus thought it possibly "the most exciting and disturbing American movie from *Citizen Kane* to *The Godfather*,"[44] and film critic Pauline Kael called it a thriller which "may be the most sophisticated political satire ever to come out of Hollywood."[45]

The film certainly satirized both Joe McCarthy and his fellow travelers on the extreme right and the Communists and their alleged American stooges on the left, but overlooked by critics was the fact that its heavy-handed and distorted portrayal of brainwashed American captives stigmatized all Korean War POWs.

Hollywood released numerous other Korean War POW films, such as *The Bamboo Prison* (1954), *Prisoner of War* (1954), *The Rack* (1956), *Time Limit* (1957), and *Sergeant Ryker* (1968), all of which dealt with themes of collaboration and brainwashing, but none had the impact of *The Manchurian Candidate*.[46]

One the first comprehensive histories to appear after the war, and still widely admired, was T. R. Fehrenbach's 1963 *This Kind of War: A Study in Unpreparedness*.[47] Fehrenbach, who commanded U.S. Army units in Korea at the platoon, company, and battalion levels, emphasized the general unpreparedness of the U.S. military. He was particularly outspoken about the lack of professionalism in the Army and the general inadequacy of its civilian soldiers, which he blamed on progressive reformers who understood nothing of military needs and training.[48] Fehrenbach painted a dismal picture of the line soldiers who landed in Korea in July 1950:

> Discipline had galled them, and their congressmen had seen to it that it did not become too onerous. They had grown fat. They were probably as contented a group of American soldiers as had ever existed. . . . They represented exactly the kind of pampered, undisciplined, egalitarian army their society had long desired and had at last achieved.[49]

In truth, the overwhelming majority of these men had come from hardscrabble backgrounds where conditions were so hopeless they enlisted in the military as teenagers, many of them as young as fifteen or sixteen. As products of the Great Depression, they were arguably the least spoiled generation of the twentieth century.[50]

As an uncompromising Cold War soldier, Fehrenbach understandably preferred the "Reactionaries," but he frequently allowed the collaboration and cowardice of a relatively few to stand for an entire generation of young men. "Whatever failures there were, in the bleak and dreary prison camps of North Korea, were no more than a continuation of the failures on the battlefield, by the same men."[51] Fehrenbach did admit that "most men, if their jailor wills, may be broken" and that "the average man was neither courageous nor cowardly," but then qualified this observation by insisting that "the iron most men expect in soldiers" had not yet been forged in the average trooper. Fehrenbach used the courage of a grizzled World War II sergeant, Charles Schlichter, to contrast with those prisoners, who for whatever reason did not conduct themselves in a similarly heroic fashion. Schlichter was indeed an uncompromising Reactionary, but Fehrenbach appears to put words in his mouth that sound more like Philip Wylie or Edward Strecker than a frontline Non-Commissioned Officer (NCO):

> Some American mothers had given their sons everything in the world, except a belief in themselves, their culture, and their manhood. They had, some of them, sent their sons out into a world with tigers without telling them that there were tigers, and with no moral armament.[52]

Fehrenbach also accepted the view that other United Nation prisoners, such as the British and Turks, had conducted themselves far better than had their American counterparts.[53] He especially praised the Turks for their willingness to eat weeds, but, in truth, so too did many of the Americans. He also described "the childlike, simple and complete religious faith of the Turks," but a similar devotion did not seem to improve the survival rate for southern Baptist or Methodist prisoners.[54]

Fehrenbach correctly pointed out that the average American prisoner was not intellectually equipped to argue with his Communist captors during the long, tedious propaganda sessions, but neither was General Dean. Fehrenbach, like most conservative critics, believed that somehow men behaved better in the past, before progressive reforms engulfed society and supposedly left those affected incapable of withstanding Communist propaganda:

> The men who had in one way or another come to hold strong, unswayable beliefs such as Schlichter's reborn faith in his God, or some old infantry sergeant's belief in his service and Colors, or even some men's firm convictions on the superiority of Anglo-Saxon institutions—were the men who were untouched, whom the Chinese soon classed as reactionaries, and segregated.[55]

William Lindsay White's 1957 *The Captives of Korea* effectively challenged many widely held views of POW misbehavior. White, who had the full cooperation of high-ranking government officials, adamantly denied that "an alarming number of our POWs, without undue provocation, disgraced themselves," and he concluded, "Our prisoners were treated with a savagery unequaled in modern times."[56] White described the lack of food and inadequate medical supplies, which he insisted were the primary reason that "as many as 60 percent of the American boys did not survive":

In February [of 1951] the diet worsened from 600 grams to 400 grams, and the death rate soared among the 17–19 year olds. They died from pneumonia, acute diarrhea, dysentery. There were also symptoms of beriberi and pellagra. Then there was the hunger. Almost all the diseases could be traced back to malnutrition. Some of these men became too weak even to go for his [*sic*] food. He might just pull a blanket over his head and even refuse to eat if his buddies brought him something. Then he would refuse water, and shortly thereafter he would die, often lying in his own feces if no buddy was willing to wipe his behind.[57]

Although White admitted there were those few who did collaborate with the enemy, he emphasized the stories of those who did not, pointing out that the twenty-one Americans who chose to go to China paled by comparison with the thousands of Communist POWs who refused repatriation:

Only 327 Koreans, 21 Americans, and one Briton did remain behind. On the other side, of the more than 171,000 only 83,000 chose to go home [and] of these probably not half were really pro-Communist.[58]

Clearly, the interminable Chinese indoctrination sessions had produced little success, either among the vast majority of American prisoners or even among their own subjects who chose not to return to their Communist homelands after the war.

Sociologist Albert D. Biderman's 1963 *March to Calumny: The Story of American POWs in the Korean War* also disputed the popular view that the POWs had conducted themselves in a less than exemplary fashion. Biderman, who spent four years as a consultant to the Air Force on POW matters and who interviewed many of the former prisoners, insisted the burdens of coping with the enemy should not be "placed primarily upon the shoulders of the most isolated and vulnerable person in the chain." He also argued, "We can learn less about the pathologies of our society from the behavior of the Americans captured in Korea than we can by attempting to understand the reasons for the complaints that have been made against them." Because of the Cold War and the resultant domestic political paranoia of the early 1950s, Biderman argued that reactionary segments of society, including many officers in the U.S. Army, wanted to use the alleged misconduct of the POWs to exemplify what they perceived as growing weaknesses in the American body politic, such as progressive education, permissive child-rearing, social security, military reforms, the coddling of the weak and poor, and a general lack of patriotism. Reacting to these negative voices, Biderman concluded, "The prisoners became the subject of another type of propaganda—propaganda by Americans, about Americans, directed to Americans."[59]

Not surprisingly, Biderman targeted the writings of Kinkead and Mayer, arguing, "By blaming the victim [they] absolve the Koreans and Chinese for any responsibility for the American deaths." Biderman also included statistics and stories from World War II to prove that the behavior of the Korean War POWs differed little from their counterparts in the Good War. Prisoners in both wars talked too much, were guilty of some form of collaboration, and often put themselves before their fellow prisoners. In fact, argued Biderman, those in Korea who devoted all their energies to helping others, whether on the long marches or in the sharing of food and medicine, often died themselves because of their selfless efforts. Clearly, asserted Biderman, conservatives who so greatly admired the survival of the fittest doctrine in other environments did not think it applied to POWs.

Kinkead had argued that approximately one in three Americans collaborated, but Biderman puts the figure at less than 5 percent. The problem was clearly one of definition. Kinkead, for example, often confused misbehavior, such as the smoking of marijuana, with collaboration. Biderman also offered rational reasons why prisoners might cooperate with their captors, particularly if doing so might cause less harm to their fellow prisoners. Before they were segregated from the enlisted men, officers occasionally ordered their men to cooperate with camp officials, particularly if they thought this might save lives. Biderman concluded that in spite of expending tremendous amounts of energy, the Chinese attempts to indoctrinate the American POWs "were a resounding flop." Hence, writes Biderman, citing how few POWs actually became Communist sympathizers, "It was not brainwashing that was the primary reason for collaboration but a sense of survival."[60]

Biderman also challenged Kinkead's assertion that no one escaped. Biderman lists forty-six separate escapes, all made before the prisoners arrived in the permanent camps along the Yalu River.[61] It is true no one successfully escaped from the permanent camps, but several men did make the attempt. A British POW, who tried several unsuccessful escapes, explains why to do so was hopeless:

Here was a prison camp. Where was the barbed wire? No fences surrounded us, no machine guns were trained on us. It was many months
before I came to realize that there was no need for these things. The
poverty of our diet, the lack of medical supplies, the high steep hills,
the lack of organization among the Koreans (to possibly aid escapes),
these were the barbed wire.[62]

Kinkead and Mayer had called for absolute noncompliance with captors
and for severe punishment for transgressors. They also insisted that those
who overtly resisted did not suffer reprisals. Biderman, however, warned
that too many Reactionaries suffered for their actions, sometimes with their
lives. "It is foolish on the basis of the Korean experience," he wrote, "to
counsel soldiers that they will be physically better off if they defy a captor."[63]
Biderman, however, did acknowledge that compliance with the enemy
raised other problems. Once the Communists had a cooperative prisoner,
they controlled him by threatening to expose him to the other prisoners.
According to Biderman, the best course for a prisoner was passive compliance or resistance, although this too could get you killed if your captors
so decided.

In 1970, historian H. H. Wubben wrote a review article for the *American
Quarterly* analyzing the controversies still surrounding published materials
about Korean War POWs. Wubben began with inconsistencies he found in
the Army's official 1955 report. On the one hand, the report concluded
that the prisoners "cannot be found wanting," but then it stated, "The
Korean story must never be permitted to happen again." The following
year the U.S. Army issued a training pamphlet which, according to Wubben, "was even more ambiguous." Because of the "lenient policy" of the
Chinese, the pamphlet insisted there had been "little or no resistance to
the enemy's indoctrination," but then it also praised the "large majority
[who] resisted the enemy in the highest tradition of the service and of our
country."[64]

Because of such obvious contradictions, a wide variety of writers were
able to use these official documents to support contrasting conclusions.
Several prominent social scientists published scholarly articles and books
arguing that the behavior of the Korean War POWs differed little from
that of prisoners in earlier wars. Among them were Albert Biderman, Walter Hermes, S.L.A. Marshall, David Rees, and Russell Weigley.[65] In 1962,
Edgar Schein and Raymond Bauer summarized this support for the POWs
in a paper, signed by twenty-one scholars, entitled "Statement: To Set
Straight the Korean POW Episode":

The behavior of the Korean prisoners did not compare unfavorably with that of their countrymen or with the behavior of people of other nations who have faced similar trials in the past.

Instances of moral weakness, collaboration with the enemy, and failure to take care of fellow soldiers in Korea did not occur more frequently than in other wars where comparable conditions of physical and psychological hardship were present. Indeed, such instances appear to have been less prevalent than historical experience would lead us to expect. . . .

It is our opinion that any serious analysis of American society, its strengths and weaknesses, should rest on historically correct data. It is unfortunate that the Korean POW episode has been distorted to make the case for one view of American society. We hope that this statement will be the first step toward setting the historical facts of this episode straight.[66]

However, the negative voices reached far greater audiences. They had the advantage of including such national figures as President Eisenhower and FBI Director J. Edgar Hoover, whose agents would badger former prisoners for years after their repatriation. It also included political scientist Anthony Bouscaren, historians such as T. R. Fehrenbach, Robert Leckie, and Harry Middleton, and school reformers Max Rafferty and Augustin Rudd, who blamed progressive education for weakening the moral fiber of America's youth.[67] Wubben concluded that the two most influential critics remained Eugene Kinkead and William E. Mayer, both of whose views seemed very much in tune with a generation ready to believe that any Communist success was an unacceptable threat to the American way of life. Nor could average Americans forget the haunting pictures of beaten men they saw in movies and newsreels or read about in newspapers and popular magazines. Conditioned by fictional heroes of film and fiction, the public, like the critics themselves, had confused perception with reality and mass-mediated images with fact.

Old images die hard. In late January of 1995, nationally syndicated columnist and retired colonel David H. Hackworth called for the reaffirmation of the 1955 Code of Conduct for U.S. POWs because of the public confession of helicopter pilot Bobby Hall, who had recently been captured after straying into North Korean airspace:

U.S. Army pilot Bobby Hall "became disoriented," flew into North Korea, was shot down and out of "fear" spilled his guts to his Communist jailers. After such disgraceful behavior, Hall returned home to all the trappings once given to real American heroes.[68]

Invoking the glorious name of Nathan Hale and his famous regret of having "but one life to give for my country," Hackworth resurrected the familiar litany of POW misbehavior: "During the Korean War, many American POWs ratted on and stole the food of their fellow inmates or allowed themselves to be used for propaganda purposes."[69]

Hackworth insisted that the men he commanded in the early 1960s "would have spit in the face of the Russkies if captured," and he charged Army Chief Warrant Officer Michael Durant, captured in Somalia in 1993, and Navy Lt. Jeffrey Zaun, who was shot down in the 1991 Gulf War, with insulting "those who stood tall such as Jim Stockdale who bashed his face into a concrete wall so the Hanoi thugs couldn't use his mug on the tube to sell their propaganda." Hackworth concluded that if we did not reaffirm and reinforce the military Code of Conduct, "we can expect a rerun of the Korean War disgrace somewhere down the bloody track."[70]

Like Kinkead, Mayer, and other critics before him, Hackworth's call for blind allegiance and total sacrifice did more to enhance cultural arrogance and popular myths concerning national character than it did to shed light on the horrific truths of being a prisoner of war.

Although more than four million human beings, including 36,940 Americans,[71] lost their lives, the Korean War was quickly forgotten, fought as it was between the Good War the Allies won against the Axis Powers and the Bad War the United States was soon to lose to a new Communist enemy. Interestingly, Vietnam POWs, who numbered less than 1,000, became popular heroes, both in the friendly confines of the movie industry and in the real world of politics and industry. Two ex-POWs of the Vietnam War became U.S. senators, including one who ran for the presidency in 2000. Several carved out successful careers lending their names to various business enterprises, and Sylvester Stallone made millions with his Rambo thrillers, punctuated by the hero's famous words, "Do we get to win this time?" The Korean War POWs, however, have been redeemed neither in popular culture nor in public discourse. With the fiftieth anniversary of the Korean War now upon us, the nation needs to reexamine the experiences of those more than 7,000 fighting men who had the misfortune to be captured by North Korean or Chinese forces. Indeed, the time for America to listen to the voices of those who were actually there is long overdue.

I

THREE PRISONERS OF WAR

It is a melancholy state. You are in the power of the enemy. You owe your life to his humanity, your daily bread to his compassion. You must obey his orders, await his pleasure, possess your soul in patience. The days are very long, hours crawl like paralytic centipedes. Moreover, the whole atmosphere of prison is odious. Companions quarrel about trifles and get the last pleasure from each other's society. You feel a constant humiliation in being fenced in by railing and wire, watched by armed men, and webbed about by a tangle of regulations and restrictions.

—Winston Churchill

Since the narratives of Robert MacLean, Robert Coury, and Akira Chikami encompass so much of what Korean War prisoners suffered in common, they appear in their entirety in this chapter. These three men describe the shock of capture, the deadly marches northward, daily life in the permanent camps, interrogations and propaganda sessions, coping with sickness and death, repatriation and accusations of collaboration, and the long-term effects of captivity, all of which will be covered in greater depth in subsequent chapters. Two of these men served in the U.S. Army; one was in the U.S. Air Force. Two became career soldiers. The other took his discharge after repatriation. Although their stories contain individual differences, collectively they serve to introduce the reader to the POW experience. Biographical sketches of these three men and all the others whose narratives appear in this book can be found beginning on page 257.

ROBERT A. MACLEAN

I'm a glutton for punishment, and Memorial Day is undoubtedly the worst day of the year for me. I used to get so drunk I wouldn't even know my own name. Now just my blood pressure gets high. All day long the History Channel runs documentaries and movies about the Second World War and

Vietnam. Then the news programs show people visiting the Vietnam Wall in Washington or feature interviews with World War II veterans. I get so goddamn aggravated, just hoping that somewhere along the line someone will sneak in some recognition for our Korean War guys.

How is it that the History Channel and A&E are always running World War II stuff? A lot of it is just a repeat of things we've seen a million times. The same thing is true of Vietnam. Why don't they put on something about our war? If I see something on World War II, I switch to another channel. If I see something on Vietnam, I get pissed off. Don't get me wrong. I don't blame the Vietnam or World War II veterans themselves. They deserve everything they've got. I just want some of our guys to get the credit they deserve.

I don't know why I'm pursuing this thing like a vendetta. It must be because I've got too much time on my hands. Even the Andersonville POW Museum portrays the Korean POWs negatively. The director heard that I was very displeased with what they had done to us. In fact, he called me. He said, "This is true information from the government that we want to teach our younger people." Jesus, I damn near blew my stack. My wife got so goddamn mad she asked, "What kind of a government do we have?"

I enlisted in the Army on August 27, 1948, when I was seventeen years old. I guess I just wanted to be on my own. I had gone to the tenth grade in a sheet metal vocational program, but I figured I knew more than they were teaching me because I had worked with metals for my father. Back in those days he was called a junk man. Today he would be a recycling engineer. I started working with him when I was six years old. He and I had a great relationship, but I figured it was time for me to see what else was going on in the world.

I also had my independent moods in the service, but during basic training I was a good soldier. I was sent to Germany, and I was going up in rank, but I got busted for hitting the CQ. He wanted me to go on KP when it wasn't my turn, so I hauled off and knocked him flat on his ass. But that didn't happen very often. For some reason or another I always had my company commander on my side. I really don't know why.

When I came back from Germany, I got into transportation and was sent to Alaska to go on maneuvers with the Canadians. That cold weather training proved very helpful when I was in Korea. When I came back in August 1950, my enlistment was up, but I heard that the 2nd Division was looking for men to go to Korea and that reenlistment would mean an automatic increase in rank. So I reenlisted.

We were sent to Japan where our company worked day and night load-
ing supplies and ammunition for what was going to be the Inch'ŏn invasion
force. Then they put us on a troop ship and off we went. During the night
the damn ship stopped, and they threw those rope nets over the side. I
thought, "Holy shit, now I know what we're going to do." I had never gone
over the side on one of those rope nets. You've got your pack, your rifle,
and everything else, and you weigh a ton. I said, "Oh man, this is disaster."
Anyway, we landed in Inch'ŏn on September 15, 1950, and it was a piece
of cake. The biggest obstacle was in Seoul, but we finally got across the
Han River and off we went.

I was captured the day after Thanksgiving in November of 1950. We had
gotten all the way to the Yalu River before we learned the Chinese had
moved into North Korea. In fact, we were cleaning our equipment in the
Yalu River when we got the orders to evacuate. We couldn't take the main
roads so we had to take the side roads out of there. We had to dump a lot
of our big equipment over the side of a cliff because it couldn't negotiate
those hairpin turns. We got back to Hamhung and then had to send trucks
up to the Chosin Reservoir. Shit, I didn't know what was going on. We
picked up D Company of the 7th Infantry Division and off we went. We
got ambushed by the Chinks, and the next morning I got captured.

You don't do much thinking about all this until years later, but as I look
back now, if those Chinks had wanted to take us out in a quick snuff, they
could have done it. There were so many of them they could have overrun
and killed all of us, but I think they wanted to take some prisoners. When
you're young, you don't think that way. You say, "Jesus, even though we
didn't have any bullets left, we put up a damn good fight. We did ourselves
proud." But later you start putting all of this stuff together and you say,
"Yeah, they needed prisoners to start their propaganda war." [*Several other
interviewed prisoners also mentioned they were convinced that the Communist forces
early in the war were ordered to take prisoners.*]

After I got captured, the Chinese pulled me and a couple of guys out
of this hut and told us we could go down and take care of our wounded.
Well, how many people would do a thing like that in war time? I think
there were four or five of us that went back to the battlefield. On the way
we passed this mud building with dead Chinamen stacked in it like cord
wood. The Chinese were very quick in picking up their dead. We took care
of any of our soldiers we could. One fellow we came across had his whole
stomach in his lap. I literally took his stomach and pushed it back inside
him and covered him up. I don't know to this day if he lived or not. I

hope he did. I wrapped up a few others with a piece of cloth. Then the Chinese ordered us back.

It took us from November of 1950 to Easter Sunday of 1951 to get to Camp One. You can't imagine how tough those marches were. You really can't. It's hard to explain to anybody. I know that later some guys wrote we never tried to help one another, but that simply isn't true. We did help each other as much as we possibly could. Such stories get me so damn upset. I never saw one GI on the march take from another guy. I never did. And we were all starving and in terrible physical shape. We would lay over during the day, and every time I got up to march at night, I'd have to bend over and open the cuts on the back of my feet so the blood would flow and I could move my feet.

We got to the point where we had to tie shoestrings or pieces of cloth from one person to the other because you would actually fall asleep while you were marching. Some of those mountains were very steep, and you could literally walk off the goddamn things. So if you felt a tug, you'd reach over and grab the guy and pull him back into line again. I remember one night I fell asleep and I heard this *clunk, clunk, clunk.* I turned around and saw a Korean kid with a rifle taller than he was. The butt of that rifle was hitting the ground every time he took a step. I said to myself, "Where in the hell do these people come from?" Of course, like in every army, there were always sadistic jerks. There was one Chinaman that wore black, and he would swing his ass over and knock a guy off the side of a mountain. But I didn't see much of that. Jesus Christ, we were starving to death. What more could they do to us? There would be days we didn't have anything to eat because we'd move into a town and there would be no food there.

I was a lot more fortunate than a lot of other guys because when I went to Korea, I made damn sure my Alaskan gear was in my duffel bag. A lot of guys froze their feet because they never realized that they had to keep moving. Even though I had snow packs, I kept moving as much as I could. They put us in a ditch one night. You know how the cold settles in low spots; well, all night long I kept going up and down the line saying, "Move your feet, stamp your feet, move them around." But a lot of them didn't, and their feet froze. Trench foot and gangrene set in, and a lot of them lost their feet.

We were the first POWs in Camp One; in fact, I was the second man in line coming off the mountain into that valley. Conditions were very, very poor. There was no food or anything else. When we got there, all the camp consisted of was a bunch of Korean houses. The Chinese simply booted the Koreans out and moved us in.

The Chinese started their so-called brainwashing very shortly after we got into Camp One. In those indoctrination sessions, some individuals would keep their mouths shut and some would speak up. I happened to be one who spoke up, and there were a few others. Most of us came from big cities. Of course, I had always been very vocal. The Chinese would rip Mellon, Rockefeller, and guys like that. "Imperialist dogs," they called them. I truly believe it was hard for them to believe all that stuff themselves. Some of the Chinese who helped us in the kitchens—the real old-timers that knew Americans from when we had troops in China during and after World War II—could speak English. We'd start talking to them, and they'd tell us, "Hey, they're full of shit. You guys don't listen to all that, do you?" I really took those sessions as a joke.

I could never figure out their philosophy. They'd ask, "Who do you think you are, MacArthur? You're a warmonger." They never made any sense. After a few hours you got so numb, it just went in one ear and out the other. They weren't sophisticated at all. If they had fed us something decent, I might have listened, but, Jesus, they were not getting anywhere feeding me cracked corn or millet or sorghum or wormy fish. That just didn't make sense.

The Turks introduced us to marijuana. We didn't know what the hell it was. It grew wild everywhere. It was a damn good thing they did because if it weren't for the marijuana a lot more guys would have died. Some of the guys just wouldn't eat. We'd get them as high as kites, and they'd think they were eating a T-bone steak. We saved a few lives that way. We used to dry it on our hibachi. This one time I snuck out during the monsoon rains because we were running low on grass. We'd pick it right out of the fields, and we eventually picked the surrounding terrain dry. Maybe we shouldn't tell these stories now, but it really happened. The marijuana made us very philosophical, and when we were stoned, we could analyze a person better than a psychiatrist could. It also took away any possible effects from the brainwashing.

I had this guy in my squad named Friday. He got really sick this one day so I told him, "Friday, you stay inside." It was early in the morning, and we had to go up into the mountains and collect wood. We had roll call and, of course, Friday wasn't there. The instructor asked where he was and I said, "I told him not to come out because he's sick." Jesus, they lowered the boom on me. They sent everybody else off on wood detail and interrogated me for twelve straight hours while I had to stand at attention with a light bulb in front of my face. Finally, I passed out and when I came to, a couple guys grabbed me and said, "You're coming with us." That was the start of Squad Nine.

We started off in Squad Nine with two or three guys and then it increased from there. They were trying to separate the agitators from the rest of the guys, so they could keep tabs on us, and that's what they did. We just refused to cooperate. One time they had a test, but none of us wrote anything down. We didn't suffer any repercussions; in fact, I think they respected us more than they did the guys they were trying to indoctrinate. Eventually, we just flat out refused to go to any of their classes. I really felt no fear that if I did something wrong I was going to get punished for it. That's the way I was brought up.

But if they wanted to kick your ass, they could, and I really got in trouble this one time. We were up in the mountains, and I was very weak. I was trying to get a log up on my shoulders, and this Chinese guard kicked me and shoved me down. This was in 1953, just before the armistice. Well, me and this Puerto Rican kid, I forgot his name, we got sick and tired of all this stuff, and I said to him, "I sure would like to get drunk!" He said, "Well, let's just not go back to camp." So we didn't. We hid in the woods until everybody else had marched off back to camp. We then went from one *yoho*'s house to another, and before we knew it we didn't have any sneakers or anything else because we had swapped everything we had for rice wine. We got pretty well shit-faced. When we walked back into camp, I spotted this guy that had given me the hard time, and I went after him. I took his gun away from him, and immediately I had about a dozen Chinamen on my back beating the hell out of me. They sentenced me to five years isolation and put me in this room all by myself. The Chinese had warned us that if we did something bad, after the war we would have to serve our term in China, so I figured, "If I'm going to spend the rest of my life in China, I'm going to have to start looking for a Chinese broad to marry." All kind of thoughts go through your mind when you're all alone. But the thought of giving up never entered my mind. I didn't give a shit whether I had to live in China or wherever, I was going to stay alive.

My grandfather had a saying, "You get used to hanging if you hang long enough." That's the philosophy I took to prison camp. You just get used to it, even the bad food. It becomes a way of life. What are you going to do about it? I had a friend who died because of hamburgers. This kid just loved hamburgers, and he talked about nothing else. This eventually killed him. He finally lost his appetite and when you lose your appetite, you begin going downhill quickly. He stopped eating all together. When he took in his last breath, he was still talking about hamburgers. I saw that and I realized I couldn't be like that.

I never dwelled on home when I was in prison camp. The only time was one Christmas. It was snowing and the air was so clear, and I did get a little melancholy. But that was the only time. If you thought too much about home, you were going to make yourself sick, and I didn't want to get sick. If you got too homesick, it would kill you.

The Chinese eventually emptied out the whole damn camp. Everybody was gone, and I was still there. Finally, this guy let me out. A truck came through to pick up the stragglers and off I went to the 38th Parallel. Maybe the Chinese had just been giving me a snow job about sending me to China.

As for the twenty-one American prisoners who remained behind, I thought they were looking more for adventure than anything else. Someone may have ticked them off in the States or in the Army. The Rats were the guys you had to worry about, not the guys who were going to stay behind or who even seemed to swallow the Communist line. The Rats wanted that extra bowl of rice and that favoritism from the Chinese cadre. And all of them came home.

I was in prison camp for three goddamn years, but I tried to put it out of my mind after I got home. McCarthy was on his rampage, we got bad press, and if we said anything, we were likely to get in a fight so we more or less just stayed to ourselves. Having said that, I don't believe there has been a single day since I returned that something from my years in Korea hasn't flashed through my mind.

I did try the GI Bill when I got out. I wanted to be an aircraft mechanic, but I couldn't concentrate. Matter of fact, I have problems concentrating today. I don't know if that's an aftermath of what I went through or what. I just knew I had to get out of that classroom. It felt like I was back in prison camp again. I couldn't concentrate on anything they were trying to teach me. So I just said, "This is not going to do me; I'm going to go stir crazy if I keep this shit up." So I got out.

I got married after I got home, and this one night I went out to have a few drinks with my brother-in-law. He mentioned that I had been a POW. Well, this guy came over and made some derogatory remarks and that led into a brawl. When I got out of that, I said to myself, "This is not good. I'd better just keep my mouth shut." So I put everything out of my mind. I got a job in a metal-spinning factory, but the walls started coming in on me. So my cousin's husband came up to me one day and said, "You want to be an ironworker?" I says, "Yeah, I want to be an ironworker." I joined the ironworkers' local. I worked outside and was able to move around. I could go several hundred feet in the air with just me and another guy and be myself. That's the way I handled myself during that time.

My family didn't know much about my POW experiences. I've got seven kids, and the oldest boy called me after a veteran he worked with began telling him about the Korean War. My son had told him, "Yeah, I think my father was a POW there." So my son calls me and asks, "Hey, why didn't you tell me about Korea when I was growing up?" I guess it was because my first wife wanted nothing to do with it. I took my first wife out for breakfast about a month ago—the first time in twelve years—and she asked me, "Do you still have those terrible dreams?" I asked her, "How did you know?" I figured she was sleeping like a rock. Hell, she could fall asleep on a picket fence. She said, "You had some awful dreams." I said, "Why in the hell didn't you tell me?" She had her reasons. Maybe she thought she was doing me a favor. She asked me, "Is that why you drank so much?" It must have been. That's what they're telling me. Drinking would knock me out and put me into a dead sleep. But after I retired, my drinking pretty much stopped, but I still had these goddamn nightmares. No question, the wives took it on the chin. My second wife is very understanding, even if I go on a rampage over some political thing—which I often do.

I didn't go to a POW meeting until after I retired in 1987. I met this former Korean POW in downtown Boston one afternoon and he says, "Have you had your POW protocol?" I said, "What's that?" He explained that it was a kind of physical and that I'd better get over to the VA. He promised to go with me and he did. I had a physical, and then we went to these POW group meetings. Back in those days one group would be made up of guys from the European theater and another group had guys who had been held by the Japanese. On the other side of the room would be a handful of us Korean POWs. One afternoon a discussion came up and all of a sudden I got so fucking mad, I said, "You sons of bitches. You lived in a goddamn Hilton for a stalag." Well, that started a riot. I walked out, and I never had anything more to do with them until I came to Florida.

I ended up in Florida because of the warm weather. All my life I had fought snow and cold steel so I moved to Florida. Then my nightmares started getting worse. [*Many of the former POWs suffered increasing flashbacks after retiring from work, often because they had more time to reflect on their horrifying experiences.*] I went over to the VA hospital and talked to Dr. Skelton, a

POW doctor. He called in a psychologist and I sat down with her. I looked at her and I thought, "For Christsake you don't know what the hell this is all about." The next time I saw Dr. Skelton, he asked, "How did you make out?" I said, "Are you shitting me? She didn't know what the hell she's talking about." Boy, did he get mad. He said, "Look, there's a PTSD [Post Traumatic Stress Disorder] clinic we started upstairs. Would you mind going to that?" And I said, "Sure." So I started going to group meetings with the ex-POWs. Naturally, most of them were flyers from Europe. We had a Vietnam guy from the VA as a PTSD coordinator. Well, with my big mouth I started in on him. I guess I kind of broke the ice. I said, "Well, I guess I am old enough. I'll just keep my mouth shut as far as these other guys go."

I've given a lot of thought to the question how all this affected me, and I've asked this question a million times at these different groups that I've gotten into. It's a hard question to answer. If I hadn't been captured, where would I have gone? I don't know. All my life I was orientated to work so I imagine I would have wound up in some sheet-metal shop or something like that. But my outlook on humanity has changed dramatically. I've gotten to a point where I can meet a guy, talk to him for a few minutes, and say to myself, "I'd like to have this guy by my side" or "He couldn't walk in my footsteps." You become very opinionated. At least I did.

I'm now the Korean War representative at the VA hospital in Tampa. My job is to get hold of Korean veterans who need medical help, or help with compensation. I also recruit volunteers to work in the hospital. I'm now sending out letters trying to reach more guys. Many of them don't even know there's help that exists for them. They are angry with the VA to begin with, and they're angry with the public. A lot of them have drinking problems, and they have a hell of a divorce rate. There's lots bottled up inside us because of what we went through, but nobody cares except us.

ROBERT "BOB" COURY

Between early May and June 10, 1953, I flew thirty-eight sorties in Korea. I had just flown a mission on the morning of June 10 when my squadron commander met me at the airplane and told me I was to fly another mission that afternoon. Photo reconnaissance had picked up a buildup about ten miles behind the lines. The photos determined the target was going to be difficult and that we should use a two-ship "pathfinder" to acquire the target followed by a twelve-ship flight. We were to dive-bomb the target, and I was to lead the twelve-ship gaggle. We found the target, I rolled into a dive, released the bombs, and was immediately hit by antiaircraft fire.

I pulled out of the dive and saw two fire warning lights glaring at me on the dash panel. The other guys in the flight began hollering at me to punch out because I had a good fire going. With the situation I had, the book says you have ten seconds to get out. I figured if the bird would hold together for two minutes I could make it back across the lines, and I was going to take that chance. I headed south, but within a few seconds I lost thrust. I continued gliding south and losing altitude rapidly. I then lost the flight controls and went into an inverted spin. I ejected and hit the ground immediately after my chute opened. I landed in a barren, battle-scarred area about fifty meters from enemy lines and some three hundred to four hundred meters from our lines. I had enough time to get out my emergency radio and talk to the deputy flight leader. He told me to head into the sun and that they had already launched a helicopter to pick me up. If I had succeeded in moving in that direction, I would have crawled right into their trench lines. I was crawling along on my stomach and all of a sudden I felt a poke in my back. I rolled over and there were two soldiers armed with rifles. They hurriedly took me into one of the bunkers. At first I thought they might be South Koreans, but when I looked around the bunker and saw a Red Star on a canteen, I knew where I was.

I was shot down about four o'clock in the afternoon of June 10, 1953. The soldiers on the frontline were very friendly and curious about the garb I was wearing. As soon as it began getting dark, they started moving me to the rear. I walked through their lines for about a mile and then out on a road. Two soldiers would take me a mile or so, and then two more would come up and continue the trek. I covered about ten miles that night, back to the area that we had bombed. I got so exhausted that I couldn't walk anymore, so for the last couple of miles they were practically dragging me.

They took me to a prisoner collecting point that was a compound of caves dug into the side of a hill. These caves were lined with timber, roofed, and covered with soil. They left one corner above ground and used it as a window and put small three-inch timbers in as bars. The first thing that came into my mind was to escape. I was not in any kind of shock. I just had a numb spot on top of my head where the canopy had hit me during ejection. I started twisting these timbers to see if I could get them loose. I finally got them to where I could take them out and put them in at will. This left me enough room to crawl out. I still had my billfold with me with some photos and a pack of cigarettes. I took the tinfoil out of the cigarettes and put it on one of the plastic picture holders, which made a pretty good reflector. I practiced with it when I got some sunshine, and it worked pretty well. I thought if I escaped from the cave, I might be able to signal one of our airplanes, or I might be able to make my own way across the lines at night.

On the eighth night of my captivity, I very carefully removed the timbers and started crawling out. The guard was pacing back and forth just a few yards from me. I was watching him and slowly making my way out when I heard people coming up the pathway to the compound. I quickly squirmed back into the cave. I didn't even have time to put the timbers back in place before they came directly into my cave, put a blindfold on me, and put me in a truck with a bunch of South Korean prisoners, and off we went.

From the collecting point we traveled all night. We were seated in the bed of a rather large pickup truck with a couple of guards standing over us. Every time I got up to relieve myself a guard would jab his rifle butt into my shoulder. The next morning we were unloaded and put into a room in a Korean hut. All of us tried to get some rest, but within an hour they came in with a huge bowl of rice and put it in the middle of the room. The Korean prisoners all had eating utensils with them, either chopsticks or spoons, and the rice vanished quickly. I reached in with my hand to get some, and the guard made us all stop. He left for a minute or so and came back with a spoon and handed it to me.

A few hours later, they blindfolded me and put me in the back end of a truck by myself. It was a cloudy day and I guess they felt they could travel without being attacked by our planes. We traveled until early the next morning when we stopped at a small command post. We woke up the soldier inside, and he proceeded to try to interrogate me. I gave him only my name, rank, and serial number, and he instructed the guards to take me away. We were in very mountainous terrain near what looked like a vacated POW camp. The guards took me down the road a couple of miles, where we stopped at a three-room family hut occupied by an old man, his daughter, and an infant child. They were moved out of one room that was then used as a cell for me. There were eight or ten Chinese guards who guarded me around the clock. It was a bare room with a dirt floor, and they insisted that I sit on the floor. They kept the door closed most of the time, and when they opened it, and I was caught standing or lying down, they raised hell with me. After about the fourth day, they began leaving the door open, and I could observe what was going on outside.

Initially they tried to interrogate me a couple of times a day. After about twelve days, they were only interrogating me once a day, but they were also cutting down on my food. During the last few days I was being fed one small bowl of rice and a can of water per day. I used the same slit-trench latrine the Korean family used. I was allowed to go down to a stream once a day and bathe and brush my teeth. They provided me with a toothbrush and toothpaste. How the Korean peasants lived really amazed me. They were hardly civilized. The daughter carried her baby on her back wrapped in a piece of cloth she tied around her waist. She also did most of the work around the house. I watched her take some kind of grain, put it in this hollow stump, and grind it with a piece of wood. She would spend a couple of hours doing this. Then she would take this meal, make a kind of dough out of it, and put it in a little tin box that had holes in the bottom. By pressing the dough through the holes she made noodles. One time the baby did its business while on his mother's back. The mother untied the sash, and held the baby out to let a small dog lick it clean. Without even cleaning the sash she put the baby back on her back. A few days later they butchered and ate the dog.

It was during this time that I was most concerned about what the future held for me. There were no sounds of ground fighting or air activity. I often thought the war could have ended, particularly since just before taking off I was told that a cease-fire was expected momentarily.

Once again I was blindfolded and hauled off in a truck. We arrived at our destination about ten o'clock at night. I was forced up a ladder, still blindfolded, into a very small room. As soon as I heard the door slam shut, I removed the blindfold and began feeling around the darkened room. It turned out to be an attic room about six feet square with a four-foot ceiling that slanted to the floor. I stayed there the rest of the night and all the next day. After dark they removed me from the attic, walked me across a courtyard into a room where several interrogators were seated. The Chinese head honcho told me, "We are very displeased with your interrogation thus far. If we don't get better cooperation, we're going to take you behind this building and put a bullet through your head. We've done it before and we will do it again." I believed him, but at that point I just didn't care.

I was then taken back across the courtyard to a cell. I could tell by feeling around the interior that this had been a horse stall. It had small double doors leading to the courtyard, and an individual entrance going to the outside. The entire room was sealed with cardboard to prevent seeing outside. There was a small opening at the ceiling. I went to the individual entrance and gave it a good kick, and it flew open. I walked outside into a bright, moonlit night, and for the first time since my capture I knew exactly where I was. I could see the city of Sinuiju and the mouth of the Yalu River.

This had to be their top interrogation center. Both to my right and left, there were individuals squatting and watching me. I immediately figured that trying to escape would be fruitless, so I walked back into the cell and went to sleep. They raised hell with me again the next morning.

The interrogation process was pretty routine. Once or twice a day they would try to interrogate me. As best I could tell, there were eight Chinese and two North Korean interrogators. One of the North Koreans tried to befriend me by telling me that he was originally from South Korea, but that he had political differences with government officials. Both he and his wife were imprisoned in South Korea. His wife died in prison during childbirth, but he was able to escape, and there was only one place for him to go, and that was to the North. I don't know whether he was sincere or just trying to get me to talk to him.

When I first arrived at this interrogation center, there were three other American POWs, all pilots. One of them had been injured and was allowed to walk the interior of the courtyard with a guard. I was able to observe this by peeling back some of the cardboard covering the cracks. Once when he passed my cell, I began humming the "Air Force Song," hoping to get some response out of him. No luck! This prisoner was moved out after a couple of days. Later I learned there were two more American prisoners there.

While at this interrogation center, it was easy to tell the war was still on because all the big air battles were taking place overhead. Finally there came a time when there was no air activity despite the good weather. I had gone out to the toilet, and one of the Chinese interrogators came out at the same time. I asked him about the status of the war, and all I got was a grin. Later, a North Korean interrogator came out, and I mentioned there had been no air activity. He said, "We expect a cease-fire momentarily. You should be going home very soon." My morale skyrocketed.

A day or two later, they blindfolded the three of us who were left and put us in a weapons carrier. They told us not to talk to each other—which lasted for about three minutes. We were heading up the Yalu River. We spent one night on the road, and the next day we went by a couple of POW camps that had already been vacated. A bit later we went by an active camp, and we could see the guys walking around and playing volleyball. We went beyond the camp about a mile, and were taken into a small command post. There someone told us the war had ended and gave us each a bottle of beer and a carton of cigarettes. We thought they would put us into this camp with the rest of the guys. Instead, they put the three of us in a little compound and left us there for a couple of hours. An interrogator showed up with some questionnaires he wanted filled out. We put down our name, rank, and serial number and handed them back. He became angry and started raising hell with us. One of our guys, Steve Bettinger, started giving the interrogator a bad time. The interrogator called a couple of guards and they moved Steve into solitary confinement. They took Don Hodges and me back to the regular camp and left us there.

We went into the compound, parked our meager belongings, and went out to watch the guys playing volleyball. Nobody made any effort to come and greet us for quite some time. The reason for this was they were divided into two groups: the good guys and the bad guys, those who had confessed to germ warfare and other evil deeds and those who had not. Finally, one guy came over and asked us some very pointed questions. We both gave him a full account of what had happened to us. He reported back to the group and they accepted us as friends. Most of them were pilots, but there were also some enlisted men there as well.

Bettinger showed up the following day. Steve was quite a character, and the last "ace" of the Korean War. He had shot down his fifth MIG and then was shot down himself. He told us they had put him in a thatched-roof hut the previous night, and as he was about to go to sleep on the floor, something dropped on his chest. He let out a yell, and the guard opened the door. A big snake had fallen out of the thatched roof.

After a couple of days at that camp, we were put on a train headed south. We went into another compound for a few days, and each day they would take a few guys out to be repatriated. I came out the next to the last day of the repatriation cycle. The thing that impressed me the most as we entered Freedom Village were two husky Military Police who were spit-and-polish from head to toe. The folks running the place questioned us a bit, fed us, and let us make phone calls home.

I was put on a hospital ship to come home. I weighed 145 pounds when I was shot down and about 105 before repatriation. On the hospital ship the head Air Force guy was Bud Mahurin, a World War II ace and a full colonel. At our first evening mess aboard ship he called all the Air Force guys together and said, "Okay, we've been through the business of being captured and tortured and all that, and there are supposed to be good guys and bad guys, but let's try to forget about that and have a good trip home."

One of my fellow prisoners onboard was a Marine colonel who was actually a staff officer. He was one of the guys who had confessed, and he told me why. He was flying up to Seoul for a meeting and had some top-secret documents with him. He was in a little twin-engine C-45 and decided to fly up to the frontlines to observe some Marines. He was shot down and captured. He told me his interrogators had all kinds of information on his family, and they threatened to harm his family members. They had the names of his children, where they went to school, and all sorts of other information. He told me, "Rather than do harm to my family, I was willing to confess to anything they wanted me to say."

My personal belief is that you can break anybody down if you really want to, given the time and the right environment. I was very lucky for a couple of reasons. I was a prisoner during the summer months when it was warm, and I knew what had happened to the guys who had already returned during the exchange of wounded prisoners in Operation Little Switch.

All of us went through a counter-interrogation on the boat. I was hospitalized after reaching the States, and went through another interrogation. When I got to my next base, I went through a third one. Several months after I got home, I received a letter from the Air Force stating that my conduct as a POW was considered commendable and wishing me future success in the Air Force.

AKIRA CHIKAMI

I was born March 19, 1927, of Japanese immigrant parents in La Junta, Colorado, but I grew up in Reno, Nevada, where I joined the Army. I got out of the service after World War II ended and became a professional boxer. There was a lot of discrimination when I used to fight on the West Coast, so they would call me an Indian, a Korean, or whatever. But I hurt my hand and had to quit. I thought I'd go back to Colorado and work in the lead mines to strengthen my hands and shoulders. I passed the physical, but when they looked at my papers and found out I was a Japanese American, they wouldn't hire me. They were very discriminatory, even though I had an honorable discharge. In the meantime, I saw a newsreel of the 1st Marine Division getting kicked out of the Chosin Reservoir. I got all excited. I had never seen combat so I thought, "Gee, that's where I want to go." I also had two older brothers who were with the 442nd Regimental Combat Team in World War II. I went to a recruiting office in Denver and asked the sergeant if I went back into the Army could I go to Korea. He said, "Sure thing." He signed me up and gave me a ticket to

Fort Riley, Kansas, where they gave me a two-day refresher course. The first day I took my M-1 apart and then put it back together. The second day I went through the infiltration course. That was my refresher course. This was December 1950. In January I was in the infantry with the 2nd Division on the frontlines in Korea, less than two months after I reenlisted.

I never had any regrets, at least not until I got captured by North Koreans in August 1951. At the time we were in the punch bowl and my company was out front as a kind of decoy but also in a blocking position, trying to get the enemy to attack us so we could call in artillery on them. We were only supposed to stay out there three days, but we got into the eighth and ninth days. I knew we were in trouble because I'd been in combat long enough to know we shouldn't be out there that long. Every night the enemy had been probing to find out where our automatic weapons were. Sure enough, on the morning of August 27 our company was overrun. We lost over 50 percent of our company that day.

We started to retreat and I got hit in the leg. My first reaction was, "Well, it's not too bad. Maybe it will be good enough to get me a trip to Japan." My company commander came by and said, "Sorry, I'm going to have to leave you." And he did [laughs]. Our medic stopped and helped bandage me up. Then two other guys came along and said, "Come on, Sarge, we'll help you." They picked me up between them and tried to carry me, but a machine gun opened up. They were both killed and fell into a stream. I started crawling, but I looked up and there was a young North Korean soldier staring at me. He was just a kid, but he had a burp gun. I still had a forty-five on me. I didn't know whether to reach for it or not. I decided not to, and I was a prisoner. He immediately took what I had: a watch, a ring, and a bracelet and then turned me over to another group where they had assembled other prisoners.

The North Koreans herded us toward our own lines where the fighting was still going on. I couldn't figure out why they were taking us in that direction, instead of to the rear. When we came to a bend in the road where our machine guns were raking the area, I realized, "They're going to make us commit suicide by marching us right into our own fire." But the shooting suddenly stopped. I guess our guys recognized we were Americans.

By then there were some thirty-five of us, and they moved us into a little ravine where it became clear they were going to use us to carry their wounded to the rear. Then, I saw one of our spotter planes we used to call in artillery. Sure enough, I heard a couple of incoming rounds, and I knew our own troops were zeroing in on us. Five rounds came in right on top of us. The guy in front of me was hit, which saved me because I was right behind him. He caught a piece of shrapnel in his chest so big I could stick my whole fist in it. When it was over, there were only about four or five of us who weren't wounded. It was getting dusk and the North Koreans were going to move us out. This American lieutenant came up to me and asked, "Sarge, are you going to go?" I told him I was. This lieutenant decided to fake an injury and say he couldn't move. There were four of our guys who stayed behind. As I moved out over the hill, I heard a burp gun go off, and I knew the North Koreans had shot them. I found out some twenty years later that the lieutenant survived, although he was the only one of the four who did. One of our patrols picked him up the next day. He was all shot up, but he lived.

I was able to walk with somebody helping me. I had to. I knew if I didn't walk they were going to shoot me. The bullet that struck me hadn't hit a bone, which was lucky. It went right through my leg. Later I picked up a tree branch to use as a crutch, so I was able to walk.

They moved us to the rear that first night. The next day we had to cross a river that was flooding and I thought maybe I would get swept away because of my leg. But I made it. They then took us into this huge cave in a mountain that was their headquarters. They tried to interrogate us, but they didn't have an English-speaking person and none of us could understand them. I was the ranking man, and they were surprised to find an Oriental. They were very curious about me because they were afraid that Japan was going to send in troops. So they interrogated me pretty closely. When they went through my wallet, they were amazed to find photos of Caucasian girls. They would look at me and then at the pictures and they would yack, yack, yack. I could only imagine what they were saying. I more or less became a spokesman for our group of POWs for what little I could communicate.

You talk about tactics. The first interrogator treated me real rough. He threatened to push me over a cliff and all that kind of stuff. Then he went away and another guy took his place. He offered me a cigarette and tried to explain that the other guy was very bitter because he had lost his family in the war. He was a little more compassionate. He told me, "I know you're just a soldier." Then he wanted to know what outfit I was in, why we were there, and things like that. They were pretty shrewd and they could get to you pretty fast. One of our guys was all shook up. He had just been married and his wife was pregnant, so he was thinking, "How am I going to tell my wife I'm a prisoner?" Someone like him became an easy target for indoctrination, and they completely broke him down. I don't know if you call it brainwashing, but men like him became easily manipulated. Of course, the North Koreans already knew who we were. I mean they knew everything. There was nothing we could tell them that they didn't already know.

They moved us out the next day farther and farther to the rear. We walked mostly at night or in the evening. In the morning we would hole up in some village or they would put us into some kind of shack. The little kids in these villages would see me and holler something that I later found out meant "half-breed." They were fascinated by me because I was an Oriental. I would be lying on the side of the road trying to rest or sleep, and these kids would pick up little rocks and throw them at me. The braver ones would poke me with sticks so they could see my face. I was an oddity to them.

About the tenth or eleventh day after we were captured, the guards wanted to know who was going to represent our group. I was the ranking sergeant so I was selected by the other prisoners. Early the next day they took me and this other prisoner, Sergeant Nehrbas, put us in a jeep, and took us directly to Camp Twelve, which was on the outskirts of the North Korean capital of P'yŏngyang. When we arrived a prisoner who identified himself as Colonel Fleming asked us how the peace talks were going. He wasn't concerned about our welfare so I was a little turned off. Fleming was one of the few prisoners to be court-martialed and convicted after the war.[1]

Camp Twelve consisted of about fifty or sixty prisoners, both officers and enlisted men. We got a real cool reception from the GIs who were already there. I couldn't understand this; it was like they didn't trust us. I had no idea what was going on. After I was released, I learned that the North Koreans had told the other prisoners they were bringing in some sergeants who had voluntarily surrendered. No wonder they viewed us so suspiciously.

The camp commander was a North Korean by the name of Colonel Pak, but not the Pak who was in charge of the notorious Pak's Palace. He was a spick-and-span officer and wore the cleanest clothes and the shiniest boots I had ever seen. He flat-out told us, "The only reason you're alive is because I'm a soldier. If I had my way, I would take you all out and shoot you because you murdered our people. But because I'm a soldier I have to take care of you and see that you stay alive." He meant it when he said he wanted to shoot us all.

The North Koreans selected us for Camp Twelve because it was a center for propaganda, and they hoped we might become Progressives and be willing to cooperate with them. Col. Paul Liles was the ranking officer in the camp. He was a West Point graduate who was also court-martialed after returning home.[2] The North Koreans took Nehrbas and me to Camp Twelve because we were the ranking NCOs in our group of prisoners and because I had been voted to represent the men and could communicate with our captors. The North Koreans also hated the Second Division. They wanted to wipe us out because we fought so many bloody battles with them.

Within two hundred yards of Camp Twelve was another compound called the Central Peace Committee. It consisted of four or six guys who were definitely cooperative. In fact, one of them was a British cartoonist named Ronald Cox who was a card-carrying Communist when he went into the British Army. He was an excellent artist and drew cartoons for the Chinese propaganda publications, one of which was a newsletter called *Towards Truth and Peace*. It originated in Camp Twelve with the Central Peace Committee, and then circulated to the other prison camps.

The North Koreans wanted to get some of us to make propaganda broadcasts over Radio P'yŏngyang. Through intimidation and threats, they forced four of us sergeants to do so. When I was scheduled to go, I didn't know what to do, so I asked Colonel Liles how to keep from going to P'yŏngyang, which was about a day's walk from Camp Twelve. He told me, "Tell them that your leg hurts and you can't make the trip." So I complained about my leg, which did actually still hurt, and they sent me to a field hospital for two weeks. A black sergeant named Clarence Covington was sent to P'yŏngyang to make a broadcast in my name. He said, "This is Sergeant Chikami."

Being in a Chinese field hospital was a strange experience. I was in a tent hospital with all these wounded Chinese and North Koreans. They knew I was a prisoner, but they didn't pay too much attention to me, maybe because I looked like them. I got the same kind of food they did, and I got my bandage changed every day. My leg had never really healed. The only thing that had really saved my leg was I got maggots in it about six days after I got captured. I could feel this pain, and I thought for sure I had gangrene, but when I opened up the bandage a big, fat maggot fell out. My medic, Bill Middleton from Texas, cleaned them out for me, but I knew they were good because I had read stories about how Western cowboys during the Indian wars had put maggots on their wounds to clean them.

Howard Adams was in Camp Twelve, and I knew him quite well. He later became one of the twenty-one who chose to go to China instead of coming home. He had been in World War II and received a Bronze Star. I knew him so well because we were both disabled. So when the rest of the camp went out on work details, he and I stayed back in the camp grinding soy beans. We used to sit there, grind beans, and talk. I thought he was a pretty good guy. He wasn't political at all. He never tried to indoctrinate anybody, and he never talked politics to me. I also knew Richard Corden slightly when I was later in Camp Five. He was another of the twenty-one. He also was not political so I never understood why these guys were so vilified. It is hard to figure what made these guys decide to stay behind. Some people say you get brainwashed, but I have no idea what people mean by "brainwashed." What does that really mean? Were we brainwashed because we had to sit there in a class listening to people talk about germ warfare, an unjust war, and all this kind of nonsense? That doesn't brainwash you. I never saw any instances of any prisoner trying to indoctrinate another into accepting the Communist way of thinking.

In December 1951 the North Koreans disbanded Camp Twelve. They told us we were going to be repatriated, and they had a big banquet for us. They gave us some wine, apples, and other good food. The next day they told us to gather up all our belongings and that we would be taken across the river on boats and be on our way to P'anmunjŏm. A group of over a hundred officers joined us from some other camp, and then all of us went down to the river to wait for the boats, but the boats never came. So the next day they loaded everybody on trucks, but I didn't get to go. Jack Caraveau was so sick that he couldn't be moved. I volunteered to stay back with Jack because we were from the same division and we were the last ones to be captured, as far as I knew. I figured that it was only fair that the other guys get repatriated before us. There was a Capt. Hugh Farler who was also too sick to move, and a Lieutenant Doherty stayed behind with him. The rest of the guys got on trucks and left, and the camp was deserted. I don't know exactly the date, but it was in early December 1951. We thought, "Well they're going to get repatriated," but the next day the planes were still flying. Somebody brought us a little bit of food, but there were no guards. We moved into what used to be the kitchen because there was a lot of firewood there. We burned it all day trying to keep warm, but we didn't get much food.

There were just the four of us there. Captain Farler was delirious and didn't know where he was. Caraveau was coughing and was in bad shape. Days went by and there was still nothing. We had nobody to talk to. Whoever brought us our food couldn't speak English, so we didn't have the faintest idea what was going on. But the planes were still flying, and we could still see dogfights, so we knew the war was not over. Captain Farler died, and we buried him in a peanut patch. Then one day a couple of fancy American jeeps came whirling in there. They were all painted up, with leopard-skin seat covers. A North Korean general popped out with a couple of female aids all dressed in their spick-and-span uniforms. He looked around the compound and came over to where we were. It was Gen. Nam Il, the chief North Korean negotiator during the truce talks. Evidently what happened was the peace talks had broken off, and I guess he just came over to see what was left of Camp Twelve. I didn't think of these things at the time, but I put it all together later. He just looked at the three of us, got in his jeep, and took off. Then a few days later they loaded the three of us on a truck and headed north. We were strafed by a Marine Corsair on the way, but we arrived in Camp Five on New Year's Eve—and that started the next couple of years.

I was put in solitary in Camp Five. I was acting crazy just to harass the Chinese. It was warm this one evening, and I didn't want to stay in this hot little hut. So I built a bench outside the hut. I was lying there, looking up at the sky, when this old Chinese guard came by and said, "Sleepo, sleepo." I didn't pay any attention to him so he went away. Fifteen minutes later he came back and again said, "Sleepo, sleepo." I still ignored him. He got ticked and ran off to get the sergeant of the guard. The sergeant of the guard came and said, "Chikami, you sleepo." I mumbled something. Twenty minutes later they got an English speaking instructor who had been sleeping. He asked me, "Chikami, why you not going to sleep?"

I tell him, "I can't sleep."

He asked, "Why, why? Regulations you go to sleep."

I said, "No, I lost my dog."

He said, "Your dog?"

I said, "Yeah."

He said, "You don't have a dog."

I said, "No, it's gone."

So he got mad and took me up to headquarters. By now it was about midnight, and they got the chief instructor out of bed and he was mad. "Chikami," he said. "Why don't you go to sleep?"

I said, "I lost my dog."

And he said, "You don't have a dog."

I said, "You're right. He's gone."

And he said, "Where did you get the dog?"

I said, "The Turks gave me a dog."

He says, "The Turks don't have a dog."

I said, "No, they gave the dog to me."

He was getting really mad, and he prided himself on knowing a little slang so he said, "Chikami. Let's call a spade a spade."

So I said, "Oh, you want to play cards?"

Oh man, he blew up. He yapped, yapped, yapped in Chinese, and three guards came in, grabbed me, and hustled me out. I still only had summer shorts on. They hustled me up on top of this high hill to a mud hut they called solitary and put me in it. It wasn't funny because it was two or three o'clock in the morning, it had got cold, and I had no blanket. The next day they brought me up a little food and water. For about two or three days they didn't say anything to me. Finally they brought me some more clothes and a blanket. I took the blanket and made a hammock out of it and attached it to these beams. Every time I saw the guard come I would jump into my hammock and swing back and forth like I'm enjoying myself. The guard would get mad and tell me to get out, but I would ignore him. Finally, he came in and cut it down with his bayonet. I didn't know what to do, but I found a little hole in the back wall. I poked my finger through it, which allowed me to look down at the Yalu River. All of a sudden I see another eyeball on the other side. It's the Chinese guard and we're looking at each other. I poked my finger in farther and he pulled back. Then he poked his finger at me, so we're playing this little game. I tried to grab his finger, but I could only get the very tip because the wall was pretty thick. Then I'm looking through the hole and wondering, "What the hell is he doing?" All of a sudden he peed on me. He peed in the hole and right into my eye. I mean, hey, I can't even rinse it out because there's no water. Burned the heck out of my eye and he was laughing.

They let me outside this hut once a day for exercise, and when they did I'd shadow box. They had never seen anything like that. They thought, "This guy really is crazy." Then the guys down in the company got together and signed a petition to get me out of solitary and took it to the commander. The Chinese had just begun to let us play a little basketball, and my buddies needed me to play on our basketball team. We had what we called a United Nations squad: a Japanese, a Puerto Rican, and a Turk on the same team. But they still kept me in there for two weeks.

Another time we were all assembled, and they were talking about how that morning their technicians in their white coats and masks had been out in the hills collecting specimens of germ warfare. They had these bugs in this dish that was covered by a glass dome. They passed it around so everyone could look at these bugs. This one red-haired kid, who was a real rebel, lifted up the lid and popped one of the bugs in his mouth before they could stop him [laughs]. Man, they hustled him out of there. They said they sent him to the hospital. We didn't know where the hell he went, but they kept him away for about a week.

Then there was the fly-killing campaign. In early 1953 my buddy and I were in the exercise yard, and we're watching this Chinese guard. He was swatting flies. Well, we didn't pay too much attention because he was always doing crazy things. But the next day there is another guard doing the same damn thing. He was swatting flies, picking them up, and putting them into a little paper envelope. We asked the Chinese in charge, "Hey, what's going on?"

He said, "Well, we have a fly-killing campaign going on in China. We're going to make China the most fly-free country in all of Asia."

The Chinese do things like that. In fact, several years before that they had a starling-killing campaign. They killed all the starlings and then the bugs ate all their grain. So we asked, "Why is he saving the flies?"

He said, "Oh, he gets credit for how many flies he kills."

We asked, "What good are the credits?" In China everybody did certain kinds of work or read so many works of Mao to amass these credits. You would get credit for all kinds of things, and these credits helped you work toward getting a Mao Zedong Badge. So they were saving the flies to get credits. One of our guys asked, "Why can't we kill flies?" The Chinese in charge thought about it and said, "I'll let you know."

A couple of days later the Chinese made an announcement at one of the formations: "We understand that some of the prisoners desire to join our fly-killing campaign. Anybody can participate on a voluntary basis. And as an incentive for you to join our campaign we'll give you one factory-made Chinese cigarette for every two hundred flies. Anybody who wants to join the campaign raise their hands and we'll issue flyswatters." A whole bunch of people raised their hands and soon everybody was out swatting flies. They're all out by the slit trench of the damn latrine swatting flies. Some guys pooled their flies and turned them in when they got two hundred. They did get a cigarette so the Chinese were living up to their end of the deal. Some of us played poker for flies: "Hey, I'll call you three flies and raise you two." This one guy unraveled the yarn from a sock and fashioned a fly trap. The flies would fly in but then didn't know how to get out. He put it over the slit trench and the first day he caught over two hundred flies. I mean just like that he caught a whole mess of them. He turned them in and got his cigarettes. So the next thing you know everybody is trying to make a damn fly trap, but nobody is as good as this guy, and they don't work. This was the only time I almost got into a fight. I went out to the slit trench to do my business. There are six slots and a fly trap over everyone of them. So I picked one up and somebody yells, "Chikami, what the hell are you doing?"

I said, "What the hell does it look like I'm going to do?"

So he says, "Well, move somebody else's trap."

The Chinese nurses had the evening duty of counting these flies, but so many flies were being turned in they couldn't keep up. It was taking up too much time so the Chinese said, "Well, we can't continue this so we're going to find a different way. We're going to weigh them." They got a very fine scale to weigh the flies, but, of course, they cheated a little. It probably now took about three hundred flies to get one cigarette, but that's better than nothing. And we're still getting this mass production. This was strictly a capitalistic idea, and the Chinese hated that, but they couldn't do anything because they had made the deal. Sometimes the Chinese would forget to pick up the flies at night and get them in the morning. But by then the flies had dehydrated and didn't weigh nearly as much as they did the day before. So all the GIs were trying to figure out how to keep them fresh. They were putting in little pieces of damp cloth to keep in the humidity so the flies would weigh more. It got ridiculous. My old friend "Sake" Cameron was out there still swatting flies. He had a piece of old goat skin that he covered with excrement and it stunk. He got a little branch and was popping all these big green flies. He was an expert flyswatter. He could hit them and make them pop over dead without crushing them. I asked him, "Sake, how come you're still swatting flies?"

He says, "Come over to my place and I'll show you something." So I went over to his hut and he's got a little bench with all his little green flies on it. He had been on work detail and had found these old toothpaste tubes made of aluminum foil. He'd cut a little sliver of that aluminum foil and then pushed it up into the abdomen of the fly. Ten of his flies weighed more than two hundred normal flies. He'd mix them up a little bit. The Chinese could never figure out how come his flies weighed so much more than anybody else's. We did crazy things like this to produce a little entertainment and to break the boredom.

I know there was a lot of criticism of us prisoners after we were repatriated, but I think a lot of this negative reaction was because of the McCarthy era. I know Colonel Liles pretty well. In fact, I went to visit him last year and I stayed at his home. You're caught between a rock and a hard spot. He was the ranking man in Camp Twelve. Well, what do you do in order to get better food and better medical treatment for the men? You have to decide if you are going to make a broadcast but keep it toned down so you're not blatantly accusing the United States of something. You have to bargain. You're in a tough, no-win situation. No matter what you do there are going to be some POWs who are going to say you're rotten, that you're no damn good. Others will realize you're in a position where you have to decide how much you are willing to cooperate with the enemy to get food, shelter, and care for your men. Take my situation. I was in charge of just a small group. The Chinese gave me the supplies and cigarettes to divide among the guys. How do you divide everything equally right down to the last thing? Apples are not always the same size. Somebody is always going to be unhappy. There is just no way to satisfy everyone.

Gen. William Dean got the Medal of Honor for doing something he never should have. He was stalking a tank. What the hell is a general doing chasing a tank? He ought to be looking after his men. That to me was ridiculous. He also wrote a letter that was turned into propaganda, but he was never singled out. Some of the Air Force POWs wrote propaganda letters admitting to germ warfare and made speeches that were far more serious than anything Colonel Liles or Colonel Fleming did.

Colonel Liles is a humble man, and that thing ruined his whole career. It's sad because I don't think he did anything wrong. He was simply trying to save his men. Yet, there were other enlisted men who really hated him for no reason other than what they had heard. We were all victims of circumstance. Being captured is nothing to be proud of, but I'm not ashamed of it because I was wounded. Yet some of these guys get carried away and think they were really heroes. The real heroes are those who never came home.

When the Freedom of Information Act passed, I sent for my POW file. I couldn't believe what was in it. If I had known, I would not have stayed in the service. They kept investigating me after I got back even though I was still in the service. And it wasn't just me. I'm sure that almost all ex-prisoners of war were watched for at least three years. I didn't know this until I got my file, and I saw they had censored who I wrote to, and who I got letters from while I was in the service. There were accusations from some people I didn't even know. Some corporal reported that Chikami was a big, mean, son of a bitch in camp, and if you didn't agree with him, he would beat the hell out of you. Where did these guys get these ideas? He also said he saw Chikami sign a good conduct pass, and that I had given up because I thought the war was going to end, and that I didn't want to get hurt. The CIC sent two people up into the mountains of Tennessee with a court recorder to take down word for word what this guy said. That was the most ridiculous thing I ever heard. At that time my ex-company commander was still living so all they had to do was contact him. He saw me get shot, he was the one who left me behind. He was later awarded the Distinguished Service Cross, although we had lost over 50 percent of our company the day I was captured. My platoon sergeant at that time threw his rifle away and ran right by me, and he got a Silver Star. I can't say I lost all respect for medals because some were given to the right people, but there were so many that were given to the wrong people and for the wrong reasons.

The worst thing in my file was from a master sergeant I didn't even know. He said that in Camp Five I tried to give the impression of being anti-Communist, but that in my heart I actually leaned toward Communism. He reported he had seen me many a night in Chinese headquarters in ernest conversation with camp officials. The only time I went to headquarters at night was when they threw me into solitary because I wouldn't go to sleep. I couldn't believe these guys. One part of the report said, "Chikami should be notified that he is being investigated." But then another part stated, "No, we can't let him know because this is a national security matter." I was eventually cleared of all allegations, but to think that it even happened, and that all that money was spent investigating us.

2

"LET THEM MARCH TILL THEY DIE"—
THE TIGER DEATH MARCH
AND BEYOND

The pitiful sight of those hopeless men, younger than I, lying by the side of the road awaiting their own execution took away all feeling of fatigue, hunger, and cold. . . . One young man, as his last earthly act, was singing "God Bless America" as loudly as his weak cracking voice was able. Tears were streaming down his face as we marched past. There were tears on our faces as well. I was staggered by feelings of hopelessness and grief.

—Larry Zellers, civilian prisoner and
Tiger Death March survivor

I wasn't going to let no seventy-year-old nun outwalk me. No, that wasn't going to happen.

—Irv Langell, Tiger Death March survivor

On Halloween 1950, some 845 North Korean-held prisoners, including approximately eighty noncombatants,[1] left Manpo, North Korea, on what would become one of the deadliest movements of prisoners during the Korean War, perhaps even in history. Called the Tiger Death March, after the brutal North Korean colonel who was in charge of the prisoners, it lasted only nine days, ending on November 8 on the Yalu River at Chunggang, approximately one hundred miles to the northeast. Its deadly effects lasted much longer; in fact, twelve months later, fewer than three hundred of the marchers were still alive, a fatality rate of approximately 65 percent.[2]

Prisoner death marches were certainly nothing new in war. After all, captured foot soldiers must be removed quickly from the frontlines, and often under extremely traumatic conditions. The most infamous such march was arguably the Japanese-orchestrated Bataan Death March, with its 40 percent fatality rate.[3] Less well known were the long marches the Germans forced on their prisoners near the end of the Second World War when Allied forces tightened their vise on the Third Reich. However, as has been true of the entire Forgotten War, the death marches in Korea are the least known of all marches involving American prisoners. There were many such marches in Korea, some lasting weeks, even months, before the men reached the permanent camps along or near the Yalu River, and all cost the lives of countless American and other United Nations prisoners.

The soldiers whose stories appear below were captured in July 1950 during the first days of the war. For some four months they had been starved, mistreated, hit by friendly fire, stricken by diseases, and moved northward under extremely adverse conditions. They had witnessed the deaths of many of their fellow prisoners, including some who had been executed by their captors. Their physical condition and morale had badly deteriorated when they were loaded on a train in the North Korean capital of P'yŏngyang on September 5, 1950, to be moved to Manpo where the Tiger Death March would begin seven weeks later.

P'yŏngyang was the gathering point for both soldier and civilian prisoners who had been picked up throughout South Korea during the preceding two months. The civilians represented more than a dozen countries and included diplomats, missionaries, teachers, and businessmen. They ranged from infants to seniors in their seventies and eighties. They too had been picked up almost immediately after the North Korean invasion and then transported to P'yŏngyang, where several of them were put in death cells. They had also suffered mistreatment and hunger, although their ensuing death rate would be considerably lower than that of the soldiers.

There was an increasing note of urgency among the North Korean captors in P'yŏngyang. American forces had made their successful landing at Inch'ŏn on September 15, 1950, and United Nations troops had also successfully turned the tide in the south. By October 9, their combined forces had pushed the North Koreans back over the 38th Parallel. Rather than losing their prisoners, the North Koreans were now determined to move them as quickly as possible to their northern border along the Yalu River.

CAPTURED!

Historically, prisoners are particularly vulnerable immediately after their capture, and such was certainly the case in Korea. Many of the men were disoriented and half expected to be shot, as had been a number of those captured. Albert Biderman concludes that 1,036 American POWs were killed in what he calls "battlefield atrocities," and "hundreds more were killed weeks after being captured," especially during the rapid advance of U.N. forces in the fall of 1950.[4] Most newly captured men suffered from a lack of sleep, food, and water incurred during the fierce days of fighting that preceded their capture. Some were wounded. All had inadequate clothing and footwear, especially when forced later to march in temperatures that plummeted far below zero. Some were also bitter because they had been forced to fight with insufficient ammunition and obsolete or inoperative weapons while being overrun by Russian-made T-34 tanks. Confusion, chaos, and poor leadership were endemic during the early weeks of the war. These were devastated men facing an uncertain future, with no assurance they would survive. The experiences of infantryman Irv Langell were typical:[5]

We were the very first troops to land in Korea when we arrived on July 4, 1950.[6] We were three undermanned companies with obsolete weapons. We had World War II M-1 rifles whose barrels were so pitted and scarred that the bullets would twist all around when they came out. Everything was so loose that those rifles were always falling apart. As I recall, we did have three new sniper rifles, and those were the only new rifles we had. We also had 2.36 grenade launchers, which were like pea-shooters against the T-34 tanks we ran into.

When we were sent up to the frontlines on July 9 or 10, we were told that only every sixth or seventh Korean had a weapon. We were also told that there were no tanks or heavy weapons, and that the North Koreans were a ragtag Army. Well, I beg to differ! Two of our companies were being overrun so we made a counterattack and got them out. Then we retreated back to our defensive position. The North Koreans hit us the next morning. I learned later we'd been surrounded for a couple of days and didn't know it. They hit us with supposedly 5,000 troops, but it seemed like there were 50 million. They just overran my company, which only had about 160 or 170 men. We ran out of ammunition and fell into a kind of, well, "retreat." "A strategic withdrawal" is what they called it. Covering your ass was more like it. We got back the Kum River, and that's where they just came from everywhere. What could we do? There were probably a dozen of us in my group, and we were sitting there with no ammunition. So they came and got us. What the hell, you can't do nothing. We were among the first prisoners, and we were kept by the North Koreans for fifteen months before being turned over to the Chinese in October 1951.

Just before I was captured, I got shot in the leg. I never got a chance to look at it for probably a week, until it smelled so bad you couldn't miss it. My leg swelled up and had a dark, hard-cased, stinky scab on it. I couldn't stand it so we conned one of the so-called North Korean medics out of some cotton, alcohol, and a pair of tweezers. I just grabbed where I was wounded and gave it one hell of a squeeze and all that pus and everything just shot out. Then I poured the alcohol on it and scrapped until blood was gone. I just kept pouring alcohol on it. It took probably three months before the last scab come off, but that's what saved my leg. By the time the Tiger Death March began at the end of October, it was better, and I could walk.

Nineteen-year-old Wilbert "Shorty" Estabrook was also part of the first wave of Americans to hit Korea. He had been living the good life in Japan and was certainly surprised to discover that real war was decidedly different than he expected:

When we arrived in Korea we had no idea we were going to fight. We were just going to go over there, march up and down, shoot our guns in the air, and that would be the end of it. We expected to be back in Japan in a couple of weeks. Then the North Koreans began fighting a dirty war by shooting back at us. I began thinking, "Hey, this thing is for real. A man could get hurt." You get this fear inside you that makes you shake all over. I've never been that scared in my entire life.

I was captured on July 16, 1950. I had run into a group of what looked like South Korean soldiers, but they were actually North Koreans in South Korean uniforms. They began shooting at me and I was yelling, "Hey, I'm an American." I was with two other Americans. I didn't know so we had to make a decision. Were we going to throw rocks at them? One guy had one round, I had my weapon but no ammunition, and the other guy had no weapon. My brain told me the only real option was to surrender. If we stayed in the hole where we were, they would throw in a grenade and we'd all be dead. So we raised a white handkerchief, and came up out of our hole. This little kid—he couldn't have been much more than thirteen—started beating the hell out of me with his submachine gun, what we called a burp gun. There were lots of insults and yelling that we didn't understand. I thought this was the end. We had all heard stories of Oriental torture, and I had already seen prisoners who had been shot with their hands tied behind them with communications wire. The death part of it didn't seem to bother me that much. In fact, I kind of hoped for that rather than prolonged torture.

I am now convinced that the group who captured us had a mission to collect POWs. If that had not been the case, I don't think I would be here today. When they moved us back through the lines, they protected us from the frontline soldiers. They were always the most dangerous. Maybe one of those guys had just lost his brother the day before or maybe he had just learned that his hometown had just been obliterated by a bomb. So people on the frontlines had a right to be pissed off. Once we got back to the soldiers who had not yet seen combat, we were more of a curiosity. Occasionally they would spit at or kick us, but there was no great desire to kill us.

Jack Browning's experience on the frontlines were similar to Langell and Estabrook's, although after he was captured he was one of the few to experience an act of kindness:

I was stationed in Japan for fourteen months before the Korean War began and I became one of General MacArthur's sacrificial lambs. The first Americans to land in Korea were with Task Force Smith on July 1, 1950. We landed the next day. On the morning of July 3, we loaded our equipment and ourselves on a train. On the way to the frontlines, we passed several trains going south, filled with South Korean civilians and soldiers hanging over the sides and top of the cars. The soldiers were bloody and all bandaged up. When we got to our destination, we jumped off into pouring rain and mud. We were standing under the eave of this old house, and we could hear the artillery rumbling in the distance. Then, I spotted this body lying on the side of this hill, kind of slumped around a small tree, and I thought, "What have I got myself into?" That's when it dawned on me, "People are getting shot and killed here." It would be a slaughter for us first guys over there. Only fourteen or fifteen guys out of my company made it, and five of them were POWs.[7]

We moved out to this little town called Ch'onan. We were just kids. None of us, except the platoon sergeants, who were World War II veterans, had any combat experience. We had nothing but M-1 rifles and carbines. Oh, we also had some bazookas, but the ammunition was either practice duds or wouldn't fire. From the edge of town, we could see the North Koreans coming across a little hill about three hundred yards away. They looked like ants crawling up and over an anthill. . . .

After we were captured, they took us out into the street and a few feet away there was a dead GI lying there. Their spokesman pointed at him and said, "Amerikanski?"[8] We nodded our heads. That's the first time I ever heard the word "Amerikanski." One of their young soldiers, he didn't look like he was as old as I was, reached into his pocket and pulled out a ripe tomato. He offered it to me and said, "Eat." So I obliged him and started eating. After taking the first bite, I started feeling dizzy. The first thing that came to my mind was, "I've been poisoned." I almost passed out, but just before I lost consciousness I started coming back around. I imagine if I would have fainted they would have finished me off, but I finished eating the tomato and it was really good. They then called for a jeep and we headed north. The date was July 8. I had been in Korea for just six days.

MOVING NORTH

Langell, Estabrook, Browning, and the rest of the American soldiers who were captured in the first days of the war would spend two torturous months moving slowly northward before eventually arriving in the North Korean capital of P'yŏngyang where they would join a large group of civilian prisoners in early September. By then hunger, thirst, mistreatment, disease, and being strafed and bombed by their own planes had ravaged their physical and mental well-being. In an unpublished memoir, Jack Browning reduced these harrowing weeks to just a few pages, but the pain has remained with him for a half century:

The jeep took Rogers and me several miles north. In the middle of nowhere we stopped and got out. I couldn't see anything. I thought they were going to get rid of us. But they took us between a couple of hills where we could see a house that gave us a little hope we might see another day. The guards sat us down on the ground and in a few minutes they gave us a small bowl of rice and motioned for us to eat. We hadn't eaten all day and we were hungry. I took my first bite of that unseasoned rice, and I thought it was the most horrible thing I had ever tasted. At home, I was used to eating sweetened rice with butter and milk. But I finally got that first bite down. I thought if I didn't eat it, it might be a long time before I got anything else. Sure enough, it was three days before we got anything else to eat.

They bound our hands and feet behind us with communications

wire and told us to lie down, which didn't make for a very comfortable night. The next morning they got us up early and took us several miles farther north. We came to a house with a well in the front yard. Our guard drew a bucket of water and filled a large gourd dipper. He took a drink and held the dipper for me and then Rogers. We then walked a considerable distance and felt the urge to urinate. The guard stopped us and unzipped our trousers and took out our penises, and we made water. He then put us back together, and we were on our way.

We came to a small village and were told to sit on a split-log bench. A soldier soon came by, looked at us, and drew out a forty-five pistol and put it to Rogers's head. In broken English he asked, "You believe in God?" We both shook our heads yes. He pulled the trigger, but it just clicked, and he walked off laughing, as if to say, "Where is your God now?" Little did he know, God was there.

They eventually took us to Seoul where we crossed the Han River on a barge. It was hot and we hadn't had any food or water for quite a while. There was all kinds of debris floating down the river, including dead humans and animals. It had also rained and washed human waste into the river, which the Koreans used to fertilizer their fields. Some of the men reached over the side of the barge and drank that filthy water. The result was dysentery and other diseases, but when you are so thirsty, you take chances, even if it kills you.

Crossing the Han River was also dangerous because of our own planes. Some of those pilots would hit anything that moved. If we had been spotted in middle of that river, there would have been sad singing and slow walking for a lot of us. Earlier a fighter plane had come over and strafed the building we were in, killing one of the prisoners.

I don't remember exactly how long we stayed in Seoul, but more POWs joined us there. We then left and started walking north until we finally got to P'yŏngyang. I remember passing ox carts filled with corpses stacked like cordwood. In P'yŏngyang the guards paraded us through the city to show their people what great things they had done. We finally got to an old two-story school building where they packed us in so tightly you could never get comfortable. The guards brought in a bucket of water. Each of us was supposed to take a few swallows and pass it on, but there was one man who wouldn't let it go. A short time later he got such bad cramps he died.

We also got our first food in days, if you call food a few heads of Chinese cabbage dumped into fifty gallons of water. Any protein came from the flies that floated on top. When I looked down at my soup, I spotted four or five flies floating on top. I called Sergeant Knowles to come over and showed him the flies. He picked up my spoon, dipped them out, and said, "Now, there's no flies in your soup." I got the message and ate the soup.

We saw what was probably the first bombs fall on P'yŏngyang. When we heard those bombs screaming down, I don't mind telling anyone I was scared. It sounded like those bombs were coming right at us, but the target was some nearby buildings. We did have broken windows and falling plaster, but the best thing was a big picture of North Korean President Kim II Sung, which fell off the wall in our room and broke into pieces. We really got a kick out of that.

We stayed in P'yŏngyang for several weeks before again moving north. They packed us in railroad cars so tightly we had to stand. The first day the guards got us off the train and moved us into a wooded area on the side of a mountain. Almost immediately one of our planes came over the mountain and strafed that train up one side and down the other. Two men died, although I'm not sure if it was because of previous wounds or if they got hit by the plane. I remember the men being laid in a very shallow grave and thinking, "No one will ever know where those men are buried." When someone died, the guards wouldn't let us mark the graves. They also had taken our dog tags. I guess they didn't want our government to know they had us. That's why there are 8,177 men still unaccounted for from the Korean War.

We again walked after we left P'yŏngyang. By this time it was October and the weather was getting cold. This one day my ear started aching, and it got worse and worse. After a couple of days my head was really hurting. I don't know who came up with the idea, but somebody said a few drops of urine was good for an ear infection. I was hurting so badly that I was willing to try anything. One of the men put a few drops of my urine in my ear. A short time later we were climbing this mountain, and I felt a sudden relief. The ear had erupted and bloody pus came running down the side of my face. It had to be the urine that did it.[9]

Jack Browning could scarcely know how bedraggled he and his fellow POWs looked after their many weeks on the road, but others noticed. It was at the P'yŏngyang train station on September 5, 1950, that captured missionary Larry Zellers first sighted Browning and the rest of the American POWs getting ready to board the train for Manpo:

I tried to look out a window from my crowded position to see what was going on. Long lines of haggard-looking young American soldiers were marching past my window to board the coaches in front of ours. I couldn't believe what I was seeing. These ragged, dirty, hollow-eyed men did not look like any American soldiers that I had ever seen! I had worn that same uniform until five years before, but I could hardly recognize it on the men walking along that railway platform in front of me. The North Koreans had provided no special consideration for the wounded. Some of the more badly injured prisoners were half-carried by companions; others limped along as best they could. Communist guards walked alongside and behind the POWs but made no attempt to assist in any way. We were all so stunned that we watched in silence.[10]

Philip Deane, who had been working as a war correspondent for the *London Observer* when captured, also caught his first view of the American POWs that same day:

After squatting in the rain for an hour we boarded a train, which was in complete darkness and seemed to be full of Americans: Brooklynese, Texas drawls, and the soft accents of New England mingled in voicing imprecations about the guards. The train rolled intermittently through the night. In the morning we left it and walked up the nearby hills to take shelter from United Nations planes.

Here we got our first glimpse of our American prisoner companions. They were indescribably dirty. They said they had not washed since their capture . . . and were crawling with lice. A large proportion of them had no shoes. They wore light-weight summer fatigues. They were traveling packed tight in open coal cars. Some had been given old cotton quilts, but even they were bitterly cold during the journey through the North Korean September days.

Then the sick appeared. Thinner even than their "healthy" companions, they walked like figures in a slow-motion film, helped along by their own medical orderlies and by Korean nurses. They were given medical treatment during the day and some extra food, which most of them could not keep down.[11]

Captured Australian missionary Father Philip Crosbie had much the same reaction when he spotted the American prisoners marching toward the P'yŏngyang train station:

On and on they came. We were touched with sadness, even with anguish, at the sight of these young men filing wearily along, some barefooted, most bare-headed, all in light summer uniforms. . . . Some had acquired Korean quilted blankets, and wore them like shawls. It reminds me how intently we must have studied every detail, when I find I can still see in my mind's eye even the bulges at the lower edges of those quilts, where the cotton stuffing gathered as the wearers moved along. I can still picture, too, the unwashed, unshaven faces, so many of them emaciated and strained.[12]

A few days later, when the train stopped for the night, Larry Zellers was again moved by the forlorn appearance of the American POWs:

Shortly after we arrived at our hillside location for the day, we looked back at the train and saw the figures of American soldiers moving in our direction. It was not a pretty sight. They moved as though in slow motion, probably because of their bad treatment. We soon found out that they were members of Task Force Smith and other units of the 24th Infantry Division of the U.S. Army who had been stationed in Japan before the Korean War broke out. The senior ranking officer was Major John J. Dunn of Rome, New York, a member of the 34th Regiment. . . . Later we learned that the POWs numbered 726 when they left P'yŏngyang in the fall of 1950. Another thirty prisoners joined them later in the year. When we last saw them on October 10, 1951— more than twelve months later—their numbers had dwindled to 292, a number easy for me to remember because my address in Kaesŏng had been 292 Man Wul Dong.[13]

Shorty Estabrook was one of those bedraggled GIs whose appearance so shocked Deane, Crosbie, and Zellers in the P'yŏngyang train station:

We moved on to Seoul and then from there to P'yŏngyang, the capital of North Korea. We had done a lot of walking, although occasionally they loaded us on these open train cars. It was on a coal car when I got wounded for the second time. I guess I didn't climb into the car fast enough, and this guard hit me with his rifle butt and opened up my skull like it was a cracked peanut. To this day, I still suffer severe migraine headaches.

By this time everybody was in dire straights because of diarrhea, worms, lice, parasites, night blindness, and all that stuff. We suffered much of this because when you're so thirsty, you don't care how bad the water is; you just drink it. So we drank from highly polluted and toxic sources, especially rice paddies that had been fertilized with human waste. If we had had decent water, many of us would have survived, but if we had not even had the bad water, we would all have died.

Unlike many of the soldiers, noncombatant Larry Zellers had not been wounded or weakened in battle. Nevertheless, he and five other civilians suffered their own crucible in the weeks between their capture in Kaesŏng on June 29 and the beginning of the Tiger Death March four months later.[14] Zellers describes his personal humiliation that began in a local jail his first night of captivity:

They started right out being as aggressive and insulting as they could. As I found out later, like all Communist officials, they want you to accept their worldview from day one. For example, they insisted this little skirmish that caused the North Koreans to move in and capture Kaesŏng was really started by the South Koreans. You couldn't argue with them. This just went on and on and on. They were playing with us.

They put us in a dungeon, removed our rings and watches and fountain pens, the whole bit, and kept us there for two nights. Each night we were interrogated. We didn't get anything to eat, just a little water. There were about fifty of us in a room about thirty by thirty, just sitting on the floor. We had half a fifty-five-gallon drum for a toilet, but it filled up and ran over, so we had to keep moving away from it to keep dry.

On the morning of July 1, we were taken out and allowed to wash our hands and eat a bowl of rice. Then they said, "We're sending you to P'yŏngyang." We figured that meant they would be sending us home. We took off in a weapons carrier with about fifteen or twenty people jammed in. There was a wooden bench on each side, and I had a guard sitting on my left with a submachine gun with the muzzle pushed right into my ribs. We arrived pretty close to nightfall, and they interrogated us again, but did not feed us. Then they put us behind steel doors in death cells. They made us remove our shoestrings, belts, ties, and anything we might use to kill ourselves.

As Larry Zellers sat in his death cell in P'yŏngyang, he knew that other prisoners were being executed, but he knew nothing of who they were or when it might be his turn. He had reason to worry. A misplaced rifle and some spent ammunition found in his house in Kaesŏng left him vulnerable to North Korean accusations that he was a spy rather than a missionary teacher:

> We heard groups of shots throughout that day and each day during our incarceration in the death cell. It was common practice for men to be hauled out of their cells at any time of the day or night. Unless you have heard the hobnailed boots stop at your cell door and the guard call out your name to lead you away, you can't imagine the terror that accompanies such a call. Some were taken out for interrogation and were later brought back. Others never returned. . . .
>
> I didn't know what to say to my two interrogators. Several times I tried to formulate some reply to their preposterous charges. Nothing I could think of seemed adequate, and I was afraid that anything I might say would only make matters worse. I have no idea how long their harangue lasted. The extreme fatigue from lack of sleep and the stress caused by the uncertainty of my fate were beginning to take their toll. The interrogation continued until the early morning hours, but I could never develop a strategy to counter their line of attack. They always had the advantage and most of the time were skillful enough to use it. I was too tired to do any more than answer their questions. . . .
>
> Somehow during that night . . . I made my peace with God and with death. My conviction was that everything would be all right, no matter what happened. It was my first victory in that prison. . . . In fact, I concluded that death might become a welcome friend under conditions of extreme torture. I didn't worry anymore about dying, but I did worry about what I might have to endure before my death. My execution: would it be painful? I was in the hands of people who had the mind-set to make it painful if they chose.[15]

After two weeks in his death cell, Zellers was moved to a schoolhouse just outside of P'yŏngyang where he met Father Philip Crosbie and another large group of civilian prisoners. Crosbie had been taken prisoner while at his parish in Hongch'ŏn, then moved north to Ch'unch'ŏn where in mid-July he became the first American to meet the man who some ten weeks later would be dubbed "The Tiger." At the time, The Tiger simply referred to himself as the "Governor of the Ch'unch'ŏn Penitentiary" but his words had a chilling effect on the young priest:

> He was dressed in a white uniform and had a pistol strapped to his hip. He made the usual inquiries and then told me that the Reds would soon control the whole country, and that I and all the other foreigners would be sent home. . . . We discussed Communism, and I told him I objected to its unjust and ruthless methods.
>
> "We don't kill good people," he said, "only the bad." Then after a pause, "Have you ever seen a man die?"
>
> "Yes."
>
> "Have you ever seen a man shot?"
>
> "No."
>
> "I have," he said, and his hand touched the pistol at his side. A few months later I was to have the opportunity of seeing a man shot—and shot by that same hand and that same pistol. When the time came I would forgo my opportunity, forced by horror and revulsion to avert my eyes. An innocent American officer would be murdered in cold blood by the man who stood before me now.[16]

After his initial meeting with The Tiger, Crosbie's captors moved him to Seoul and then, on July 19, to just outside of P'yŏngyang where he and the other assembled civilians remained until September 5. They were then joined by the POWs at the train station and spent the next five days on the train before arriving in Manpo. In Manpo the civilians were put in a quarantine station, which had previously been used for immigrants coming in from Manchuria. The GIs camped out on the Yalu River. On October 7, everyone once again moved out, this time downriver to Kosan. Two weeks later they walked some twelve miles to the south of Jui-am-nee. The GIs left Jui-am-nee on October 26, marching back in the direction of Kosan. The civilians departed the next morning. Both groups ended up on October 30 just south of Manpo in an area the GIs dubbed the Cornfield. It was the day before the start of the Death March, and for the first time since they met at the Ch'unch'ŏn Penitentiary in mid-July, Father Crosbie once again saw The Tiger:

> The Tiger wore knee breeches and a tight-fitting jacket that gave him a lithe appearance. He was tall for a Korean, slim, quick, and nervous in his movements. When he walked he leaned forward a little. His

features were regular, but protruding teeth gave him a perpetual grim-
ace. His bright eyes were keen and restless. His age we could not
guess.[17]

The next day, when Jack Browning got his first view of The Tiger, he
realized that life was going to get even worse for himself and his fellow
prisoners:

> The new man was a major who was a little taller than the average
> Korean, but little did we know we now had a crazy man in charge of
> us. Before we started marching, he told us, "The ones too weak to go
> can stay here and be put in the People's Hospital." Well, it didn't take
> no Einstein to figure what the People's Hospital was. We'd already
> heard and seen too much, but Ray Rogers was getting weak with dys-
> entery and he decided he would stay.
> I told him, "Man, don't stay. I will help you."
> He said, "No, I want to just stay here. I would be nothing but a
> burden on the other men."
> I never again saw him or the other thirteen or fourteen who decided
> to remain behind.

Pfc. Wayne "Johnnie" Johnson also knew their situation was desperate.
Although he did not consider The Tiger to be insane, he quickly recognized that he had no respect for human life:

> I thought he was going to shoot everybody. I felt he wouldn't have
> hesitated. Before we left the Cornfield to start the march, he had us
> lined up against this rock cliff with machine guns set up in a crossfire.
> We pretty much thought that was the end of us right there. We could
> hear artillery rounds; that's how close our own troops were to us. They
> must have been within twenty or thirty miles of us. I think he had
> orders to keep us at any cost from being liberated, and that's why he
> was planning to execute all of us; instead, we started on the Death
> March going up through the mountains farther to the north.

No one ever learned The Tiger's real name, but after observing the first
of his many atrocities, one of the prisoners simply labeled him "The Tiger,"
and so he is known to this day by the survivors of his deadly march.

OCTOBER 31, 1950—THE DEATH MARCH BEGINS

On October 31, 1950, The Tiger stood up to speak before his assembled prisoners. Using captured English Salvation Army Commissioner Herbert Lord as his translator, he warned that the march would be long and difficult and that no one would be allowed to fall out:

> We are going on a long march. I am in command, and I have the authority to make you obey. From now on, you will be under military orders. . . . Everyone must march. No one must be left behind. You must discard at once anything that can be used as a weapon. After all, you are my enemy, and I must consider that you might try to do me harm.[18]

When The Tiger announced that the march would cover sixteen miles that first evening, Commissioner Lord warned him that many of the elderly civilians could not survive such a distance. The Tiger contemptuously responded, "Let them march till they die!"

The Tiger then moved down the line of civilians. He approached Father Paul Villemot, an eighty-two-year-old French priest who was leaning on his cane. He knocked away Villemot's cane with his swagger stick, saying, "Throw that away. That is a weapon." When he came to Larry Zellers he pointed to the rolled-up straw sleeping mat on his shoulder and repeated, "That can be used as a weapon. Throw it away."[19]

When the march did not begin promptly that ill-fated Halloween, Father Crosbie concluded that The Tiger was more determined than ever to show the prisoners he meant business:

> I evolved a theory that The Tiger had worked out a schedule for the march, and had decided on specific places for our overnight stops; that our late start, and this delay near Manpo, upset his schedule; that the upsetting of his plans enraged him, so that he drove us mercilessly on in an attempt to catch up with his schedule; and that his failure drove him to greater fury, and blinded him to any regard for health or even life. . . . *Bali, bali!* (Move quickly) became the dominant feature of our journey that first evening, and all the days that followed. And it was this inhuman driving more than any other cause that made our march a march of death. Most of those who died were killed by

the gruelling pace. The length of the journey, the lack of sleep, the bad and inadequate food were all contributing causes; but many, perhaps all, could have endured these hardships if they had not been continually hurried along during the hours given to travel. . . . This merciless pressure was especially weakening for the many who were suffering from severe dysentery, which seemed to be rife among the POWs. It was pitiful to see poor, emaciated lads who had fallen out, trying to regain their places in the lines, stumbling hurriedly and unsteadily along with a guard at their heels.[20]

Larry Zellers suggests another possibility why The Tiger was so uncompromisingly cruel:

In September or October 1950 General Shih-lun Sung issued an edict that anyone caught not doing his duty, wherever he was and whatever the rank, could be shot on the spot by anyone else. A private could see a major not doing his job and he could shoot him. He had also ordered that no prisoners were to be retaken by our side. Apparently that order was followed. The only ones who really got out were those in the Sunch'ŏn Tunnel Massacre who faked death. Some of those guys were rescued. I thank God we didn't know about that massacre. We didn't know they would do that.[21]

Shorty Estabrook suggested one reason the civilian prisoners had to move out of Manpo was because Chinese soldiers had moved in and taken over everything. Even before the Tiger Death March actually began, the GIs were living in the open just south of town in an area Shorty called the Cornfield where it was already so cold "we had to hollow out a place in the dirt as best we could and then lie side by side to share our body warmth." It was here, says Shorty, that The Tiger took over.

It was already night when the prisoners moved out of Manpo on the road traveling east. After a short time, they circled back and again marched through Manpo. They certainly did not make the sixteen miles The Tiger demanded, stopping after six or seven miles where they spent the night in the open. Larry Zellers describes the first day:

We left on the march very late in the afternoon. I'm not making this up, but it was Halloween eve, October 31. We marched through Manpo. If you read General Dean's autobiography, he spoke of being in Manpo and looking out one day and seeing a group of staggering prisoners. He knew from the distance that they were Americans. He said he saw them only for an instant but that was our group.[22]

We did not mix with the soldiers during the march, but we did at night. They would put a perimeter guard around us. The whole idea of us escaping out of that thing was so remote that I think even they didn't believe we could get away. The soldiers were in the front, and this is where The Tiger did most of his marching up and down and haranguing them to move faster. No matter how fast we marched, it was never fast enough for him. I suspect he thought, and indeed they were quite close, that the American soldiers would take this area, and he wanted to get out of the way before they arrived.

During the march, first came the soldiers. Then came the South Korean politicians. There were, I believe, seven of them. They never got out. They were followed by the diplomats, the British minister and the French consul. Someone asked if the diplomats were given special consideration because they were diplomats. I said, "Well, they were allowed to march in a group by themselves." The rest of us brought up the rear, including the older people. It wouldn't have been so difficult except for the fast pace. We tried to assist some of them. That first day we were not allowed even to bury the dead. That didn't present us with any problem in the civilian group because not one of us at that point was near death, but the GIs ran into that problem.

At first the guards were making sport of the weaker POWs. They took turns kicking the stragglers in the rear, laughing and jumping up and down as they did so. They were not yet using their rifle butts to beat the prisoners over the head; that would come later when this first game was no longer considered fun.

When you begin a trip you're supposed to start in the morning, but we had started almost at nightfall. We marched until about midnight, covering perhaps six miles; then The Tiger ordered us to stop in an open field where we tried to sleep until morning. The snow was falling when we started marching but it never built up. Real snow came later, but during the night it got very cold, and when you don't have proper food and you're cold already, it goes right through you. For warmth, people huddled together on the cold, wet ground, praying for the morning to come. I did not try to sleep that first night, though moving around to try to stay warm was not permitted.[23]

NOVEMBER 1—DAY TWO

After that sleepless and frigid first night and a tasteless morning meal of boiled corn, The Tiger, whose mood had only worsened because of the previous day's delay, ordered the prisoners to begin marching at a faster pace. When Philip Deane noticed the naked bodies of several GIs that morning, he asked what had happened to their clothes: "I was told," he later wrote, "while they were dying, some of the others wanted them."[24] Deane also provided a vivid picture of the civilian and GI prisoners as they began the second day of the march:

> The eighty-two-year-old French missionary [Father Villemot] was being carried by Monsignor Thomas Quinlan. Miss Nellie Dyer, an American Methodist missionary, was carrying Sister Mary Clare, an Anglican nun, in her arms. Father Charles Hunt, the Anglican missionary, suffering from gout, was being dragged along by his companions. Commissioner Lord, the column's official interpreter, had tied a rope around the waist of Mme. Funderat, a seventy-year-old White Russian, and was pulling her along. Two White Russian women walked with crying, cold, hungry babies on their backs, holding their other young children by the hand. The children who were not being carried had to trot because the pace was too quick for their gait. Two Carmelite nuns were coughing up blood. They were shod in rough wooden sandals they had made themselves. Norman Owen, procounsel at the British Legation, Seoul, had as his only footwear Father Hunt's chasuble, divided in two with a half for each foot. The septuagenarian French fathers, obliged to stop because of their dysentery, were egged on by the guards, who fired off their rifles near the old men's ears.
>
> Ahead, the GIs, still in summer fatigues, a large proportion with no shoes, marched in a long, straggly column of threes; soon many were being carried. Frequently the exhausted carriers would drop their charges and we would pass creatures, hard to recognize as human, prostrate on the road. During the morning of November 1, too many dropped out. The Tiger called the American platoon commanders together. Speaking through Commissioner Lord, he said, "No one must drop out. I order you not to allow anyone to drop out." He pulled down his epaulette. "I have authority to make you obey. If you do not,

I will punish you with the extreme penalty of military discipline. Even the dead must be carried."[25]

The Tiger ordered the prisoners assigned to groups, whose leaders he held responsible for everyone keeping up. When the lines nevertheless lengthened and more stragglers began to drop out, a furious Tiger called a halt and angrily ordered the group leaders to his side. Jack Browning describes the scene and the resultant execution of Lt. Cordus H. Thornton:

The morning of November 1, The Tiger made a little speech translated by Commissioner Lord. He said, "Everybody stays together no falling behind." At that time there were about eight hundred of us, and we hadn't yet lost many men. We took off about daybreak that morning, and it was The Tiger's job to see that we made our destination one way or the other, and he was going to make it easy on himself. We walked about a half a day, when The Tiger gathered up the American officers. He wanted to know whose men were falling behind, but no-body stepped forward. Then, real angrily, he said, "I'll kill you all." Lieutenant Thornton from Texas was singled out because more of his men had fallen out. The Tiger blindfolded him, but Thornton chose not to have a blindfold. He was wearing an old cap he had picked up somewhere. The Tiger put him down on his knees and raised the muzzle of his gun, which was a funny-looking old nine millimeter with a round handle. He then stood back a couple of feet and shot him in the back of the head.

Larry Zellers, who averted his eyes during the actual shooting of Lieutenant Thornton, could never forget the grisly details surrounding the execution and the effect it had on the prisoners:

The Tiger moved smartly to face the victim and ordered him to turn around. Pausing for a moment, the Tiger pushed up the back of Thornton's cap and put his pistol against the back of Thornton's head. I noticed right in front of me a little Turkish girl who was probably fifteen or sixteen. She was sobbing softly to herself. Some people were averting their eyes. I kept looking, at least I had my face turned in that direction, but when I knew the gun was going to fire, I shut my eyes for a brief two or three seconds until it was over.

When I opened my eyes, I saw that the brave young man lay still without even a tremor. The Tiger knew his business well. Quickly putting away his pistol, The Tiger called for Commissioner Lord to come to his side and translate for him. "You have just witnessed the execution of a bad man. This move will help us to work together better in peace and harmony."

The Tiger waited for a few minutes for the impact of his words to sink in before ordering, "Bury him!" It was an order given to no one in particular, and for a few horrifying moments it seemed that no one moved or spoke a word. Out of nowhere a tall blond sergeant appeared, moved down the steep slope to a level place about fifteen feet below the road, and began to dig away the stones with his bare hands. When someone threw a shovel down, Sgt. Henry Leerkamp began to dig a grave with it. The Tiger stood on the knoll by the side of the road, watching but not saying a word. The digging was very difficult in the hard and stony ground, and finally the sergeant looked up and asked, "Won't some of you come down and help me?"

The calm appeal for aid by this one brave man in the midst of horror spurred the others into action. Immediately, several people moved forward to assist. They finished the shallow grave, laid the body of the victim in it, and piled large stones on top.[26]

According to Zellers, The Tiger then ordered that all dog tags be turned over to his guards to make it more difficult to identify bodies. He also forced Commissioner Lord to sign a paper certifying that those who dropped out, including Lieutenant Thornton, had died of heart failure. That done, The Tiger ordered the prisoners to resume marching, although, says Zellers, "This time the guards were not playing their innocent little game of kicking the stragglers in the rear as they had done the day before. They were now using their rifle butts as clubs to drive the GIs like cattle."

Father Crosbie also noticed the increasingly impossible conditions of the march:

We kept on hour after hour, knowing that it would be inviting further tragedy to allow anyone to fall out now. . . . Our own plight was bad enough, but it was evident that the POWs were in a worse state. Again and again we heard the shout going up along the line: "Send back more strong men." As with us, the weak who could still walk were being supported by their comrades. But already many of the POWs were unable to walk at all; they had to be carried bodily. But the pace was so gruelling, and pauses for rest so infrequent, that even a team of

four could not carry a man for more than ten or fifteen minutes without relief. As each hour passed there were more and more men to be
carried, and the number of those fit to carry them was steadily reduced. If The Tiger continued to force this pace, it was only a matter
of time until it would be physically impossible to obey his orders that
no one fall behind. What then?[27]

By the end of the second day, the prisoners had covered more than
fifteen miles.[28] When they finally stopped to rest, a cold wind had come
up, and the prisoners had to huddle together on the cold ground trying
to keep warm. For the second consecutive night Zellers could not sleep:

Because we had all been captured in the summertime, no one was
dressed for the cold. In an effort to stay warm, several of us followed
the example of the Russian prisoners in stuffing our clothes with straw
and tying a rope around our pant legs at the ankles. Throughout the
period of the Death March and until January of the next year, I wore
only a pair of seersucker slacks, a shirt, and a lightweight coat given to
me by the Koreans at Jui-am-nee. The American military prisoners were
equally ill prepared for the cold with their fatigues and lightweight
coats, though thanks to the kindness of the North Korean quarter-
master at Jui-am-nee, most of them had warm fur hats.

All the POWs and civilian prisoners slept on the knoll of a small hill
that night. It was possible to move around to some extent without
bothering the guards, most of whom who had been withdrawn to form
a perimeter. The remaining guards had built a fire at the top of the
hill, and a number of POWs had come to it to try to get warm. The
guards did not seem to object to the presence of the POWs at the fire
as long as they could find places for themselves. Whenever one returned from a round of inspections to discover that he had been
squeezed out, he would use his rifle butt to batter his way back to the
fire. Those he knocked out of the way would crawl back to the fire as
soon as the guard had cleared a path for himself. This scene was repeated over and over throughout the night. Each time we saw a guard
returning to the fire, Danny [Louis Dans, an American civilian] and I
would try to persuade some of the men to move out of his way, but it
was no use. Even at the risk of being struck on the head with a rifle
butt, no one was willing to give up his warm place. . . .

Occasionally I could stand the cold no longer and would turn and
walk slowly among the sleeping POWs scattered about the hillside.

Near morning, I stumbled as I stepped over a form lying on the ground, and my foot struck the leg of a POW whom I assumed was asleep. The form began rolling down the incline, turning over and over, finally coming to rest some ten feet farther down. On investigating, I discovered that the man was dead. When I reported what had happened to those gathered around the fire, one of them replied, "Shoot, a little while ago I woke up and tried to move Bill. Me and Bill had been sleepin' under the same blanket, and Bill was dead. He was already cold."[29]

NOVEMBER 2—DAY THREE

On the morning of November 2, Father Crosbie reported there were about a dozen dead American soldiers and at least eight more who were unable to walk. Those not able to march were ordered to remain behind. According to Crosbie, "Commissioner Lord overheard the instructions given to the local people about burying the dead. . . . It included every man we had left behind."[30]

November 2 was to be a long day, with only a few brief rest stops. All the civilians survived, even the eighty-two-year-old French priest, Father Villemot. According to Father Crosbie, the endurance of the civilian prisoners "amazed" many of the GIs who "asked how it was that we had many aged folk still walking, while they were carrying men of nineteen and twenty. And some of our elderly ones had kept going even without aid from others." By the end of this third day, however, Crosbie noticed that many of the civilians were also failing, especially after a horrifying night with both civilians and GIs crammed into a schoolhouse:

Then began a night that seemed an age. Soon after the doors were closed, the room became a bedlam. Cramped and twisted limbs began to ache. Men moaned with pain, tried to get some relief by movement, and were cursed by their tortured neighbors. Officers called for order, but their voices only added to the ever-growing din. Exhausted men keeled over, and were pushed aside by the stifled men on whom they had fallen. Some struggled to get out of the room, walking perforce over their comrades' bodies. Outside, others hammered at the doors and begged to be let in. Guards shouted through the windows, threatening to spray the milling prisoners with machine gun bullets. Time

stood still. One's whole world had become a chaos of noise and suffering.[31]

As dreadful as that night seemed to Father Crosbie, his narrative neglected to mention what Larry Zellers considered the most unforgettable
happening of that terrifying night:

After about thirty minutes of this madness, someone screamed from
somewhere in the darkness. The efforts of others to quiet him met
with no success, and soon others—possibly some of the wounded—
also began to scream. Suddenly the door was thrown open by a guard
wielding a submachine gun, and by means of Lord's translation we
were warned not to make any more noise. For a brief period there
were no screams. When the guard was required to return the second
time, he was obviously angry at our disobeying his order. Nevertheless,
the screaming soon broke out again. At the guard's third appearance
there was a difference: "This is my last warning. You must be quiet. If
I have to return, I will open the door and fire into the room with my
weapon." He slammed the door shut, leaving us alone.

Maj. John J. Dunn, senior ranking American officer, spoke up from
somewhere in the near-total darkness. "Men, you have heard what the
guard said. I order you to be quiet for your own sake. Do any of you
have any doubt that this guard means what he says? Let Commissioner
Lord tell you what he thinks about it."

"I agree! This guard is under orders from The Tiger, and you all
know what he did to Lieutenant Thornton. We have got to be quiet,"
concluded Commissioner Lord.

Major Dunn spoke again. "I don't know where the officers and non-
coms are in this room, but you must be scattered all over. From now
on, when anyone screams, he is to be picked up and thrown outside."

For a time there was quiet in the room, but after about thirty
minutes someone cried out. Following Major Dunn's orders, those
around the offender picked him up and passed him overhead to the
door. Probably a total of two or three were ejected in this manner.
Those who were thrown outside were not punished by the guards; they
simply had to wait out a very cold night with those who had not been
made to fit into the room in the first place. Again, there was quiet
inside for a short time.

The next person who cried out did not want to be thrown out in
the cold and fought back. From the darkness came the sound of blows,

followed by a shout: "Now throw him out!" When the offender had been ejected from the room, there was some whispering in one corner. "That officer hit this man," someone spoke up. Immediately, the quiet of the room was broken by a loud clear voice stating name, rank, and serial number and adding, "If anyone ever wants to make anything out of it before some board of investigation after the war, then go ahead." There was no response. No one else cried out.[32]

NOVEMBER 3—DAY FOUR

After the previous night's terror, Father Crosbie reported that The Tiger greeted the exhausted prisoners with an early morning speech on the fine care they were receiving, and he assured them everyone would be well cared for:

First, he told us that the People's Government had in mind . . . only the preservation of our health and our ultimate release. We should appreciate, therefore, the interest the authorities were taking in our welfare, and should cooperate with their efforts. Secondly, we need have no anxiety about the people who fell out during the march. They would be taken to People's Hospitals and would be well cared for. Thirdly, from this morning there would be transport for the women who found difficulty in walking.[33]

After The Tiger's speech, the male prisoners left the women behind and started to march. Unfortunately, the women did not get to ride and had to march under the leadership of Nell Dyer, an Arkansas missionary who had to help several of the elderly women. The only man to accompany them was Commissioner Lord, who was himself over sixty and had a bad heart. When the seventy-six-year-old Mother Beatrix could go no farther, the others were ordered to leave her behind. They left in sorrow, and soon the sound of a rifle shot rang in their ears. Mother Beatrix was the first civilian to die. There would soon be more.

That afternoon Commissioner Lord, dragging the seventy-year-old Mme. Funderat behind him with a rope, rejoined the main group for a midday break. When it was time to resume walking, the guards ordered Lord and the others to leave the exhausted Mme. Funderat behind. No one saw her again.

During the afternoon march, Larry Zellers noted the difficulty the stronger prisoners had trying to help those who could no longer help themselves:

Normally, two people would have had no difficulty assisting a third, but all of us had been on a starvation diet for about a month. Although our bodies had not yet wasted away as much as they would later on, we were little more than living skeletons. Our bones were covered with cracked, dry, dirty skin; we had scruffy beards and long, dirty, matted hair. Our ragged summer clothes and hollow eyes completed the testimony of our depleted condition.

Little clusters of people from our various groups were scattered up and down the road for miles that afternoon. Monsignor Quinlan and Father Crosbie were trying to assist the oldest member of our group. Father Villemot, who had come to Korea in 1892, was then eighty-two years of age. Not having teeth, he could not eat the half-cooked corn that the local villagers prepared for us. As the old man's strength failed, Bishop Quinlan and Father Crosbie were required to carry more and more of the burden. Slowly, these three men dropped behind and were soon out of sight. At one time Father Villemot begged to be left to die in a farmyard. Finally, he was permitted to ride in an oxcart that was provided for Madame Martel [a French diplomatic prisoner] after Georges Perruche [also a French diplomat] made a strong appeal to The Tiger. . . .

Toward evening, more POWs fell out of line, unable to keep up. As we walked past them, we tried to encourage them to keep walking as long as possible. Some did make a new effort, but others remained by the side of the road. Later, we heard many gunshots behind us; we knew what was happening.[34]

Although there were few acts of kindness during the March, Larry Zellers does mention one sympathetic guard:

On this particular afternoon I noticed something different. The guard who marched by my side was not like most of the others. My burden became greater near nightfall, and I was obliged to fall behind rather than abandon the malnourished, weak, and frail Anglican nun by the side of the road to die alone. The main body of marching prisoners was miles ahead. Darkness was fast approaching, but this guard stayed by my side, offering encouragement. As other groups of two fell behind—one stronger, one weaker, but together trying to trade a little time in exchange for a life—each couple was assigned a guard, and the decision was his whether to tolerate the delay. Many did not. The sound of the gun was heard in the gathering darkness.[35]

At the end of this death-marred fourth day, the POWs spent the night in another schoolhouse, while the civilians slept inside a church. Crosbie writes that they had covered another twenty miles, but it probably only seemed that far. By this time, it had become increasingly clear that un-healed wounds and disease often dictated who lived and who died, but there were others who had, consciously or not, decided to take the line of least resistance and simply give up. Irv Langell describes what pushed him to survive the march:

We knew we just had to keep up. If you dropped out, you were a dead man. In my squad, Pop Wilson, an older man who was in World War II, told me, "Langell, you keep going. I'll stick my boot up your ass if you don't." That's how I survived, although he died that first winter. I was also inspired by the courage of the nuns during the march. Some of them were in their seventies. We even had one who was blind. They were stepping it up, and some of our punk twenty-year-old kids couldn't keep up with them. Well, I wasn't going to let no seventy-year-old nun outwalk me. No, that wasn't going to happen. Your mind-set was everything. Some guys complained, "Oh, I can't make it. What am I going to do? They're going to kill me." And they did. It was as simple as that. I can still picture this one guy. He was probably two hundred pounds, over six foot tall, and he was crying because he couldn't walk any farther. I knew he was one of those momma's boys. He said, "They're going to kill me anyway. I might as well give up." I can still hear him saying this. You couldn't get through to those types. You couldn't even shame them into trying harder.

In addition to willing yourself to survive, as Irv Langell did, Shorty Estabrook credits the tough lessons he learned during his childhood in rural Maine:

I guess each man has his explanation for being able to survive. I know that some definitely gave credit to their belief in God. But I think it goes a little deeper than that. I was born in northern Maine. I can't even remember how young I was when I first picked potatoes. In the potato fields if you got hungry, you just wiped off a potato and ate it. This would also help quench your thirst. At home we ate out of the fields and our garden. My mother made bread. We had deer, moose, and bear meat. It was very rare to go even to a small store to buy any food. So I think my stomach was in a lot better shape than those guys who were used to processed food.

NOVEMBER 4—DAY FIVE

The fifth day of the March fell on a Sunday. According to Father Crosbie, it was the worst day of all, in part because they were now marching in a snowstorm over steep mountains but also because of the mounting death toll:

Of all the days we had spent in bondage, none had left us more bitter, painful memories. In the early hours of the morning it had begun to snow. Now, at dawn, the guards told us we must leave immediately, for today we would have to cross the mountain range that lay ahead, and we must hasten to reach the passes before they were blocked with snow. Our supper of the evening before had been meager. Now, without breakfast, we began a hurried, uphill march through snow. Mercifully, Father Villemot and Madame Martel were allowed to ride on a supply cart. The rest of us struggled along as best we could, the stronger helping the weak. . . .

Shots sounded somewhere near us, but caused us no alarm. We had often known the guards to amuse themselves by firing off their rifles. As we passed the mouth of a ravine we saw an officer and some guards returning toward the road. Larry Zellers remembers distinctly that they were laughing, but like myself he thought nothing of the incident at the time. Somewhere ahead of us more shots sounded. If the thought entered our minds that there were more shots than usual, it was soon dismissed from our attention as we labored on, anxious to overtake the others.

We came upon an exhausted GI sitting by the roadside, then another. Beside each of them a guard was standing. We passed around a bend, and then two shots rang out behind us. We knew at once that they had been fired on by the guards we had just passed. I remember still how my head reeled and my knees went weak as the shocking truth came home to me. We recalled now the first shots we had heard, remembering the guards emerging from the ravine. We recalled, too, the shots that had sounded ahead; fired perhaps in another ravine.

Our hearts ached with helpless pity as we came upon more and more men sitting or lying exhausted by the roadside, attended always by guards, who waited ominously till we stragglers passed. Then, each time, we listened in dumb anguish for the sound that always came— the sound of a shot behind us on the road.[36]

Father Crosbie argues that these men need not have died if conditions had not been so appalling and their own will had been stronger:

A few months ago they could have made the march with ease. Captivity had transformed their vigorous young bodies into feeble, tottering skeletons. Half-starved and ill-clad, they had lived in almost arctic cold, sometimes in unheated buildings, sometimes under the open sky. They had covered the miles behind us in long, forced stages, with sleepless nights and all but foodless days. And if they weakened now, they would have gone through all this in vain; for the penalty for weakness was death.

We passed them by as closely as we could and as slowly as we dared, and I spoke a few words about God's love and mercy. God was near to us in this dark hour . . . beyond this night of pain and hate. His love was real . . . His mercy . . . His forgiveness . . . His reward was waiting for us. . . .

Some nodded as if they understood. One poor lad just looked blankly up at me, and asked me if I had a cigarette. I remember the trickle of blood that ran from one man's mouth. There was one, with eyes wide and bright, who stared defiance at the guard standing over him. I watched another struggling to his feet, to stagger a few paces and then sink down again. . . .

My eyes fell again on the road beneath our feet. The white carpet of snow was flecked with red. Blood on the snow. . . . Other sights of that morning may fade from memory with the passing years, but the picture of blood-flecked snow is etched too deeply ever to be erased.

Twenty-two men fell out that morning. Knowing what had been their fate, we had no doubt now of what had happened to Mother Beatrix and Madame Funderat and the eighteen soldiers who had fallen out the day before, and the sick men who had been left behind on previous days. And we knew now what "People's Hospitals" meant in the language of The Tiger.[37]

The march over the mountains on this fifth day was indeed fatal for the weak. Larry Zellers observed, "When a GI would drop out, a North Korean guard would stay with him; then as soon as we marched by, the guard would shoot him and roll him over the side of the road. Later, when we were on those steep mountain roads, the guards would just throw them over the side and their bodies would roll maybe a hundred feet." Philip Deane also witnessed what it meant to lag behind:

On November 4, we crossed a mountain pass in a bitter blizzard. More and more GIs were dropping out. They lay by the side of the road, mutely looking at the departing column. A young, red-headed kid, who could still walk, was trying, weeping, to carry a dying friend. A guard kicked him on. He stumbled on, sobbing. We heard many shots. At one point in the serpentine windings of the road, stopping because of dysentery, I looked down to the lower bend. The Tiger was pushing one of the dying with his foot into the ditch. When the GI was completely off the road, The Tiger shot him. I saw two more killed this way on the lower bend of the road before the guard kicked me on.[38]

Wayne Johnson offered a possible reason why The Tiger was determined to leave no live stragglers behind:

The Tiger was determined he wasn't going to let us be overtaken by our troops. At all costs he wasn't going to let anybody live to be liberated. He could have just as easily let the guys that fell along the side of the road lie there, but he was not going to let any of the POWs be saved by our forces. I don't know whether that was an order he was given or whether he did this on his own. I don't think anybody can answer that, but it meant that if a guy dropped out even to defecate or whatever and didn't stand up or get his pants up fast enough, he was shot.

Exhausted himself and certainly in shock after seeing so many men die, Larry Zellers tried to make sense out of the what was happening:

I had seen the first of many American soldiers to drop out that day because they could not keep up with the grueling pace through the snow. For a moment the realization that these young men would soon be in the presence of God filled me with awe and almost succeeded in converting this barbaric scene into one of tranquillity. Then I was brought back to reality: someone was dying—someone was responsible for this outrage.

It is impossible for me to describe my reaction to what was occurring. We had known for some time that prisoners who could not keep up had been executed, but this was the first time that we had seen the horror firsthand. There was such a searing of sensitivity that no one spoke for a few minutes. Then from somewhere behind me someone said, "They are shooting those boys." Kris Jensen turned partway around and shouted, "Yes, and they will shoot us too if we don't keep up."

In the face of such jarring reality, I was out of touch with my own feelings for a time. I had never felt this way before because I had never seen anything like this before. The feeling came across as a nausea in the pit of my stomach and a weakness affecting the entire body. There are no words. Feelings don't even have a name. Soon we came upon other young men who could not go any farther. They were awaiting execution as soon as our group had passed them. I could tell by looking into their eyes that they knew what was coming. I looked back a second time at the sound of another shot to behold the same wretched scene as before. I didn't look back anymore.[39]

The weary survivors made it down the other side of the mountain pass in the late morning of November 4, and stopped to rest at a schoolhouse in the village of Chasŏng where they remained the rest of that day and part of the next. For once there was even straw on the floor, and the prisoners felt a little better. That evening a truck and a bus arrived to transport the women, children, old men, and five very sick GIs to the next stop. The remaining prisoners left the schoolhouse the following afternoon.

NOVEMBER 5—DAY SIX

The rest in Chasŏng was most welcome, but it was certainly insufficient to restore the prisoners' spirits or strength. Jack Browning thought back on what going without proper food and shelter had done to him and the other prisoners:

Some of the days we wouldn't get a bite to eat. A couple of days we got feed corn that you would give to animals. It consisted of hard, little kernels that had been partially boiled, but still had the husks on. It destroyed many of the guys that had bad stomachs and who had dysentery. Those husks cut them all to pieces, and they would pass blood.

This one night we stayed in a little small schoolhouse a short distance from a village. They packed us in there as tightly as they could, but they still couldn't cram all of us in. You couldn't sit or lie down. If you did you would be sitting or lying on somebody else. There was moaning and groaning going on all night long. People were hurting. Their legs were cramping and people were lying on top of them. It was just impossible to get any rest. Some of the men had to stay outside, and some of them froze to death. The temperature supposedly got down to thirty-six below zero that November. When we had to sleep outside, we would try to use a rock or anything else we could find to scoop out little holes in the ground to get below the wind. We'd then hunch down and huddle together. We'd try to cover up with these old bags made of rice straw that we picked up along the way. You have to understand we weren't wearing anything but the summer fatigues we were captured in. I still wonder how any of us survived.

On the afternoon of November 5 the more able-bodied GIs and civilians left together in a group. Those who were too sick and weak left later. The prisoners only covered ten miles, and those who made it stayed in another schoolhouse that night.

NOVEMBER 6—DAY SEVEN

Once again the prisoners left in two groups and again covered approximately ten miles. Still two days from the end of their march, they were becoming progressively weaker. By now, everyone was physically and mentally numb, but, as Larry Zellers later wrote, it was still impossible to escape the terror:

My mind seemed to float after a time. I seemed strangely out of touch with my body. I didn't have to make any concerted effort to remember what happened yesterday or the day before that—it was all there, instant recall in bold relief. As if looking through a camera with a wide-angle lens, I could see it all.

There was no physical pain as I walked along. The pitiful sight of those hopeless men, younger than I, lying by the side of the road awaiting their own execution took away all feeling of fatigue, hunger, and cold. There were a million things to think about, but my mind refused to make a choice—perhaps because any choice would involve pain. One young man, as his last earthly act, was singing "God Bless America" as loudly as his weak cracking voice was able. Tears were streaming down his face as we marched past. There were tears on our faces as well. I was staggered by feelings of hopelessness and grief. . . .

Some of these young men were so stunned that they were not fully aware of where they were or what would soon happen to them; others were not so fortunate. We were horrified not only by the thought of what these young men were facing but also by the look in their eyes, the sound of their voices, what they said, and what they asked for. They were not asking for very much, but it was beyond our ability to deliver. One young man sitting by the side of the road asked for a cigarette. Another American soldier, waiting to be shot, asked for a speedy death at our hands: "Will someone please hit me in the head with a rock?" he pleaded. We heard this request over and over, from the time we came within hearing range until we were out again. . . .

Up ahead, one POW had fallen behind to help a buddy who could no longer continue on his own. They were urged on by the guard, but at last the weaker one fell to the ground and remained there. After a few moments, the guard shoved the stronger man away and motioned for him to go on by himself. The young man stood for an instant, then turned and went running up the road. He was barefoot. After a few paces, he stopped and returned to his fallen comrade. He knelt down, removed the shoes from his friend, and, holding them in his hand, ran forward to rejoin the group. The man sitting calmly on the ground made no effort to stop his friend from taking his shoes, and neither did the guard. At that moment his action seemed cruel to me. Thinking about it now from the vantage point of many years, I am not so sure that it was.[40]

NOVEMBER 7—DAY EIGHT

The prisoners spent the night of November 6 in another schoolhouse. In the morning they set out on what would be the next to last day of the march. That evening, Father Crosbie noticed a Korean officer come into the schoolhouse where they were staying. With him were Maj. John Dunn, Commissioner Lord, who did the interpreting, and Dr. Ernst Kisch, an

Austrian Jew who had survived Buchenwald and Dachau. The officer wanted to compile a list of the dead or missing:

> For hours the three men struggled with figures and dates, trying to get the record straight. It would be interesting to see the report that was finally drawn up by that Korean officer. Did it mention, I wonder, that The Tiger, at some point during the march, had ordered the guards to take all identification discs [dog tags] from the POWs? Did "missing" and "dead" have separate meanings in the report of the march itself?[41]

Dr. Kisch, who had been required to do similar things in the Nazi death camps, was forced to put down the cause of death as enteritis, a comparatively mild inflammation of the intestines, which was rarely fatal and then only to children. Dr. Kisch himself would not survive the effects of the march, dying at Andong in June 1951.

NOVEMBER 8—DAY NINE—THE MARCH ENDS AT CHUNGGANG

The Death March ended November 8 at Chunggang, which would be the first of several temporary camps where the emaciated prisoners would continue their ordeal. Those who had the good fortune to travel by truck and bus had arrived three days earlier, although one of the nuns died her first night in Chunggang.

It had been a terrifying nine days. The survivors of the march had, as Philip Deane writes, "left behind a hundred dead, buried without mounds in 'People's Hospitals.' "[42] Many of the survivors were more dead than alive, and their suffering was far from over. At seven o'clock that first evening in Chunggang, The Tiger insisted exercise would improve the condition of the prisoners and ordered them to perform calisthenics. He repeated his order the following morning. Exercising in freezing November weather was the final blow for many of the men who had already contracted pneumonia during the march. Arguably, the dead were the fortunate ones. The survivors would endure eleven more months of hunger, sickness, and death before conditions gradually improved during their final year and a half of internment.

NOVEMBER 16, 1950–MARCH 29, 1951– HANJANG-NI

The prisoners stayed in Chunggang for only a week before leaving on November 16 for an overnight march that took them a few miles up the Yalu River to Hanjang-ni where they would remain until March 29, 1951. Although their harrowing days of marching were over, the death count continued to mount during the long winter months. According to Larry Zellers, without proper clothing, shelter, and food, the prisoners simply could not overcome the debilitating effects of their days on the road. Then too chance continued to play a role in who survived and who did not:

> The weeding out of the weaker ones that had begun during the march continued at an accelerated pace. Nor were all the ones who died among the weakest; some of the POWs were fortunate enough to be quartered in homes with heated floors while others, through no fault of their own, were placed in the schoolhouse. Those who had to live in the schoolhouse with inadequate heating had a much more difficult time of it.[43]

Pneumonia was a deadly killer in a camp such as Hanjang-ni, although adequate housing and medicine would have prevented many of these deaths. The civilian prisoners received only one shipment of antibiotic drugs, which arrived just after Father Crosbie contracted pneumonia and undoubtedly saved his life. To make matters worse, North Korean medical personnel, apparently ignorant about which illnesses were contagious, moved all the sick into their so-called hospitals, which was tantamount to a death sentence. Larry Zellers estimates that 99 percent of these men died. He and Monsignor Thomas Quinlan were occasionally allowed to visit the hospital, and when they did they observed that some of the GIs refused to eat:

> We noticed POWs sitting around not eating their food. When we inquired about it, they answered, "Leave us alone. We know what we're doing." I suppose they did know. They were in the process of escaping from their brutal circumstances in the only way that was available to them. We tried to talk to them, but they pretended not to hear us; after a time they refused to look in our direction."[44]

Philip Deane also concluded that although many of the men died of pneumonia, there were reasons other than disease and hunger for the growing death rate:

Some caught pneumonia because they were made to kneel in the snow. From our house we could see GIs on their knees outside their billets. The guard, walking up and down, frequently kicked the kneeling men. We wondered why this was done. We were soon to find out for ourselves that it could be done on the flimsiest pretext. On December 5, 1950, an interned South Korean politician asked George Blake and me, who were on water-carrying duty, to fetch four twenty-five gallon drums of water instead of three, because, he said, he wanted to so some laundry. We answered that we were too exhausted. The South Korean politician complained to the guard, saying that we "looked down on the Korean people." The guard ordered George Blake and myself to kneel down in the snow. . . . He beat us with the butt of his rifle, kicked us and slapped us. . . .

But disease and privations were not the only killers. There were GIs who would give up a day's food for one cigarette rolled in old newspaper, and—I am sorry, it is true—there were GIs who bought food at the price of another man's life. There were those who worked in the cook house and stole their comrades' food. There were those who stripped their skeletic, dying companions, hours before they died. But, by and large, those were the exceptions. There were those who not only succeeded in preserving their human dignity but tried to explain—to me, a journalist—the others who had failed.[45]

According to Deane, even a trip to the river to get water could be a deadly experience:

The Yalu River was less than a mile away, but the guards would not allow water to be fetched more than once a day. I was told there were GIs—I could not check this personally—who did not have water for five days and who died of thirst. The water was brought in fifty-gallon drums on a cart pulled by GIs. The pull was over a bumpy road, and the men on duty were thoroughly splashed. The water froze immediately, and the GIs pulling the cart returned looking like weird creatures from Scandinavian folklore. Frequently, frostbite followed, and infection, then death.

A room was set aside for the sick. The frostbitten were put into it. There was no fire in the room and the floor was bare. The door was nailed shut, and the patients were left alone. No one went near the room for two days. When the door was opened, all the occupants were dead.[46]

Jack Browning suffered a similar experience in December 1950 when a guard punished him and another prisoner for stealing a rice ball:

The guard stripped us to the waist in below zero weather and made us stand there for what seemed like an eternity but in reality was probably twenty-five or thirty minutes. In that weather it doesn't take long to freeze to death. The guard poured ice water on us and then beat us with a tree limb which was much larger than just a switch. He struck us several times each. It felt as if he was bringing up blood every time he struck me. I thought I had suffered some bad pain with my ear infection, but it was nothing compared to that beating. But the worst was when he let us go inside, and we began to thaw out. We rubbed our bodies to get the blood circulating, and that was the worst pain I've ever experienced. My joints felt as if they were going to explode. It felt like every fiber in my entire body was being torn apart. All we could do was scream. About three days later my friend died.

Being doused with freezing water was not the only indignity Jack Browning and his fellow prisoners suffered during the winter of 1950–51:

We stayed in an old schoolhouse that first winter. There wasn't any such thing as changing clothes and taking a bath. It was so miserably cold and you couldn't get water to wash your clothes or body. When we went outside to the toilet, we had to alert the guard and ask him in Korean, "Can I go to the toilet please?" If you didn't, you were subject to a beating.

When we went outside to urinate, it was so cold our urine froze as soon as it hit the ground. There would be these big stacks of urine. . . .

One man had dysentery and had to go out, but he didn't make it to the door. He lost control, and the watery stuff ran down his legs onto the floor. A guard came in and took a small stick and raked it through the mess, and then wiped it across the man's mouth.

When a man suffered from chronic dysentery, he would often lose his appetite and quit eating. What time he didn't spend at the toilet, he usually stayed lying on the floor, kind of curled up in a fetal position or humped up against the wall in the same position. He would get sort of hollow-eyed with a far away look in his eyes. In less than a week he would be dead.

We were burying five or six or even more a day that winter. I wasn't on this one particular burial detail, but those who were told me that they had to bury this real tall guy. They scraped out a little hole in the burial area, but when they tried to put him in the ground, he was too tall. They started to take him out to enlarge the hole, but the guard ordered them to break the man's legs so he would fit.

In spite of the terror and death that was an every day occurrence, it was food that dominated the attention of those who remained alive. The diet that first winter consisted primarily of under-cooked millet, which, according to Larry Zellers, lacked the protein needed to rebuild damaged tissue while severely damaging their digestive tracts. To make matters worse, some of the prisoners did not have teeth to chew the millet and the occasional field corn, and literally starved to death:

Our ration of grain that first winter was 600 grams of millet per person per day, or approximately one average water glass full. When cooked properly, it swells to about three times its normal size. About twice the size of a pinhead, each individual grain is surrounded by a hard shuck; hence, cooking millet thoroughly enough for human consumption is difficult. If diarrhea is to be avoided, it must be well cooked so that the shuck is split open by the swelling of the grain inside. Improperly cooked millet caused great problems for us during that first winter. The excessive diarrhea caused us additional weakness at a time when we were being starved by the poor diet. We had no way of knowing how many people died because of diarrhea.

Getting up off a heated floor that was sometimes too hot and going outside to answer a call of nature when the outside temperature was forty below zero was very stressful. Just how often did we have to go outside? For me the average was from six to twelve times each night. I hasten to add that this relatively large number of bathroom calls was true of the first winter only. After we had gained more experience and had better control of the firewood, the problem was not nearly so great. We simply added more water to the grain and cooked it longer.[47]

Going to collect the daily food ration also provoked Zellers, especially when he had to witness guards mistreating GIs:

> The job that we dreaded more than all the others was that of going to collect our food rations. There were two reasons: one, waiting for more than an hour in the bitter cold; and two, watching the guards abuse the American soldiers as they also waited in line. Some POWs were struck occasionally with a rifle butt; others were sometimes kicked, often until they fell to the ground.
>
> Watching the North Koreans sport with the Americans was one thing; standing by helplessly as some of the POWs cooperated with their enemy in humiliating themselves was another. The guards knew what to do; they would often throw down a cigarette butt and watch the POWs fight over it. Some who were thus wrestling on the ground were so weak that they could not stand by themselves. The American officers were powerless to do anything because they were being held in separate huts.[48]

The arrival of spring in Hanjang-ni temporarily raised the prisoners' spirits. With warmer weather the guards allowed them to go to the river and take their first baths in almost a year. The men were shocked when they looked at each other's foul, emaciated bodies, covered with all kinds of sores from sleeping on filthy dirt floors and not bathing. The spring thaw also produced a grim reminder of death. The rising waters of the Yalu River washed out the shallow graves of those who had been buried along its bank during the long winter months. It was, according to Jack Browning, a most unpleasant sight and smell: "Decayed human flesh has a distinctive odor, one you never forgot. In fact, the stench was so bad they had to move us."

The prisoners' stay at Hanjang-ni came to an end on March 29, 1951, when they were moved a few miles back down the Yalu to Andong. They were leaving behind some 222 bodies, but, as Larry Zellers later wrote, "Even though we were still losing people daily, our departure from that terrible place seemed a sign that we would one day see the land of the living. Any change has to be interpreted as a change for the better when one has so little else to go on."[49]

MARCH 30–OCTOBER 10–ANDONG

The prisoners moved into an old Japanese Army camp at Andong. By this time The Tiger had been replaced by a North Korean major, and the death rate began to diminish, although another sixty men would lose their lives in the little over six months they spent at Andong. Larry Zellers refers to the months at Andong as a "holding action":

> The line between life and death became blurred, as did our emotional response to that which it separated. We shed few tears for those defeated by death. We experienced precious little joy for the victory of life. Daily existence was just you and your witness against whatever they and nature and circumstance could throw at you.[50]

The physical treatment of the prisoners did improve in Andong. By then, the Chinese had certainly urged the North Koreans to step up their indoctrination programs in order to exploit the propaganda opportunities their captives afforded and interrogations were frequent. There was also more direct contact between the GIs and the civilian prisoners, a practice the North Koreans tried to stop. Insisting the civilians were "a bad influence" on the POWs, they moved the GIs to a nearby private house on May, 10, 1951. By this time, however, the GIs were doing better on their own. Hardened by the events of the past ten months, and slowly regaining a measure of their strength and confidence, most now were determined to survive. Jack Browning describes their renewed spirits:

> I had the attitude if I died over there, it would be because of one of two things: they were going to have to shoot or starve me to death, although they were doing a pretty good job of the latter. My thought was as long as there was breath, there was life and hope. I scrounged, and I stole from them. All of us did, anything we could get our hands on. When things began going a little better, we began playing cards and talking about our girlfriends and wives. James Duncan, Shorty Estabrook, James Moore, and several others always were doing something to get the rest of us to laugh.

Larry Zellers also noticed that the GIs were "beginning to give a better account of themselves [and] to stand together as a team." Clearly, slowly

improving conditions allowed these men to regain their self-respect and
their ability to survive.

The GIs were turned over to the Chinese after leaving Andong in October 1951, an act that might well have saved their lives. The officers were
sent to Camp Two, while the rest of the soldiers ended up in Camp Three
at Changsŏng where they remained until repatriated after the armistice
was signed on July 27, 1953. Their treatment and food greatly improved
in the permanent camps and, predictably, the dying finally stopped. In fact,
during their almost twenty-two months under the Chinese, only ten additional GIs died, and even their deaths could be attributed to the long-term
effects of the Death March and their fifteen-month incarceration under
the North Koreans.

The civilian prisoners left Andong for Manpo on October 10, 1951,
where they stayed in a North Korean civilian prison. Zellers calls it the
"Place of Learning" because the North Koreans tried constantly, albeit with
little success, to indoctrinate their civilian captives. They left Manpo on
August 13, 1952, arriving three days later in Ujang.

The Chinese refused to accept control over the civilian prisoners, as
they had the soldiers, but they did agree to provide them with food. From
then on, explained Zellers, the civilians had plenty of rice, flour, vegetables,
bean oil, and even some meat:

> The Communists at Ujang, aware that we were going home soon, did
> two things for us to try to win our favor: they gave us all we could eat
> so that we wouldn't look starved when we were displayed to the world
> press, and they told us that we had religious freedom—but only among
> ourselves. It was the final irony: as prisoners we were not only supplied
> with more food than the ordinary North Korean citizens enjoyed but
> we were now given a degree of religious freedom that they were de-
> nied.[51]

Ujang was the final stop for the civilians before leaving on March 21,
1953, for the North Korean capital of P'yŏngyang, where Communist jour-
nalists attempted to persuade them to admit their treatment had been
good. Fearing reprisals against the POWs who were not yet freed, no one
said a word except Nell Dyer. When asked if there wasn't something for
which she could thank the Korean People's Government, she replied, "Yes,
as a matter of fact, there is. I thank the North Korean government that I

am still alive. Knowing how little they value life in this country, I feel fortunate that I still have mine."[52] At least twenty-five of the eighty-seven civilians were not so fortunate.

POSTSCRIPT TO THE TIGER DEATH MARCH

Without someone to record what actually happened, historical events and individuals too often slip through the cracks of time. Fortunately, such has not been the case with the Tiger Death March. Larry Zellers, Philip Crosbie, and Philip Deane left comprehensive accounts of what the civilians endured and also provided generally sympathetic descriptions of the GIs who were with them during the Death March and after. Nevertheless, given the negative treatment domestic critics accorded the Korean War POWs, it was imperative that these men have the opportunity to tell their own stories. It was equally important that they establish a support system that would meet their needs both individually and collectively. Tiger Survivors Wayne A. "Johnnie" Johnson and Wilbert "Shorty" Estabrook have been responsible both for preserving the historical record, and for keeping track of the survivors.

"JOHNNIE" JOHNSON'S SECRET LIST

Arguably, the most incredible story to emerge from the horrific Tiger Death March concerned a secret list put together by an eighteen-year-old infantryman from Lima, Ohio, named Wayne "Johnnie" Johnson. Captured near Choch'iwŏn after only nine days in South Korea, Private Johnson began keeping a list of those who died or were killed during his thirty-seven months as a prisoner. In fact, he fortuitously kept two lists. After the Chinese discovered one, he stuffed the remaining list into an empty toothpaste tube and smuggled it out during his repatriation. U.S. military authorities, however, showed little interest in his list so he told no one about it until his first ex-POW convention in 1989. Finally, in August of 1996, the U.S. Army awarded him the Silver Star for "exemplary courage and selfless determination to provide a record of deceased soldiers, even in the face of death by a hostile enemy." The following year, *Reader's Digest* told his story.[53] Since then, literally hundreds of families have contacted him looking for loved ones who remain Korean War MIAs. Some weeks Johnson received as many as a dozen letters asking if a particular name was on his list. This young soldier's decision to risk his life to chronicle the fate of his fellow prisoners is indeed a story in courage and determination:

When we were originally sent to Korea, we were told it was a police action that would probably take just a couple of weeks to clean up. So when we were captured, I thought it might be maybe a month or two, and we would be back in Japan. That's what most of us thought. I was captured on July 11, 1950, after having been at the front for maybe five or six days. We started walking, I don't know how many miles before we finally stopped. At that time there were probably about six hundred of us. The guards put us on the second floor of this building which was pretty much burned out. One of our planes came down and strafed the building and hit about twenty of our men. A couple of them died immediately, and two or three others later on. Because many of us were from different companies and regiments and didn't know each other, I thought that somebody would want to know who they were and when they died. So I wrote down their names and what information I had on them.

I had a little stub of a pencil, and I wrote these first names down on a piece of paper that I had ripped off the wall. I thought that would be the end of it, and that when we were freed in a month or so I would have this information for their families. I didn't know that I would be a prisoner for another three years and that I would add almost five hundred names. That never entered my mind.

Once I started I thought there was no sense stopping. I just thought it was the right thing to do. So when somebody else died, I added his name. I got most of the names from friends of those who died. Of course, there were guys who died whose names I don't have because I didn't know them and no one else did either. There were also some names on my list I later could not make out because they got smudged in the toothpaste tube I used to smuggle the list out past the Chinese.

We had sixty to seventy guys die in those almost four months while we were moving north before the Tiger March began at Manpo on October 31, 1950. Some died from wounds, but the majority from malnutrition and the diseases that were made worse by not having enough to eat. These men were just not able to adjust to what little food we did get. Just being able to swallow was difficult, but if you couldn't get the food down, you died. It was that simple.

The Tiger Death March covered just over 100 miles and we lost approximately one man for each of those miles. It ended on November 8 at Chunggang where we stayed for a few days and then moved on to Hanjang-ni for the rest of that first winter when the largest number of our men died. In March of 1951 we were moved to Andong where we stayed until October of 1951 when the Chinese took us over and moved us to Camp Three. Approximately 300 men died in Hanjang-ni and Andong.

All during this time I continued writing down the names. Whenever I got the opportunity, I would talk to guys about who had died. I would try to find out their first and last names, their unit, rank, home town, and when and where they died. I even kept up the list after we were turned over to the Chinese in Camp Three because we were still losing a few men. I think the last names I recorded were of the four or five men who died in April of 1952.

The Chinese discovered one of my lists while we were in Camp Three. It had taken me a long time to compile my first list, and I got to thinking what would happen if it got lost or destroyed. So I decided to make a duplicate copy. That was fortunate. We lived in these mud shacks, and I stuck one list in the wall and buried the other in the floor. This one day we were out in this field where they fed us their propaganda bull. We spent a couple of hours listening to that malarkey, and when we got back to our shack, I discovered that the doggone wall was busted out, and my one list was missing.

I don't know how the Chinese found about it. Somebody might have slipped up. I don't think anyone directly told them. Anyway, that's what I would like to think. It was not very long before the guards came and took me to the commandant's office. He wasn't too pleased about the list. There were four of us living in that room, but I told him it was my list. I figured there was no sense in dragging the other three guys into it. He thought I was going to use the list to make his government look bad for its cruel treatment of us, and he did a number on me. He made me sit in this chair and started hitting me with his riding crop. After an hour or two, he really got perturbed. He was ranting and raving, and he took out his pistol and hit me a couple of times in the head. Then he put the pistol to my head and cocked it. Well, fear didn't even begin to do justice to my feelings; it was more than fear I can tell you. I thought that right there was the end of everything. But eventually he calmed down. I guess I finally convinced him that the list was just for humanitarian purposes, that I only wanted the information so that the families could have some kind of closure on what had happened to their loved ones. In any case, he must have bought my story because he didn't shoot me.

I still had the other list hidden in the floor. When we were told that we were going to be repatriated and to get on these trucks, I dug my other list up and put it in my pocket. It was a little scary because the Chinese commandant had already told me that I would not be released if I did anything else, and there wasn't much doubt in my mind he would have lived up to that. I still had this list in my pocket when we stopped at this processing camp where the Chinese wanted to make us look more presentable before turning us over in Freedom Village.

We were issued a green bag that had a red cross on the side of it, and there were toilet articles in it. That was the first time we ever had any contact with anything like the Red Cross. We were able to shower and shave, and that's when I got the idea that they would never look inside a toothpaste tube. I took the tube in the shower with me. Fortunately, toothpaste tubes were not made then like they are now. They were lead and when you unfolded the end, there was this big opening, and that's where I stuffed the list. Unfortunately, when I put the list in the tube, some of the names became smudged, and later I couldn't read them. The guards were only about ten feet from me, and I was trying to wash it out without them seeing what I was doing. I did the best I could, but I didn't get out all the residue, and it messed up some of the names. Later the Arizona Department of Safety used an infrared scanner to restore some of the names.

We were debriefed on board the ship coming home and asked if we knew the names of any of the prisoners who had died. When these officers questioned me, I took out my list and laid it on the table and started recording the names. I had scarcely begun when one of the officers decided it was going to take too long and said to me, "Never mind, we don't need all this." Fortunately, a lieutenant wrote on his report that I had this list of POW dead and should be commended for my actions. If it wasn't for that one sentence, none of the official recognition and the Silver Star would ever have happened.

I kept the list to myself after I got back to the U.S. until 1989 when I attended my first ex-POW convention. About a dozen of us were sitting around a big table talking about different guys and when they died. I can't remember who it was, but somebody's name came up and nobody could figure where or when he died. So I said, "Well, I can tell you." I went to my room and got my list. I brought it out and told them that this fellow had died in a freezing cornfield outside of Manpo just before the start of the Death March. The guys were amazed. None of them even knew my list existed.

In August of 1995, Sgt. Victoria Bingham, who worked in the Pentagon's POW/MIA Office, came to our Korean War ex-POW reunion in Sacramento. She was looking for information on MIAs. She interviewed me and found out about the list. She was so overwhelmed. She just couldn't believe all this information on MIAs existed and nobody knew about it. That started it. She took the information back to Washington and checked out the names. Then she got the idea that somebody ought to show their gratitude. I'd always said all I wanted out of this was for somebody to say, "Hey, thanks, I appreciate what you've done," but that had never happened before.

"SHORTY" ESTABROOK AND THE TIGER SURVIVORS ORGANIZATION

Wilbert R. "Shorty" Estabrook, who founded the Tiger Survivors in 1970, has devoted his considerable energies these past thirty years to accumulating all possible information on those who were with him on the Tiger Death March. In this undertaking he has been greatly aided by "Johnnie" Johnson's list and by retired Command Sgt. Maj. Timothy F. Casey, who, although not a prisoner himself, possesses great expertise on Korean War POWs. Shorty Estabrook, who also publishes a newsletter, credits Johnson and Casey for their indispensable help, but, without question, it has been his own tireless efforts that have been primarily responsible for completing the story of the Tiger Death March. As Shorty puts it, "I am trying to get something going so this organization can live on after the originals are all gone":

I am the unofficial, unelected, and unappointed president and founder of the Tiger Survivors. I am all this because no one else wanted to do it. So over the past thirty years I have lived and breathed this project.

It all started after I retired from the Army in 1970 and had a little time. I thought it might be nice to try and contact some of the old guys. I had a few names I had written down. Then I got hold of the *Stars and Stripes,* which listed guys who were returning and their hometown. I would just call information or write letters to the editor. The first Tiger Survivors reunion took place in Albuquerque in 1976 as part of the general American Ex-POW Association reunion.[54] I think there were seven of us Tiger survivors there. We started talking, and from there it just boiled and boiled.

When Johnnie Johnson came to his first reunion at Evansville, Indiana, in 1989, we knew nothing about his list of names. Some of us Tiger Survivors were sitting in the lobby. I had been compiling my list for some time by then, so I asked the guys if they had any additional names and addresses of prisoners who died with us. Each of the guys came up with a name or two. Then Johnnie, who is very quiet, said, "Oh, I've got a list with over four hundred names." I said, "Well, I'll be darned!"

After that I worked on getting the spelling of the names and hometowns correct, as well as adding any additional information. Some of this was quite easy, but some of Johnnie's names had been obliterated in that toothpaste tube he used to smuggle out his list. Johnnie then went through the Forensic Department of the State Police in Arizona and they recovered more of the names. We could have done better, using a new procedure the FBI had, but the FBI wanted to charge for this service, so that was the end of that. Anyway, we finally pieced together the entire list, a copy of which is now on my website.[55]

I have to mention Com. Sgt. Maj. Tim Casey, who at the time was retired from the Army. He came to us out of the blue. I can't say enough about this guy. I met him at one of the reunions. I'm not sure why he was there because he was not a former POW. But he became our analyst. He turned out to be the most knowledgeable man on Korean POW/MIA issues. He's just brilliant and he knows so much. In fact, the Defense Department's Prisoners of War and Missing in Action Office should have hired him, but they didn't have the money.

I put out our newsletter four times a year. We now have a mailing list of about 350. I answer and ask questions. I help guys find old buddies. Even those who weren't prisoners will write trying to locate an old friend. I've also added to our list the names of relatives of those who died in Korea. We are now at the point where there are more relatives who come to the reunions than there are of us. They have so many questions. Even now some of them don't know anything about what happened to their loved ones. The Pentagon often doesn't know much beyond their unit and sometimes the date they were listed as missing and their place of capture. How would they know anything else? There's no coverup. You get into combat and get hit by something as large as a .155 artillery round, there's not going to be anything left. There are all these stories about guys being kept in Russia, and some of them are laughable. But the families, of course, grasp at straws, and I just try to help.

3

THE SUNCH'ŎN TUNNEL MASSACRE

I sure do want to make this statement to everybody. I'm not a bit ashamed of being a prisoner, but I'm not proud of the fact that I was taken prisoner when the country needed me.
— Melvin Rookstool, survivor of the Sunch'ŏn Tunnel Massacre

Every war has its shocking atrocities involving prisoners of war. The Malmédy Massacre of World War II, in which S.S. troops executed more than seventy American POWs during the Battle of the Bulge, comes immediately to mind. However, as has been the case with the entire history of the Korean War, similar mass killings of prisoners in Korea have not received the same kind of historical inclusion.[1] One of the worst was the Hill 303 Massacre of August 14, 1950, in which forty-five American POWs were shot, and only four survived. Former POW Glenn Reynolds, whose further experiences appear in chapters five and eight, tells of burying the dead:

One of our companies found twenty-six 5th Cavalry soldiers in a ravine where they had been overrun when the North Koreans took Hill 303 away from them. They were tied up with communications wire and were all shot in the back of the head. Supposedly the North Koreans later said we were pushing so hard they didn't have time to get those guys out of there so they just shot them. The next morning, a bunch of us had to go to the scene. It was probably a quarter of a mile away, and it was the most gruesome sight I've ever seen. These young guys were seventeen, eighteen, nineteen years old. It was unbelievable. You can't imagine the feeling you get seeing your buddies all murdered like that.

Equally shocking was the Taejŏn Massacre of September 1950 in which approximately sixty American prisoners were forced to sit in a Taejŏn prison yard, again with their hands tied behind their backs, and shot. Only two survived. In addition, some 7,000 South Korean bodies were also found in mass graves in Taejŏn.[2]

Former prisoner Dr. Gene N. Lam, more of whose experiences appear in chapters four and six, witnessed the results of another mass killing at a Chinese roadblock near Kunu-ri on December 1, 1950. Years later, in an interview with the *San Antonio News,* he said, "The systematic starvation that they seemed intent on carrying out against us and the massacre of the litter patients to me represent the most terrible things that I know of which happened over there." He was referring to over one hundred wounded, who had been placed on litters and loaded on ambulances, trucks, and jeeps:

> The column of trucks stopped and when it became evident that the convoy couldn't get through, our officer in charge ordered us to leave the vehicles and to try to escape on foot. It was about one a.m. and the weather was well below freezing. We took off, but six of us were captured. I didn't see them actually shooting the litter patients, but I heard the machine guns fire, and then when they marched us back past the convoy, I saw the bodies. There's no doubt about what they did.[3]

However, no slaughter of helpless prisoners could be more horrifying than the Sunch'ŏn Tunnel Massacre. On October 30, 1950, North Korean guards shot and killed at least sixty-eight American prisoners outside a tunnel near Sunch'ŏn, North Korea. There were only twenty-one survivors.[4]

Several days earlier, with American troops closing in on the North Korean capital of P'yŏngyang, the guards hastily jammed more than one hundred American POWs into four open railroad cars and started moving them northwest toward Sunch'ŏn. Because American planes and artillery were constantly bombarding the tracks, the train took almost a week to cover the thirty or thirty-five miles, during which several prisoners died from malnutrition and disease. Finally, on October 30 the train stopped in a tunnel some ten miles north of Sunch'ŏn. The prisoners were ordered off the train and then taken in groups into nearby ravines and fields to be killed.

Why the Sunch'ŏn Massacre? Such atrocities defy rational explanation, but American planes had destroyed the tracks leading out of the tunnel to the north and United Nations troops were closing in from the south. The North Korean guards might well have been under orders to block any rescue of their prisoners, or they might simply have decided the prisoners were slowing down their retreat northward.[5]

The morning after the killing, Brig. Gen. Frank A. Allen, Jr., the Deputy Commander of the 1st Cavalry Division, reached the grisly scene. Liberated POWs in P'yŏngyang had told General Allen about a train moving prisoners to the north. Allen had also heard rumors about the killing of prisoners in a tunnel. Pausing to pick up a guide from the Republic of Korea's 6th Division, Allen jumped in his jeep and drove north to investigate. In 1954, while testifying before the Senate Subcommittee on Korean War Atrocities, General Allen described what he found:

> I heard a cry from another source, of an American, so we came down the hill, and there we came across the most gruesome sight I have ever witnessed. That was in sort of a sunken road, a pile of American dead. I should estimate that in that pile there were sixty men. In the pile were men who were not dead, who were wounded. . . . We, incidently, found a very shallow grave; it must have contained at least sixty bodies on the other side of the road, down maybe fifty yards from the place.[6]

Melvin Rookstool and Valder John were two of the twenty-one survivors who lived to tell the story of the Sunch'ŏn Massacre.

MELVIN D. ROOKSTOOL

I enlisted in the Army in 1949 when I was sixteen years old. I was just knocking around, and I got involved in some problems, half of which were my own fault to be sure. The judge gave me a choice: "Go in the Army or go to reform school." It wasn't too long after that I wished I had chosen reform school.

I was in the infantry stationed in Okinawa. We were supposed to go to Japan for more training, but General MacArthur decided we needed more troops in Korea immediately so we went directly to Korea. That was early in July 1950.

We landed at Pusan, and we were in a camp there for a couple of days. I remember one guy shot himself in the foot. I heard his rifle go off. Supposedly he shot himself so he could go home. Anyway, we were loaded on trucks and went about forty miles north above Pusan toward Taejŏn, and that's where I was taken prisoner on July 27, 1950. We had been fighting for a day and a half when the North Koreans simply overran us. A half dozen or so of us were going down this road, thinking we were heading in the right direction. Some North Korean on the hill must have yelled "Americans" because all hell broke loose. I was lying in a shallow stream and shots were hitting the water all around me. That's a good way to wake up in a hurry. I started running down this stream, trying to get away, and I got hit in the shoulder. Then I ran into one of their machine guns, and I said to myself, "Hell, I can't outrun that," so I just threw up my hands and climbed out on the bank.

The first thing that happened was this one guy ripped off the chain holding my dog tags. He threw the dog tags away, and then attached my chain to his uniforms as a kind of decoration. Then they had us carry some boxes—ammunition, I think—up this hill where they just kept gathering more and more prisoners. After that they headed us toward Taejŏn. It was in a police station in Taejŏn where I got my eye knocked out.

Like everybody else, I was asleep on the floor. This guard came in, and I don't know whether he tripped over me or what, but I came up off the floor right quick, and I guess he thought I was going to jump him. He had a pistol in his hand, and he hit me in the side of my face and took out my eye. They never did anything for me, and I carried my eye around in my hand for sixty-three days. This is difficult to explain, but I grabbed that eye and pinched it real hard between my thumb and fingers. You know you have cords—I'll call them that—running back into your head from your eye. Each time I would bounce up and down while I was walking, man, that would hurt. But I hung on to it for sixty-three days. After pinching it so hard, it would go numb—or whatever the hell you want to call it. My eye finally came completely off from my cutting those cords with my fingernails.

I got wounded again on the march northward. We were walking from Taejŏn to Seoul and this Korean woman was sitting alongside the road holding some apples in her lap. I jumped out to get one, and the guards shot me in the foot just as I jumped back.

[*Rookstool and as many as four hundred of his fellow prisoners were held in a schoolhouse in Seoul for several weeks, but when American forces began closing in, they were again marched northward, this time to the North Korean capital of P'yŏngyang. After another four weeks, Rookstool and 239 other prisoners were loaded on the train that ended up in the tunnel outside of Sunch'ŏn, North Korea.*]

In Sunch'ŏn I got shot in the back of the head and the thigh and bayonetted in the right arm and right leg. It's called the Tunnel Massacre, but we were shot outside the actual tunnel. We were on a train heading north when it stopped in this tunnel, and they unloaded us. The guards said they were going to feed us. They lined us, say three abreast, between the end of the train and the opening of the tunnel. They then told us they couldn't find a place big enough to feed all of us at once, so they separated us into groups and marched us by group into these draws. I was in the second bunch. I would guess there were about twenty in the first group, but only twelve in my group. They ordered us to sit down, and, boy, did they feed us!

The first bullet hit me in the thigh, and I fell over toward this bank that the guards were standing on while they shot us. I just shoved my head right up into the bank. They then shot me in the back of the head, but the bullet went in just a little ways and came out. After that they walked over and stuck us with bayonets. When this guard stuck his bayonet into my arm it was the first time it really hurt. It went right into the bone. When he pulled out his bayonet, my arm went right up with it into the air. So he kicked my arm off his bayonet. Goddamn, that hurt! But I didn't yell out.

They just left us there. Every time I tried to stand up, I would just topple over backward. They told me later that was because of the loss of blood. Two other fellows and I had crawled under a shock of corn. All of a sudden I felt one of them feeling around my body. I asked him, "What the hell are you doing?" What he was doing—well, I would have done the same thing—he was looking for any food I might have had. I'm not sure how much time passed, but we heard a Korean running around hollering for us to come on out because the Americans would soon be there. We figured it was a trick. But, finally, we said, "The hell with it." We crawled out and this Korean ran up to us. We couldn't tell a South from a North Korean, but he had an American second lieutenant's bar on his uniform. He was an ROK soldier. He told us the Americans would soon be there. And an airborne outfit did come in and pack us out. They took us back to P'yŏngyang, and then flew us to Japan.

VALDER "VAL" JOHN

I was born March 15, 1931, just outside of Green Bay. I lived there until my father came home from World War II and we moved to Milwaukee. I joined the Army in March 1948 when I was seventeen and was stationed in Japan when the Korean War broke out. We were taken out of the Eighth Army as replacements and sent over with the 24th Division. I was captured in Taejŏn on July 19 or 20, 1950.

We were just overrun. Our officers had told us before we got to Taejŏn that we were going to stay there and fight until the last man. We knew we weren't going anywhere because we were already surrounded. We took quite a pounding for about five days. By then the North Koreans had just about leveled Taejŏn, and we didn't have many people left. General Dean ordered our officers to get everybody in line because we were going to try to break out one way or another. Of course, he was captured there. We tried to break out, but it didn't do any good. They hit us on a road leading out of Taejŏn. They were just machine-gunning the heck out of the place. They got our trucks, jeeps, and whatever was left. They just blew them off that road. I was in the back end of one of the trucks when the driver got hit, and the truck crashed into a building. I was thrown out and a jeep ran over the back of my legs. I also got hit in the hip. I managed to roll into a rice patty alongside the road and stayed there all that afternoon. When it started getting dark, the North Koreans were going around with lanterns, bayonetting and shooting people. Somehow, I squeezed through this rice patty and finally got up in the hills.

I could walk with a stick. Then I met this other guy who was wounded in the foot, and we started walking. We went into this little hamlet up in the hills and tried to get some food and water. They were bringing it to us when the North Koreans came in and captured us. They took us back to Taejŏn and put us in a little jail cell with I guess eight others. I don't know how many days we stayed there, but not many. There was this little crackpot of a guard who came in everyday, pulled the bolt back on his carbine, pointed it at our heads and said, "We've got to shoot you because your troops are getting closer." You couldn't tell whether he was joking or not, but I didn't think we were going to get out alive. He would get so carried away with his Communist thinking that he'd break out in tears and get terribly angry with us. I was very happy when someone told us we were moving out.

They took our boots, and most of us had to march barefoot until we were able to wrap our feet in rice bags. We marched toward Seoul and on the way we picked up other prisoners. Even more POWs joined us in Seoul where they put us in a schoolhouse. We stayed there until about the time of the Inch'ŏn landing in the middle of September. Our guards forced us to march through Seoul with banners denouncing the United Nations. They took movies of us, including some taken by Russians. We had some guy standing at a podium reading a script they gave him. If you didn't cooperate they'd torture you.

They wanted us to become Communists. They would run down the

American government, and being an Indian, they'd say to me, "Look how you've been treated." I tried to tell them I wasn't into politics, that I didn't know anything, and that I had joined the Army because I didn't have anything else to do. Surprisingly, they knew a lot about Indian history. They'd say, "That was your home the government invaded. They killed all your ancestors." Oh, they knew our history real well—better than I did.

They also used physical force on me. Some guy I didn't know told them that I had seen them shoot prisoners with their hands tied behind their backs during the first days of the war. So they pulled me out, cut me up, and pulled out my fingernails. If they wanted you to confess to something, that's what they did. Actually, I had never seen them killing those particular prisoners, but somebody had shown me a photo of dead prisoners from the *Stars and Stripes* newspaper. We all saw those pictures, and they made a great impression on us. Our officers told us, "Don't get captured because they don't take prisoners."

I constantly expected that they were going to kill us. This went on and on, day after day. I remember falling asleep while we were marching. Some guys were holding me up while I slept, because they had been interrogating me for about three days straight, with no sleep. But I didn't give up. I just blocked out of my mind all that stuff they were telling us. It was like a tape recording; every time it was the same thing. To try to warm up to you, they'd say, "Here's a cigarette." And if you resisted, they got tougher and tougher.

When troops from the Inch'ŏn landing moved closer, the North Koreans moved us from Seoul and marched us north to P'yŏngyang. We had a bunch of wounded with us. We had started with 373 men in Seoul, and a lot of them were wounded. By the time we reached P'yŏngyang there were only 250 of us still alive. Again, the guards did the same thing they had earlier. Guys who couldn't walk or couldn't be moved, they'd shoot. They had given us some food in Seoul, but on the march to P'yŏngyang we got hardly anything to eat.

The North Korean guards put us on a train in P'yŏngyang because so many prisoners were dying—dozens at a time. They packed us in these open gondola cars like sardines. Everybody was so weak. We couldn't have made it much longer the way we were living. The train stopped in the tunnel, and the guards ordered us off. One of them told me to get twenty-five men together because we were going to eat. They gave us these little bowls for our food and told us to line up and follow them. They put us in a small ravine and told us to sit down and wait for our food. We sat down, and they started shooting us. I was shot in the arm and fell down. The guy next to me got hit in the leg and his blood splattered all over my face and head. When they got through shooting, they came around and stepped on everybody and pounded on them with their rifle butts. If anybody moved or they thought you were alive, they shot or bayoneted you. They pounded on my back and stuck a bayonet in my side, but not very deep. I just laid there. I guess what saved me was all that blood spattered on me. Then they hurried off to the other groups.

I was unconscious for quite a while. I guess it was the next day when I came to. I heard someone speaking English. They were on the hills looking around. I started yelling and they yelled back. One other guy and I were still alive in my group, but he died that night. Gen. Frank A. Allen from the 1st Cavalry was with the rescue force. I told him I was cold, and he covered me with his jacket. He said, "I am promoting you to a one-star general." I mumbled something like, "I'm awfully dirty, sir, and I'm also pretty lousy." He told me not to worry about that.

Only twenty-one of us came out alive. I really don't know why the North Koreans did this to us. Maybe because we were dying off so fast they didn't want anything more to do with us. Or maybe we were holding up their progress northward.

I spent more than a year and a half convalescing. I had double pneumonia and almost died in Japan. I also had dysentery, but I was lucky because it had just started. Many of those on the march who got it lasted only a matter of days before they died. I weighed less than ninety pounds although I had weighed 227 pounds before I was captured. I ended up in a hospital in the States for eighteen months. My arm kept me there the longest. I had been shot twice in the left arm, and the muscles were all torn up. My arm was just a little piece of bone with a hand stuck to it. They didn't know what to do, and finally one guy operated on it, and put me on these exercises, and my arm started filling out. After that they were going to discharge me, but I said, "No way." I knew if I stayed in the Army they would have to take care of me. I ended up spending twenty-six years in the service.

Maybe they kept me in that hospital so long because they were still investigating me. I found out after I got home that while I was a prisoner some members of I guess a Communist organization came to my parents' house and told them that I wasn't dead but alive and a prisoner. My parents had already received one notice that I was missing and then another that I was dead. My mother didn't want anything to do with these Communists. They just came that one time and left again. After I got back I received a notice that I was to appear before an investigating board. No press would be involved. So I went up there and stayed about a week. My Army counsel told me to answer the questions with a simple yes or no, and not to give them anything more than I had to. Some way or another it came out in the newspaper, including my picture, that I was one of the people being investigated. All this was kind of mysterious and upsetting. When I think back on it, it was degrading to have to go through all this, but, as I told my wife the other day, I've made my peace with all that stuff. I don't even hate the guys who shot me. That was part of my upbringing. My Oneida grandmother had a great influence on me. She taught me spiritual things, such as being at peace with myself. I think that's why when the North Koreans started shooting me, I said, "Forgive them for they know not what they do."

4

DEATH VALLEY AND
THE TEMPORARY CAMPS

In capture, the individual separates from his primary culture and begins the journey into a world of chaos. The prison landscape is the body of that chaos; it represents a place of evil, a place so horrible that only the most graphic terms can describe it.

—Robert Doyle, author of *Voices from Captivity*

Their names were Death Valley, Mining Camp, Bean Camp, or simply the Valley. Their occupants were several thousand United Nations prisoners captured after 300,000 Chinese soldiers secretly flooded over the border into North Korea during the last two weeks of October 1950. In the ensuing weeks the Chinese forces overran the surprised and ill-prepared U.N. troops at such places as Unsan, Ch'ŏngch'ŏn River, Kunu-ri, and the Chosin Reservoir. Unprepared to deal with such large numbers of prisoners, the Chinese put them into temporary holding areas until the permanent camps opened along the Yalu River in the early spring of 1951.

Like those U.N. soldiers captured south of the 38th Parallel during the first months of the war, these new captives also had to endure deadly marches marked by little or no food, debilitating diseases, climatic extremes, and the psychological effects of having seen so many of their buddies killed. There was also the uncertainty of their own fate. Surrounded by death, including the killing of wounded prisoners, the captives gave little credence to those Chinese officers who announced, "Don't think of yourselves as captured, but as liberated." The prisoners did, however, hope their lot would improve once they reached their final destination; indeed, their captors had promised this very thing. Unfortunately, the temporary camps became places of terror and death, with the men reduced to basic instincts for survival.

DEATH VALLEY

Located near an abandoned mining camp some sixty to sixty-five miles south of Pyŏktong and the Yalu River, Death Valley was also known as the "Mining Camp."[1] More prisoners passed through Death Valley than through any of the other temporary camps, and more of them died.

Robert Jones was captured on November 28, 1950, some thirty-five miles north of Kunu-ri near the village of Unsan. Jones and his group of prisoners spent several weeks winding their way north before reaching Death Valley, where thoughts of food and death dominated their existence:

> After we were captured, they made us get on our knees and put our hands behind our heads. Then they walked up and down the line and fired a couple rounds. At the time I thought they were shooting every fifth person. I don't really know if they did or not, but they said that's what they were doing just to let us know they weren't playing and that we had better come peacefully or we wouldn't be coming at all.
>
> At the time, I don't really think they were prepared to take prisoners, and we sure as hell weren't prepared to be prisoners. They just sort of threw us all in together, all ranks, and started marching us. I don't know if it was north, south, east, or west, we just marched. It was colder than hell, but it was going to get a lot colder. I guess we walked for about five weeks. We marched primarily at night. It seemed like the only time I woke up was when we stopped marching. I learned how to sleep while walking.
>
> The Mining Camp or Death Valley, it was all the same—just a group of huts sort of joined together, about six in a row, and about three or four rows deep. They put anywhere from fifteen to twenty men in each hut, which only seemed fifteen by fifteen feet in size. We had to lay down in two lines, and there was only enough room for you to lay on your side and that was it for sleeping arrangements. I got some terrible bedsores on my bad hip. I look back now and think maybe that wasn't all bad because they formed some nice scabs that I used to eat for meat to keep me going. We really had almost nothing to eat in the two months we stayed in Death Valley.
>
> People were dying nightly. It was just too big of a shock to a lot of the guys. I wasn't raised where you ate three meals a day, so I could make it on one, but I wasn't even getting that so I was also having it

rough. But those guys who had been used to eating two or three meals a day just couldn't make it on one. They knew they were going to die, and we knew they were going to die. So someone would ask them, "Well, you ain't going to be around tomorrow, can I have your shoes?" Someone else would say, "I'll take your jacket." Another guy would ask, "How about your ring?" The poor guy would make that kind of agreement. He'd be dead in the morning, and they'd strip him, worse than vultures, and drag him out and throw him into an empty room next to the latrine; just throw him in there. We might not even know his last name. We didn't act like we were Americans—we were just bodies.

We started lying about how many of us were alive so we would get more to eat if we got anything at all. They would give you so much according to how many were alive so we told them more of us were alive than there really were. We even kept dead bodies in the rooms so we could get additional rations, until we couldn't stand it anymore.

Capt. William R. Shadish was a battalion surgeon with the 9th Infantry, 2nd Division, when taken prisoner on December 1, 1950, at the infamous Chinese roadblock near Kunu-ri. The Chinese marched Shadish and approximately one hundred other prisoners in a generally northward direction, picking up another four hundred or so prisoners before arriving at Death Valley the day after Christmas. According to Shadish, "These men had been stripped of all medical supplies and equipment and many had their overcoats and shoes taken away." Many were wounded, and approximately fifty of them died before reaching Death Valley. Based on Shadish's observations, the American Ex-Prisoners of War organization published a 1981 pamphlet that included a brief description of Death Valley:

Death Valley was divided into two sections, north and south, about two miles apart, and officers were placed in the south section. The north section was approximately half the size of the south section. In the south section there were six barracks-like buildings with four to six units per barracks. A unit consisted of a room and a kitchen area. There were twenty-five men in Captain Shadish's unit—so crowded that two-thirds of the group had to sit with their knees under their chins while the remaining one-third lay down. The men rotated positions. Korean-type floor heating was used, but wood was so scarce that heat was available for only one hour each day. Food consisted of 400 grams [14 ounces] of cracked corn per man per day.[2]

Capt. Gene N. Lam was a battalion surgeon with the 2nd Infantry Division when he was captured on December 1, 1950, and witnessed the killing of the wounded litter prisoners (see chapter three). Lam later estimated that less than half of the approximately 1,200 2nd Division men who were captured with him at the Chinese roadblock near Kunu-ri survived:

The Chinese obviously hadn't anticipated holding a large number of captives and had no confinement area prepared. We were subjected to night marches in sub-zero weather for about three weeks while they searched for a suitable place to confine us. On Christmas night, 1950, we arrived at a deserted mining camp, which we soon named Death Valley. The wounded with us at the time of capture had been taken away from us; their fate is unknown. No medical supplies were available. Pneumonia, dysentery, hepatitis, and malnutrition were the leading causes of death. Our food consisted of cracked corn and millet. On New Year's Day, the Chinese produced a hog's head for a treat for the entire camp, which held about 1,100 men. Housing consisted of rooms about 12' × 12' into which twenty to twenty-five men were crammed. The temperature hovered between twenty and thirty degrees below zero. Body heat helped keep us from freezing. . . .

Facilities for sanitation were practically nonexistent. There were three small pit latrines around the camp, but they were soon filled and frozen. The men then relieved themselves whenever and wherever the urge moved them. As a result, in a few weeks the area was littered with frozen feces and frozen urine. We attempted to keep the area clean but could not do this due to a lack of cooperation. The water supply was the nearby river. It ran on a lower level from all the latrines of the camp and consequently was contaminated at all times. The men were instructed to boil the water for drinking, but many did not heed this advice, with subsequent diarrhea and dysentery. No facilities were made available for personal hygiene. The only way the men could wash was to use snow or the river water. . . . No clothing was issued; consequently, when a man died his clothing was stripped from him and given to the other men without proper clothing. . . .

The Chinese used the local school as a hospital. It was a place to die. After thirty days in Death Valley, twenty to twenty-five men died each day. In the bitter cold of the North Korean winter, the dead were stacked like cordwood away from the camp. I remember passing the stacked bodies when we left in March of 1951. Of the 1100 men who arrived in Death Valley, fewer than 500 left the camp three months later. All the rest had died. Of the 110 members of my medical company taken to Death Valley, thirty-five were alive to be moved to another camp three months after their arrival.[3]

Most of the rooms were too small for all the men to sleep comfortably at the same time, so they took turns standing, sitting, or sleeping. There was also no heat except that generated by the close proximity of so many bodies. However, the resourceful Captain Lam and some of his men were able to get some heat in the makeshift hospital the Chinese allowed the prisoners:

They let us set up this little hospital. They gave us two fifty-five gallon drums to make a stove . . . but they didn't give us anything to burn. Right next door was one of the few buildings in Korea built with boards. Within two weeks every board and every piece of straw in it had disappeared; in fact, the whole building had disappeared. When I was called in, the commander asked me what had happened to the building. I told him, "Well, obviously you are mistaken. There is no building there." They knew we stole it, but they didn't know how.[4]

The exact number of prisoners held in Death Valley is difficult to ascertain. Lam put the number at 1,100, but historian Raymond Lech estimates there were 3,000 prisoners, of whom approximately 500 died.[5] David Polk, who gathered materials on Death Valley and other camps for the Korean War Ex-POW Association, puts the number at between 1,000 and 2,000, with 1,200 surviving.[6] All agreed, however, that a few ounces of cracked corn or millet a day were insufficient to keep the men alive. In order to survive, the prisoners had to take desperate measures. In 1954, after returning to active duty in Nevada, Captain Lam lectured young soldiers on prisoner survival techniques and described what he and his fellow prisoners were forced to eat in Death Valley and in the permanent camps as well:

When you are captured, you are not going to be fed very much. And if you miss one meal because it doesn't look good to you, it will take you over a week to make up for what you've lost. You are on a bare subsistence level and you can't afford to miss any meals. If you are going to walk out, you have to be in shape to do it.

You've got to eat any- and everything they give you, anything that grows, anything you can steal—and I mean anything. We ate cats and dogs and rats and weeds, and, the *pièce de résistance,* maggots. Cats taste just like squirrels. Dogs are like strong beef. A rat has a slightly wild taste. But maggots taste like no comparable food I know. Just delicious [laughs]. You may have to choke a little to get them down, but they are meat. They gave us rotten meat that was loaded with maggots. The Englishman we had cooking for us said, "My God, I can't do it." He wanted to wash them off the meat. I told him, "No! Just throw them in with the meat." And they turned out extremely good. You will be repulsed by the food they give you. You look at it and think, "I can't possibly eat that." The only time you really have to look at it is when it looks back at you. When it does, just grab a stick, beat it, and eat it anyway [laughs].

We ate weeds. In the spring of 1951, every man in our camp had severe beriberi. We were swollen up like a bunch of balloons. The weeds started to come up and we gathered every weed that grew. We didn't know what they were, but we tried them all. Within a month we had completely cleared up our beriberi. So from then on, weeds were added to our diet. There wasn't a weed growing in our compound. They used to take us down the river on wood runs, but it wasn't how much wood you could bring back, but how many weeds.[7]

On January 21, 1951, those Death Valley prisoners who could walk left for Camp Five at Pyŏktong. The sick and wounded would spend another seven weeks in Death Valley cared for by men like William Shadish and infantry medic Sgt. Charles B. Schlichter.

Schlichter was captured during the retreat from Kunu-ri on December 1, 1950. He and fourteen other prisoners marched through snow and cold for almost four weeks before arriving on December 26 at what military historian T. R. Fehrenbach, who told Sergeant Schlichter's story, describes as "a snow-covered bauxite mining camp they would call Death Valley." According to Fehrenbach, the Chinese immediately began their attempted indoctrination of Schlichter and his fellow prisoners:

A slender Chinese officer addressed them in broken English. He told them that the People's Volunteers had decided to treat them not as war criminals, but under China's new Lenient Policy. Though the officer did not say it, the average Army POW would be treated much like an average Chinese felon or class enemy. No great pressures would be put on him, other than those of starvation, lack of medical care, and a certain amount of indoctrination. . . . The officer told the shivering, tired, fearful POWs one thing more: "Everybody here is the same. No officers, no NCOs here. Everybody is equal!"[8]

In accordance with their deliberate policy of humiliating the officers, the Chinese assigned Sergeant Schlichter the responsibility for the camp hospital rather than putting in charge an Army doctor such as Captain Shadish. However, the two men worked together:

The crude "hospital" had pallets for only sixty men, among the hundreds who had untreated combat wounds, dysentery, pneumonia, jaundice, and psychic disorders. The Chinese allowed Shadish exactly enough medicines to give four men one sulfa tablet four times a day. Each day, Shadish and Schlichter, crawling from man to man, had to play God. To the four men who had the best chance to live, they administered the sulfa. The worse off, Schlichter said later, "We committed to God's care."[9]

Caring for the sick and wounded in Death Valley was an impossible task. According to William Shadish, less than 10 percent of these men would survive captivity:

Of the 250 to 300 sick and wounded left in Death Valley on January 21, 1951, only 109 survived to make the trip to Camp Five on March 13, 1951. Fifteen ox-carts were furnished as transportation, and the trip took seven days during which eleven more lost their lives. It became difficult for many of the prisoners to continue the march after the third or fourth day. The guards used rifle butts on those who fell behind. On the last day of the march a truck picked up twenty-four of the prisoners and took them to Camp Five. Seventy-five percent of the sick and wounded group died soon after arrival at Camp Five on March 19.[10]

Sergeant Schlichter accompanied twenty of these sick prisoners on a mule cart. As the last to leave Death Valley, the young medic looked back and saw "three starving Korean dogs, snuffling warily in from the hills to feed on the bodies of the young Americans they had left behind."[11]

THE VALLEY

The Valley was located near the village of Sombakol, some six or seven miles from Pyŏktong, where several of the permanent camps would open in the spring of 1951. Some of the prisoners thought the Valley had also once been a mining camp. Mountains towered above the Valley, closing out the sun and pushing temperatures down to thirty and forty below zero. The men were put in small, mud-walled huts with straw roofs that did little to keep out the cold. Army physician Sidney Esensten, who was captured on November 27, 1950, describes the scene:

> The Sombakol camp was in a valley where the prisoners from the First Cavalry had been captured on November 4, 1950. Then we joined them about the middle of December. We stayed there until about the middle of January of 1951 when they moved us to Pyŏktong, which became the major camp for all the prisoners of the war. The valley was three miles long, a half mile wide, and surrounded by cliffs that were 8,000 feet high. There weren't any buildings that were treatable, because they were all damaged.[12]

According to Raymond Lech, the death rate was much lower in the Valley than in the other temporary camps, with only twenty-four deaths occurring among the 750 American prisoners. Lech credits the organizing efforts of Lt. Cols. Harry Fleming and Paul Liles with keeping the men alive.[13] Both Fleming and Liles, however, would later be court-martialed, largely because they worked too closely with their Chinese and North Korean captors in their efforts to keep their men alive. Fleming later explained to his court-martial board, "The most futile thing in the world was a dead prisoner of war in North Korea. I had determined that I was going to do everything in my power to keep those people alive."[14] Liles, who as ranking officer supported Fleming's efforts, later told his court-martial board, "I was more concerned with keeping myself and my men alive than in preserving my own honor and reputation."[15] Some of the prisoners had, however, turned against Fleming, perhaps because their captors encouraged such behavior but also because under such abysmal conditions starving men tend not to trust anyone else to look after their own welfare.

Before ending up in the Valley, Lt. William H. Funchess was captured by the Chinese on November 4, 1950, near the town of Anju in North

Korea. A bullet had gone through his foot, and it was badly swollen and bleeding, but he was determined to walk after witnessing what the Chinese did to those prisoners who could not march:

> We came across some wounded GIs lying on the ground. The enemy soldiers kicked and prodded them with bayonets in an effort to get them on their feet. When the GIs were unable to stand, the enemy soldiers forced us to walk past the wounded. In a few seconds I heard several rifle shots. I turned my head and saw the GIs had been killed. Right then I made up my mind that regardless how badly my foot hurt I would keep going. I knew I would be killed on the spot if I was unable to walk and became a burden to the guards.[16]

With only a stick-crutch to aid him, Lieutenant Funchess spent three weeks stumbling over increasingly steep and icy terrain before he and some fifty other prisoners stopped outside Pyŏktong, which the Chinese told them would be their permanent camp.[17] The day after their arrival, however, Pyŏktong was badly bombed, and they were moved several miles to the Valley where they would stay from late November until the end of January when they returned to Pyŏktong and the newly opened Camp Five:

> As darkness fell, we were assembled and told to move out. . . . We went cross-country for a while before reaching a dirt road. After getting on the road we walked uphill for an hour or so and then it was downhill for a couple of hours. Finally we reached an isolated snow-covered valley about six or seven miles northwest of Pyŏktong. It was sparsely settled and I saw a small group of mud huts with thatched roofs and another group of shacks several hundred yards away.
>
> They took me to a room and pushed me inside. The room contained a number of GIs and I was the last one to arrive. A guard threw in a bundle of dried corn stalks as bedding. The stalks were about three-fourths of an inch in diameter and were too hard to sleep on. Closer inspection revealed some of the stalks still had a "nubbin" ear of corn attached. We ate the dried corn immediately and threw the corn stalks out the door. This was to be our home for the next eight or nine weeks. We called it "The Valley" for lack of a better name. . . .
>
> Temperatures were far below freezing, but . . . we were given no clothing or shoes and had no blankets or anything to use as cover. All we had were the clothes on our back. [Our] summer uniforms did little to protect us against the bitter cold. The only way to keep from

freezing to death was to cling as tightly as possible to the man nearest you. . . .

[In] a little more than two months the Communists never gave us any type of vegetable or meat. We had no water to drink but there was a bountiful supply of snow outside. Needless to say, they gave us no salt, sugar, eggs, seasoning or anything else—just a cupful of grain twice a day, except for some occasional soybeans.

I would not call the toilet facilities primitive. They were nonexistent. We went outside a few feet from the shack to answer the call of nature. Those who were seriously wounded were lucky to make it to the porch. Fortunately there were no odors outside because everything froze immediately. The stench of pus-filled wounds and decaying flesh inside the shack was sickening, however. The fact that nobody had a bath for a couple of months didn't help any. The odors were worse after going outside in the cold fresh air and then returning to the room with the wounded. I knew my foot stank because I could smell it whenever I sat down. I couldn't see the extent of the injury caused by the machine gun bullet because my foot was black with pus, dried blood, and dirt. . . .

The Chinese guards never came inside the room to search us because they couldn't stand the odor. They counted us several times each day and night. Instead of coming inside, the guard would throw the door open, hold his breath, hastily count and then slam the door shut. Usually the guard had a sick look on his face if he ever took a breath inside the room. Several times one little guard threw up after taking his head count inside the room.

I told the men in the room I had a Bible and asked if they wanted me to read to them. All of them answered in the affirmative. . . . I started at the beginning of the Bible and read one chapter. After a few hours I read another chapter. I kept it up as long as I was in the room. It gave all of us a feeling of comfort in the strange land so far away from home.[18]

THE BEAN CAMP

It was called the "Bean Camp" because of the small soybean balls that made up the daily food allowance. It was located near P'yŏngyang where it too had evidently once been a mining camp; in fact, some prisoners also referred to it as the Mining Camp. According to Lech, it held some nine hundred prisoners, approximately one third of whom would die in part because of "a gross lack of discipline." So bad was the chaos, writes Lech, that the soldiers "became a mob." Officers were "required to remove their insignia of rank, and camp administrators commanded captured enlisted men to neither talk with the officers nor take orders from them."[19]

Sgt. Don Poirot, who was captured on February 13, 1951, does not recall being part of "a mob" or refusing to talk to officers in the Bean Camp, but he certainly remembers conditions so filthy and seemingly hopeless that many of the prisoners gave up their will to live:

It must have been two or three weeks, possibly more, before we arrived at what was called the Bean Camp. It consisted of a configuration of buildings that must have been set up for a special purpose. There was a main street that had long buildings on each side of the road. As best I can remember there were five or six rooms in the long building and a kitchen at one end. There must have been six or eight buildings on each side of the road. About in the middle of the buildings which were meant to be lived in there was a larger building that was used to cook meals. There were six or eight water wells, and all water was boiled before being drunk.

The meals consisted of a purplish seed. When cooked it became swollen like rice. To this was added some cooked soybeans which were then placed in a little bowl. The ration was one bowl per man per day as I remember. The soybeans weren't always completely cooked and this, plus using water that had not been boiled, caused a very high rate of dysentery. There was human feces all over the place from those that couldn't make it to the latrine areas. Men died every day. The living conditions were terrible, and men just gave up the will to live. I saw men say, "To hell with it," and just lie there and die within a couple of days. I saw this not just once or twice but many times. Survival was based on a saying that has become common today: "Take it one day at a time."

There was one room designated the "sick room." If one of the Chinks decided a man was sick enough, we would carry him down there. In this so-called sick room were millions of flies. When they settled on the wall there was almost no place that was not occupied by a fly.

On two or three occasions I was chosen to go on burial detail. We carried and dragged the deceased to a designated place and with an old shovel and a pick we dug down about eighteen to twenty-four inches, which was as deep as we could go in our poor condition. We dropped the corpse in the hole and someone read a few words from a Bible. We shoveled the dirt in and went on about our way. It wasn't a job that any of us liked, but someone had to do it.[20]

Billy Joe Harris was captured February 13, 1951. After some four weeks of marching, he ended up in the Bean Camp, where he admits his spirits hit rock bottom. He felt so desperate that even when given the opportunity to write home, he refused to do so:

Our morale reached an all-time low in Bean Camp. We lost a lot of men. They were dying of starvation and dysentery. We just didn't have anything to eat, and we had no medical supplies. That was in April 1951. While we were there, the Chinese came in and told us they would give paper and pencils to anyone who wanted to write home. They told us the mail would go back through China and on to Switzerland and then to the U.S. I had made up my mind that the condition I was in I wasn't going to write because I didn't think I was going to make it. I'd just as soon my folks not know what had happened as get a letter from me and then I'd die. So I didn't write. But a friend in the same room did, and I guess he mentioned my name and address. During the peace talks his name never showed up, but his parents had received this letter stating that he was a POW. The truth was, he had died shortly after he wrote that letter.

In mid-April of 1951 Harris witnessed one of the deadliest "friendly fire" tragedies of the war, when two P-51s strafed and bombed several buildings in the Bean Camp:

The main supply route from the north was just a little west of us, and our Air Force kept attacking us because the place wasn't marked. One of those planes hit and killed seventeen or eighteen of our guys. I was one of the guys who had to pick up what we could of those guys and carry them up to two holes where we buried them. We weren't even able to take their dog tags, so they are still among the missing. I only knew the names of two or three, and I turned their names in when I got back, but there were also guys nobody knew. At the time you weren't really interested in anybody's name unless they were in your squad.

Lech writes that the Bean Camp closed shortly after the deadly bombing. Of the six hundred survivors who began marching northward toward their final destination at Camp One near the village of Ch'ŏngsong, less than half of them would make it.[21]

At least 4,000 United Nations prisoners passed through the temporary camps.[22] The fortunate ones spent only a day or two; others spent as much as three months. For those who spent most of that dreadful winter of 1950–51 in these camps, a death rate approaching 50 percent was not uncommon. Historians Raymond Lech and T. R. Fehrenbach argue that more of the enlisted men might have survived if they had better supported one another and had been more accepting of those officers who remained committed to the welfare of their men. Perhaps, but this is also blaming the victim. If there had been sufficient food, clothing, and medical care, without question the prisoner death rate would have been closer to the 2 percent figure suffered by American POWs interned in Nazi Germany, where enlisted men also tended to be self-centered, disorganized, and isolated from their officers.

5

LIFE IN THE PERMANENT CAMPS

You just had to take it one day at a time. I opened my eyes each morning in the hope I was going to close them that night.
—Douglas Tanner, Korean War POW

I knew that somehow I was going to get out. I had made my mind up regardless of how bad it got, I was not going to succumb and holler, "I don't have the will to live." I was going to hang in there until I got off that peninsula; then if I fell dead I figured that I had accomplished my mission. I didn't want my body buried over there in that God-forsaken land.
—Glenn Reynolds, Korean War POW

The majority of American prisoners ended up in five Chinese-administered permanent camps along the Yalu River that separated North Korea from Manchuria.[1] By far the largest was Camp Five, which was located just outside of Pyŏktong. It contained approximately three-quarters of the American POWs and eventually contained only enlisted men. Camp Two was an officers' camp located just northeast of Camp Five. Camp Four, which was for sergeants, was located farther up the Yalu near the village of Wiwŏn. Camps One and Three contained enlisted men and were to the southwest of Pyŏktong, near the town of Changsŏng. The North Koreans continued to run the two interrogation centers known as Pak's Palace and Camp Twelve, as well as Camp Nine, which the prisoners referred to as the Caves. All three of these camps were located near the North Korean capital of P'yŏngyang.[2]

The prisoners in these camps suffered from bitter cold and inadequate shelter, insufficient and filthy clothing, dangerously contaminated water, unsanitary conditions, lice and other pests, boredom and lethargy, debilitating diseases, uncertainty about their future, and, above all, acute hunger. According to the international governing principles of the Geneva Convention on Prisoners of War, "The food ration of prisoners of war shall be equal in quantity and quality to that of troops at the base camps of the detaining Power." Neither China nor North Korea, however, were signatories, and even if they had lived up to the spirit of the Geneva accord, many American prisoners would have had trouble surviving on the meager rations and mostly vegetarian diet of the average Communist soldier.

In earlier twentieth-century wars, the International Red Cross periodically inspected POW camps and often furnished supplies to the internees, but its representatives were not allowed in the North Korean camps until the final days of captivity. Without any kind of outside help, the U.N. prisoners remained entirely at the mercy of their captors who, until the summer of 1951, made little effort to keep them alive.

Chance was all important in determining who survived. Between three and four thousand Americans died in captivity, and the overwhelming majority perished during the first nine months of the war because of exposure, disease, mistreatment, and starvation.

As had been the case in the temporary camps, the prisoners were stuffed into crowded, filthy, and often unheated quarters. They were also subject to disciplinary measures for various transgressions and endless indoctrination and propaganda sessions. Momentary respite came from infrequent mail calls, visits to camp libraries (which unfortunately contained mostly pro-Communist literature), occasional games of cards or chess, and, above all, from long conversations and friendships with fellow prisoners. According to Michael Cornwell, if you made it through that first winter, when the death rate far exceeded 50 percent, your chances for survival greatly improved:

When we were under the administration of the North Koreans in Camp Five, they didn't give a damn. They would have just as soon killed us all. They could care less if we lived or died. We had hardly anything to eat. No blankets. Very little heat. No medicine. Zero. So we lost half our men: 1,500 people. Nobody knows what really killed most of them. Exposure. Dysentery. You could catch a bad cold and it would kill you. Bad water. We drank out of the Yalu River. They told us not to, and they were right. A lot of people also just gave up.

Eventually in the summer of 1951 they moved some of us north to Camp Four. If you could make it until May 1, 1951, chances were you would survive. That's when the Chinese took over the camps. They immediately cleaned us up. We were filthy, dirty, and covered with lice. All we had were the clothes on our backs. So they started improving things, but that's also when they started their indoctrination sessions.

They sort of planned it that way. See how good we are to you? Now we are going to get something out of you. I always felt the North Koreans had reduced us to animals, and that's just about what we were. We were little better than wild beasts. Hunger is a horrible thing to live with, and we were starving. Our diet, morning and evening, before May 1951 was cracked corn. They cooked it, but not always long enough to get it soft. By April 1, 1951, I imagine I didn't weigh 115 pounds. We were all just skin and bones.

In addition to starving their prisoners, the Communists fomented chaos by not allowing the officers and NCOs to give orders to the enlisted men and by eventually isolating the upper ranks into their own compounds or camps. According to historian Raymond Lech, this segregation policy had "a devastating effect on morale because enlisted men had no one to follow and officers and NCOs had no one to lead." Lech further argues that because of this lack of discipline, "The groups of Americans degenerated into rabble. Each man felt himself alone and isolated, unprotected by his fellows and fair game for anything the Chinese might choose to do to him."[3] Arguably, Lech over-emphasizes this lack of leadership, but many enlisted men admit they were reduced to basic survival instincts that often did pit one man against another; however, most cite a lack of food as the causative factor rather than diminished leadership. After all, once the quality and quantity of food improved, so too did their mental outlook, organizational skills, and willingness to help each other.

FOOD AND WATER

Whether awake or asleep, food dominated the thoughts of all prisoners except those who had given up and were waiting to die. Until the final months of captivity, there was never enough food, and what did exist was either lacking in nutrition and vitamins or so coarse it was difficult to digest. The Chinese argued that the prisoners could expect to eat no better than their average line soldier, but there is also ample evidence that they initially deliberately withheld rations in anticipation that starving prisoners would be more susceptible to their propaganda efforts. Whatever the motivation of the captors, the result was prisoners so hungry that, according to Billy Joe Harris, they acted like "raven wolves":

Starvation is the second worst death you can have. Only a lingering death from being burned is worse. It's a slow death. The pain is always there, and you think about it all day long. Food is all that sticks in your mind. When you go to sleep, you dream about it. You get up the next morning, and it's the same thing. It's a miserable way to die. In hard times people normally pull together, but when times get too bad, they go the other way. At a certain point humans become like raven wolves, and that's where we were as prisoners. Whatever you could get—and however you could get it—that was it. Basic survival was what it amounted to. When you get down so far, you don't think of anybody but yourself. It's a terrible state to be in, and I saw it in Korea.

Many men died because they could not force themselves to consume food that looked so unpalatable, but Roy Hardage understood he had to eat anything he could scrounge if he were going to survive:

All of us had some form of dysentery, but I always ate the burned crust off the bottom of the pot. We set it up so the burned stuff would go to one squad one day and to another the next. I had heard World War II POWs say this was good for dysentery. Besides, it was chow.

There were a lot of guys who just couldn't eat all their food because of their condition. After you eat only straight corn or barley day after day, month after month with no salt or bread to accompany it—well, this "horse feed" really gets hard to force down. But I knew damn well if I didn't eat it, I'd die. So I would try to keep my mind on something else. I would never look down at my food so I could ignore the worms in it. If you look at the same chow day after day, it will eventually crack you up. When eating it was best to get in a big argument; then, before you realized it, you had swallowed your food.

Some of the guys just couldn't eat so they'd take their food down to the creek and throw it in. When the Chinks discovered this, they would chew our ass out at roll call and then cut our chow. They'd tell us, "We give you too much to eat because you throw the People's food away." They were always talking about "the People's this," and "the People's that." It was just more of their propaganda.

It really made the Chinese feel good to tell us that they must be giving us too much food, so I began going around the platoon like a hungry dog raiding a trash can, picking up all the chow people didn't want and eating it myself. I knew I should eat everything I could find because the time might come when I could no longer eat. Some of the guys made fun of me. They'd say, "Boy this *go-hung* really agrees with you. They must eat the same thing back in Oklahoma." I would answer them with a little slogan I'd always say when eating: "Eat *go-hung* and go home."

The Chinks would come snooping around and watch us eat, and that really pissed me off. Sometimes I'd get so mad I'd say, "Look, you bastards, I'll eat this shit and stay alive, but when I reach the United States I can laugh at you poor bastards because you'll have to eat this for the rest of your life." It would really piss them off when you told them, "*Grunt-grunts* eat better chow than this." Then you'd grunt like a hog.[4]

Wayman Simpson, who survived the Tiger Death March and ended up in Camp Three, also understood a tenacious spirit and a willingness to eat anything were mandatory for survival:

When I first got captured I made up my mind that I was not going to give in or give up. There were some who told themselves over and over, "If I die I am out of the mess." But I was going to eat everything I could beg, borrow, or steal—clean, dirty, or otherwise. If I thought something had a little nutrition I ate it. And that just stayed with me. I think it helped that we were raised during the Depression and didn't have much to eat. We knew how to tough it out. We knew how to adjust if something different came along. A lot of guys couldn't adjust to their changing circumstances. I can remember these guys on post before we got to Korea. They'd skip lunch and dinner and go to the snack bar. We called them "snack bar babies." Guys like me ate all three meals in the mess hall. You had to have a will to live and to eat whatever there was.

The men began to do better when the Chinese took over the camps and allowed them to do their own cooking. Richard Bassett, who was captured on October 6, 1951, after conditions had begun to improve, describes how the men in Camp Five learned to prepare their meager rations in ways that would do the least harm to their bodies:

The method of preparing our food was very primitive. Each company had its own kitchen that was simply a long shed with a series of fireplaces over which hung a huge black pot. Everything was boiled in these pots although occasionally our cooks, who were affectionately called "belly robbers," would get enough bean oil to fry the chow, which was something special. Each kitchen had its own crew and chief cook who were supervised by one Chinese officer and two Chinese soldiers. There were water carriers who did nothing but carry water, wood choppers who chopped the wood, and firemen who built the fires and kept them going. All of these men were volunteers, and they enjoyed certain privileges such as not attending roll call, pulling company details, or having to attend certain lectures. As a group they were a good bunch of guys who did everything they could to make our food go as far and as equitably as possible.

The men rarely had meat in the camps, and certainly not until overall conditions began gradually to improve in the spring and summer of 1951, when they would occasionally get pork. Bob Carman describes the challenge of preparing and eating a pig:

Before we'd cook a pig, we'd call one of the camp doctors and he would examine the pig for trichinosis—we called them triggers. He would say, "Cook him real, real good!" These triggers looked about the size of a grain of rice. When you'd stick the pig, they would just pour out in the blood. The doctor said, "They're just extra meat as long as they're cooked." At first, I just could not eat it. I flat out couldn't. We'd boil him first; then we would take him out and skin him, and chop the skin up real fine. Then we'd clean the bones off and clean the head up. We would even clean the brains out. Man, we didn't leave anything. Then we'd throw the rest of the carcass in the pot and make gravy for the morning meal of rice. If we had enough cabbage, potatoes, or soybeans, we'd throw them in as well. We ate an awful lot of soybeans. That's where we got our protein.

Almost all prisoners suffered from dysentery. On the long marches they often drank water from contaminated rivers, rice paddies, and wells. In the permanent camps they learned to boil their water; in fact, according to Don Poirot, in Camp Two the Chinese eventually demanded they do so:

Our captors insisted that all water be boiled before drinking. I suppose this was due to the lack of purified water or a means to purify it before using. It was not uncommon to see one of the Chinese drinking hot water from a cup just like you would tea or coffee. But to an American used to drinking water with ice in it, the very thought of drinking water hot or warm just didn't sit too well. A lot of times we drank water from one of our wells or some other source. Some men came down with dysentery which was probably caused by that water. If one of the guards, or other Chinese personnel, caught one of us drinking water that had not been boiled they would raise hell with us.

Poirot also learned to eat his food without looking too closely at what kind of creature might be sharing his meal:

We were still eating that purplish stuff in Camp Two that we called maize. There was also a side dish of maybe a little Chinese cabbage or, from time to time, some pork or fish. A few times I happened to be down at the kitchen when the rations came in. This one day it was salted fish in a wooden box, but there were a lot of maggots on the fish. We still ate it after it was cooked, but I quit going near the kitchen when the rations came in. I guess there is something to that old adage about what you don't know won't hurt you. We did receive rice from time to time, but that other stuff was still our staple.

Several developments in mid-1951 impacted the quality and quantity of the food in the permanent camps. With so many prisoners continuing to die, the Chinese became increasingly alarmed about public opinion in a war that was also being fought through international periodicals and news-reels. By this time, the Chinese were also using food as an inducement during their indoctrination sessions. Finally, as Robert Fletcher reports, the start of the truce talks in June 1951, and their stormy two-year history, also had a pronounced effect on living conditions in Camp Five:

By the fall of 1951 we were getting a little better diet. They were oc-casionally giving us a little rice. On Chinese holidays we'd get rice and maybe a little piece of pork. By 1952 I'm sure the Chinese realized they had to fatten us up. Peace talks were progressing, and if we went home in this sorry condition, the world was going to condemn the Chinese.

SMOKING

Many prisoners' addiction to tobacco was so strong that some were willing to give up anything, even their food, for something to smoke. According to Don Poirot, the Chinese regularly gave the men a small amount of tobacco, but it was clearly not enough to satisfy the needs of heavy smokers.

We were given a tobacco ration. It came in a little package about one inch thick, two inches wide, and approximately five inches long. No cigarette papers were issued. Some men made pipes out of various items and others used any and all kinds of paper, including the small Bibles that someone had been carrying. I didn't smoke so I gave my ration of tobacco to a different person each time it was issued. I think we received five or six packages a month. There was always a market for the tobacco if you wanted to sell it.

Jack Browning was shocked that some of his fellow prisoners, who like him had survived the Tiger Death March, were now willing to risk even death for a cigarette:

With such a meager diet it was absolutely essential that you ate what little they gave you, regardless whether or not you had any appetite. Some of the men, who would rather smoke than eat, traded their meager bits of food for tobacco, which contributed to several of their deaths.

Philip Deane, who was one of the civilian survivors of the Tiger Death March, also witnessed the power of tobacco:

Once a guard dropped a cigarette butt. Two of the dying youngsters, moving with horrifying slowness, got down to the ground and crawled like insects towards the smoking butt. They reached their objective together. Slowly, they raised their arms, and slowly, they hit each other. You could hear bone hit bone, and you could see the brittle skin part, uncovering the bone. They gasped and moaned as they fought. When one of them fell to the ground, the other moved to pick up the spoils. The cigarette butt had burned out.[5]

Jeff Erwin had his own solution to the tobacco problem:

Some of the guys who smoked about went crazy. About the second spring we were there this Korean gave me and another guy a handful of tobacco seeds. We planted them alongside this little creek that ran through the camp. It got up waist high with big old leaves. Guys were drying it on pieces of tin and rolling cigarettes. Those seeds and the residue of the soybeans was the only thing I got from the Koreans or anybody else.

There was another kind of smoking in which many of the prisoners indulged, although, according to Robert Fletcher, no one had to barter or bribe anyone to get a supply:

Marijuana grew wild in Korea, bushes as high as this roof. I didn't know what it was. In the frontlines we had used it for camouflage. Guys would say, "You've got a million dollars over your head." I would look up and say, "Where?" They would shake their heads because I didn't know what was going on. We would go out on wood detail, and some guys would come back with bulging pants. I would ask, "What you got, onions and stuff in there?" And they would say, "Oh, we got something better than that." I'd ask, "What are you talking about; that's nothing but a weed; you can't eat that stuff." I was still a dumb, little country boy. I didn't know nothing about it.

Don Poirot was equally naive about these abundant "green-looking weeds" that seemed to grow wild all over Korea:

On one of our details to collect wood we were passing a crop of some green-looking weeds when someone said, "That's marijuana." Most of our detail walked right into the field and started pulling up stalks of this stuff. In the meantime, the guards were having a fit. They didn't know if we were starting a riot, getting ready to escape, or what. The stuff was green, but it didn't take long for someone to get a sheet of tin and dry the stuff out over the embers of our cooking fire. What they didn't dry, they put up on the roof of the huts to dry normally. I wasn't going to try this stuff and after the initial trial, all but a few of the guys let the stuff go.

Jim Crombie only tried marijuana twice, but discovered that it did have a pronounced effect on him:

I smoked marijuana twice around the holidays while I was in POW camp. The Turks would go out of the camp and get it. I don't know how to judge marijuana, but the stuff I had, well, you didn't give a dang whether anything happened that day. We'd pass that joint around and everybody would lie there laughing and hollering. You'd never know we were in a POW camp.

MAIL

Nothing could do more to raise a prisoner's spirits than a letter from home, but until conditions gradually improved in mid-1951 there was little or no mail. The Chinese then decided that, like food and cigarettes, the mail could be used to reward or punish prisoner behavior. The Chinese also wanted to use the mail to convince the world of their "lenient policies," but they tightly censored incoming and outgoing letters, and many never reached their intended readers. For Bob Carman, this was an untenable situation:

> My wife never received any of my mail. I received two letters from her, one from my mother, and one from a friend of my mother's. That was all the mail I received so I quit writing. I just quit because other people were getting ten, fifteen letters a crack, and I wasn't getting zip. When I quit writing, this Chinese official came to me and asked, "Why don't you write?"
>   I told him, "Because you don't send my letters."
>   He said, "Oh, we don't hold up your letters; they are sent out."
>   I told him again, "No, I'm not writing any more letters."
>   He said, "Oh, but you must."
>   And I said, "No, I mustn't." So I did not write another letter.

Incoming mail could take months to arrive unless, explains Douglas Tanner, the letter contained "demoralizing or depressing" news that the Chinese hoped to exploit:

> A letter to us at Camp Four would take anywhere from three to six months. I got one letter telling me of my grandmother's death and it came in only three weeks. I hadn't even finished reading it when the Chinese took me to camp headquarters and asked, "Do you feel sad, do you feel bad at having lost a loved one and you're so many miles from home, fighting this unjust war?" Any letter that contained anything that they felt would be demoralizing or depressing came through quickly.
>   One of the guys in Camp Four received a letter from his father who was a car salesman, and he had enclosed this business card showing a new 1953 Oldsmobile. I have no idea why the Chinese allowed that letter to come through, but they called him in and said, "You don't

have anything like that in the United States; that's propaganda." Well, when I got home I bought one of those pieces of propaganda.

All letters were censored, but, according to Tanner, there were ingenious ways of fooling the censors:

They started letting us write letters home in 1951, but if there wasn't something in there about being well treated and well fed, the letter never got out. Well, I had a little thing going. My grandparents raised me, and when my grandmother felt I wasn't quite telling the truth, she would say, "Go tell it to the Marines." So I put in my letter to her, "The treatment isn't bad, the food is all right, and please go tell it to the Marines."

Robert Schaefer also used deception to dupe the censors in Camp One:

When you wrote letters home you could put in a code. You could say, "I'm being well treated, even better than I was in high school. Even Coach Jones never treated me this well." Everybody back home would know that was a lie.

Jeff Erwin neither received nor successfully sent any mail, but one of his buddies did manage to get the truth past the Chinese censors:

I had been married for a year and a half, but the Chinese wouldn't let any mail go out, especially if you were someone who didn't agree with them. So I just remained an MIA. We had a Marine captain there, I can't remember his name, but he wrote a letter home saying we were having really good food and that he was looking forward to getting home and having dinner with Joe, which was the name of the family dog. The Chinese ate that up and let his letter go through, but they didn't send any of mine.

Richard Bassett also noted how your standing with the Chinese often dictated whether you received or were able to send letters:

The letters of the Progressives went directly home through China. They were also nearly always assured of plenty of letters at mail call. They were living proof of the lie that under Communism everybody shares and shares alike. As long as they worked for and agreed with the Chinese, they received decent care.

During the latter part of January 1952 the Chinese presented us with our first large mail call, which was an extremely happy occasion. They started letting us write home three times a month, but it depended a lot on what you wrote whether or not your letter ever left camp. At the end of February I received my first letter. My mom had written it on New Year's Eve. One of the happiest moments a POW can have is to hear the mail clerk call his name. It was even wonderful to have fellow prisoners receive mail, even when you did not, because we shared our news from home with each other.

Until this first big mail call in January, only a few guys had received letters from home. Within a few months, we started having regular mail call every ten or fifteen days, and most of the guys got letters. Of course, their families had been writing; it was just that so many of these letters never reached us. I eventually received about forty letters, over half of which arrived during my last three months of captivity, and nothing did more to raise my morale. However, I can safely say I did not receive one tenth of the letters that were written to me.

Michael Cornwell describes an instance when the Americans used the mail to work together against the Chinese:

We didn't pull together very well that first winter. A lack of leadership was part of it. If the Chinese could identify our leaders, they immediately took them away. The state of discipline and training in our Army was pretty sorry at that time. I saw a guy go up to a lieutenant after we got captured and say, "Now, you're no better than I am." . . . A couple of times we did stick together. If you wanted to send a letter, you had to put as a return address "Chinese People's Committee for World Peace and Against American Aggression." We told them we'd go along with the Chinese People's Committee for World Peace but not the rest of it. We stuck together on that, so for two months we just didn't write any letters. Then they changed their minds.

GUARD-BAITING

Prisoners of war lose more than just personal freedom and control. A sense of self and time can also be lost. For such men the future appeared painfully uncertain, and often a kind of lethargy and fatalism began to dominate their thinking. In the most extreme cases, a despondent individual simply turned his face to the wall and gave up. One way desperate men could retain a semblance of self-pride was to use humor and guile to make life difficult for their captors. Harry Falck and his buddies in Camp Five took particular delight in doing so:

> One morning this guy said, "Hey, everybody get a long stick. When we go out for roll call, run that stick along the ground. If one of the guards comes by, say, 'Arf, arf!' " The guard, of course, didn't know what we were doing. He would point and ask, "What you talk?" We'd bark some more. He'd walk off. Can you imagine a thousand people coming out with sticks and barking like dogs at roll call? Another time we fell out for roll call on our imaginary motorcycles. We tried to disrupt them one way or another with our little tricks.

Glenn Reynolds describes the "mysterious whistler" who drove the guards in Camp Five to distraction:

> This guy named Copeland from Waycross, Georgia, was the biggest cutup you ever saw. He never took anything serious. He once stole three chickens from the guards' kitchen. The guards demanded to know who stole their chickens. Someone then wrote a note stating, "The Whistler did it." Nobody knew Copeland had written the stupid note. The guards kept hassling us and carrying on. Then Copeland would go down by the river and start whistling. The guards would hear it and they'd charge down there with their bayonets at the ready. They'd just about get there, and somebody in another part of the camp would begin whistling. Those Chinese ran up and down that compound for at least thirty minutes. Then they told us all to go to bed. Copeland was lying there laughing. Then he said, "We've got a surprise for them tonight." Every hour on the hour a guard would come in with a flashlight and take a head count. He'd count all the heads: 120 heads. He'd leave and then come back an hour later. At the twelve o'clock bed-check we had 120, but at one o'clock we only had 119. Then the guard found Copeland. He had tied a rope with a hangman's noose around his shoulders and had managed to pull himself up into the rafters so all the guard could see were his feet. The guard ran back to get the commander. In the meantime, Copeland cut himself down, got rid of the ropes and climbed back in bed. So now we've got the full 120 head count. This drove them nuts. About five or six of them

made the count. So then they hauled us out in formation and asked us what we'd done with the body. Stuff like that would keep us going for two or three days.

Lt. Bob Carman and his fellow officers in Camp Two took great satisfaction in baiting the guards during the great germ warfare scare when the Chinese accused American pilots of dropping deadly viruses on the civilian population:

The Chinese made us look at all these water color paintings that were supposed to show the bug warfare that allegedly was going on over there. These paintings showed bugs crawling out of bombs and doing this and that. They wanted us to pass them around, but we got some wet rags and began messing up the water colors. . . .

Then this one night some B-29s flew over and dropped all this foil to confuse the radar. The next morning there was foil all over the place. The Chinese said it was bug warfare. So the guards were out there using twigs like chopsticks to pick up these pieces and put them in a can. We walked over and picked up some foil, held it up in the air, then put it in our mouths and chewed it. Then the Chinese guards rushed over to the hospital and washed their hands in iodine. When they came back, we pointed at them and laughed. Well, to point at a Chinese is the worst thing you can do, so they just kind of ducked their heads and walked away.

One day we got a dead rat, put him in a parachute harness, and hung him on the front gate. When the Chinese saw the rat, they really started jabbering. They thought they had discovered proof that we were guilty of germ warfare. Doing things like this helped keep up morale.

The taunting process could go both ways, as Don Poirot discovered when some guards took great pleasure in turning the tables on their prisoners:

The area we slept and lived in was a row of buildings on each side of a little dirt road. Our latrine was located behind the last row of houses. Almost everyone would get at least one call of nature every night. So you had to get up in the dark and go down to the latrine. The latrines consisted of a pit dug into the ground and then boards put over the top. You walked out on the boards, squatted down, and took care of your business. There was usually a guard or two nearby, I guess to make sure we wouldn't wander out of the area. One or two of the guards took great delight in hiding and jumping out and hollering what I suppose was the Chinese version of "boo!" It would scare the living daylights out of us. To retaliate, we would stand on the side of our hootch and throw rocks over the building hoping to hit a guard. In counter-retaliation the guard would then refuse to let anyone use the latrine for the rest of the night. We eventually came to a truce. The guards quit trying to scare us, and we quit throwing rocks.

In the final analysis, baiting the guards was a healthy response to an untenable situation. Of course, as Michael Cornwell makes clear, one had to know his limits:

We baited the guards and played tricks on them and each other. This made life a little more interesting and helped break up the boredom. There was a line between being feisty and going too far, which could get you in a hell of a bunch of trouble and even lead to your demise. I was a little bit of a hell-raiser, and I did like to aggravate the guards, but I always knew when to stop.

PUNISHMENT

In spite of their self-proclaimed "lenient policy," the Chinese were not adverse to administering both physical and mental punishment if they thought doing so would produce cooperative prisoners. Some men were forced to stand for hours at attention or were unceremoniously dumped in "the hole," where in winter, water would seep in and turn to ice. The irrepressible Robert Blewitt had often been in trouble with American authorities even before he was captured, and certainly nothing changed in Camps One and Three:

I often ended up in the hole, but you're not supposed to be good in jail. It was just a hole in the ground that had pieces of wood stripping over the top for bars. I got in trouble for all kinds of things. Sometimes I would liberate this stuff from the Chinese, requisition so to speak, and then I would sneak out of camp and trade it for whatever I could get. We didn't have a wall, but the Chinese could always see you except behind their headquarters, and that's where I'd sneak out. I'd go down to a nearby village and trade whatever I had. Of course, I often had to pay the price, but it was a way of amusing myself.

We'd also steal food out of this giant wok the Chinese cooked in. We'd go by and flip out a piece of meat or whatever and take off. Of course, I had to do all the dirty work because if any of us were going to get caught, it was going to be me. I didn't like getting caught, I just liked doing those things. I also stole chickens whenever I could. This one time I had herded them into this little building, and I'm chasing them around. They're clucking and feathers are flying. I got this one, and I'm trying to strangle him. I'm planning to smear him with mud, stuff him in our chimney, and bake him. While I'm strangling this chicken, I look out the door and sure enough here comes a Chinese guard. This chicken is just about dead, so, man I'm trying to revive him. I'm kicking the chicken and saying, "Come on, come on, wake up, get back to life." And it did. It hopped up and started running around. The guard asked me, "What are you doing with the chicken?" What was I going to say? I told him, "I'm playing with the chicken." The guard said, "The chicken cannot play with you." Off I went to the hole again.

Wayman Simpson was another American prisoner who frequently found trouble and solitary confinement:

Unlike the North Koreans, the Chinese did not bother us too much physically. But they went to work on our brains, which can be worse. If you are damaged physically, you can recover, at least to some extent. If they break you mentally, you're broken for life. Their favorite deal was to put you in solitary. I spent more time in solitary than I did with the troops. I done everything but make them shoot me. And they came close to that a couple of times. We had this ravine behind the camp headquarters that we called "Rock Gully." They had these boxes lying on these ledges, a little bigger than a casket. You could sit up in them if you bent your head down. They were maybe three to four feet high and about seven feet long. It was pitch-black in there, and I could feel something crawling on me the entire time I was in there. The walls were made out of mud and cornstalks, and I would make a mark on the wall for every day I was in there. The longest I ever spent in there was sixty-two days.

Most of the prisoners went on work details, usually to gather wood for fuel, but Glenn Reynolds points out that meaningless work could also be used as punishment:

The Chinese showed us no mercy. The first couple of weeks after we got in Camp Two the Chinese selected maybe forty prisoners for punishment. They gave ten of us hoes and shovels. Another ten got a burlap sack, tied a rope to all four corners, and then stuck a yahoo stick through it. We called them "yahoo sticks" because it took one yahoo at each end of the stick to carry things. They scratched out a line on the ground maybe sixty feet long by three feet wide. They then ordered us to dig a six-foot deep hole. To tell the truth, we actually thought we were digging our own graves. One group had to dig up the dirt and put it into these sacks. Then the next group had to carry this dirt two or three miles away and drop it in the mountains. The next day another group would go up into the mountains and shovel the dirt back into the sacks, carry it back, and refill the hole that had been dug the previous day. Then another group would begin digging all over again. I think they were trying to make us believe there was going to be a mass burial.

Speaking up or challenging camp authorities always got one in trouble, as it did Douglas Tanner in Camp One:

They kept telling us to speak freely, and as long as you said what they wanted to hear, it was fine. One day when this interpreter said, "Speak freely about what you feel," I told him, "Well, you keep saying that the Russians are such peace-loving people. If that is true, why do they maintain the largest standing army in the world, and why have they not returned the war vessels we loaned to them during World War II?" For that I spent fifteen days in solitary.

Solitary confinement consisted of a jail cell, well away from the other prisoners. There was a jail in that town, and I was put in one of its cells. I was allowed out about 11:00 at night for about fifteen minutes to take care of nature, and then it was back in. If you had to go more than once a day, you just cleaned up during that fifteen minutes you were out. The second time I was in solitary, I was put in a box about four-foot square. After you crawled in, you couldn't turn around, so you always backed in so at least you could look out. You could roll over, but you couldn't sit up.

A favorite Chinese punishment was forcing the offender to confess his transgressions in front of his fellow prisoners. Of course, as Bob Carman explains, if you were clever with words, your confession contained something more than the Chinese wanted:

> There was not much mistreatment in Camp Two. However, Hector Cadero, who is now a judge in Puerto Rico, was punished. The guys were all the time stealing chickens that wandered loose outside our camp. They would split the bamboo fence and throw a little bit of rice outside with a noose made of shoe laces around it. When the chicken would come over to eat the rice, they would jerk that string around the chicken's neck. We had these fifty-five gallon drums for our wash water, with a fire box underneath to heat it. They'd take the chicken, pack it in mud, and then stick it down in the fire box to cook. Several of the guys did this, but only Hector got caught. The Chinese put him in solitary confinement for a couple of days and told him he could return to us if he confessed. So he "confessed" in front of all of us. He said, "I will not be caught stealing chickens again."

DEATH AND DYING

Surrounded as they were by the dead and dying, the prisoners had to develop defense mechanisms that would aid their own struggle for survival. Some became immune or insensitive to death, knowing full well that if they became too preoccupied with death, they would soon lose their own will to live. For others, the senseless and unnecessary deaths made them even more determined to survive in order to inform the outside world what they had seen. Some men tried to avoid the pain of losing a close friend by never getting too close to anyone. Others withdrew inward, but, in truth, no one could escape the dreadful truth. For Jeff Erwin the pervasiveness of death brought out the best and worst in people:

> A lot of the guys in the camps lost their perspective and sense of values. Let me give you an example. We had this guy in our squad who died. The chaplain came in our mud room and said a few words over him. When the chaplain left, it was dark, and we noticed that the guy's socks were gone. We had already worked it out who in our squad would get his socks, pants, etc. That damn chaplain had taken his socks with

him. I went over and made him give them back. That chaplain died. There was a Catholic priest there who had more damn guts than any man I've ever known. He would go out at night and try to steal food for the sick. He was always going from room to room comforting the sick. The most unselfish man I've ever seen in my life. But he also died. A lot of guys didn't want to waste any of their strength on others because they knew it would be hard to replace. So they did no more for anyone than they absolutely had to.

There were many reasons why prisoners died, but, as Michael Cornwell makes clear, there were usually telltale signs of impending death:

> If you saw a guy who was really desperately sick—couldn't eat or hold food down—you knew he was a goner. Then there were the guys who wouldn't go on details or do anything for themselves. They'd sit around and talk about home and their mothers. They took the attitude that their captors should look after them. Well, that wasn't going to happen.
>
> I was determined I would not be one of those who died up there. I told myself, "No way am I going to be one of these guys I bury every day." It was depressing as hell, and you were hungry and cold and filthy dirty, but you had to think, "Tomorrow is another day." That's the attitude you had to have.

Glenn Reynolds also thought he could predict who was going to die. One indication was when a man became preoccupied with a single thought:

> One of our guys talked about nothing but beer and ham sandwiches with mustard. That's all he talked about, nothing else. One day he just lay down and wouldn't eat. I told him to get up and move around. But he told me, "No, I'm giving up. I don't have the will to go on." The next morning we picked him up and carried him out for the cart to pick up. When you say, "I give up. I don't want to go on," you've sealed your fate. I saw too many of them do that.

Capt. Sidney Esensten, who was a physician/prisoner in Camp Five, also noticed that men who announced their impending deaths were invariably correct:

Another phenomenon was premonition of death. People who were relatively well would tell the men in their rooms, "Don't bother to wake me in the morning, because you will not be able to get me up." One hundred percent of the time they were right."[6]

Harry Falck and others in Camp Five tried desperately to keep the sick from dying. When their efforts failed, they also learned to be fatalistic about their fallen buddies:

When we first got to Camp Five that winter our guys immediately started dying of beriberi, dysentery, and pneumonia. We tried to keep the guys alive any way we could. If someone got down or sick, or looked at the wall all day, we'd force him to eat. Some made it back, but others just completely gave up and died. We could usually tell if a guy was not going to make it just by watching his reactions. He might be talking to you one day, but the next day he wouldn't say a word, and he'd be wandering aimlessly around the room. Then he would say, "I'm not hungry." So we'd force his mouth open, stuff food in it, and make him swallow, but he would vomit that up. When he started vomiting, we knew he wasn't going to live long. We hardened ourselves for when he died. If you slept next to him, you'd shake him. If he said, "Yeah, all right," he was still alive. If he didn't say anything, well, he was gone. . . .

They'd die, and we'd stack their bodies in this little shack for two or three days, until we got maybe a dozen or so. We'd take their clothes so we could use them ourselves. That was the only scavenger stuff most of us ever did. If they had dog tags we would try to take and hide them. We then carried their bodies out to this hillside. We would dig a trench about four feet wide and maybe four feet deep and put their frozen bodies in it. Sometimes the bodies would break when we put them down. We'd cover them with dirt from the frozen ground that we dug up with our fingernails and stones, or whatever we had, and then we'd pile stones on top. The guards wouldn't let us say a prayer or nothing, so we'd go back and say our little prayers to ourselves. Then we'd continue with our day. . . .

All the camps had their daily burial details, but in winter burying the men in such rocky terrain was all but impossible. According to Jeff Erwin, it was also difficult to keep any record of the dead:

We would go on burial details to bury our own, but this was absolutely impossible in winter. So we'd take them out to the side of the mountain and cover them up with rocks. Hell, with the first spring rain they'd go rolling out to sea or wherever.

We didn't keep a record of those who died and that's why there are so many MIAs. We couldn't bury the guys and with the first spring rain the bodies were gone. We tried to collect their dog tags, but a lot of them didn't have dog tags. My barracks commander died, and I brought his wedding ring home. He lived in Seattle. So I called his wife and went down to give her the ring. There was a big, evil-smelling old pipe still smoldering in the ashtray. I'm sure she wasn't smoking it.

COPING AND SURVIVAL

What conclusions can one draw about the men who did survive those first deadly months and beyond? Good health was, of course, of great importance, but not easy to maintain. The first American troops sent into Korea from Japan had allegedly been living the soft life of an occupying army. Many were in bad physical shape, as were many of the reservists and draftees. Such men could not march fifteen miles under the best of conditions, and they died by the hundreds during the forced marches that characterized their first weeks of captivity. Many of the career officers and NCOs insisted that the discipline they learned in the service helped them survive. However, many of these men already had a maturity and sense of discipline on which the military could easily build. Some men argued that the hardscrabble times in which they grew up prepared them to survive almost anything, even the prison camps. Several who had been raised in rural and impoverished areas suggested that city boys did very poorly in the camps. On the other hand, urbanites argued that surviving the tough streets of their impoverished neighborhoods provided invaluable training for captivity.

More important than geographic origins was a strong sense of self-preservation. Those men who had earlier enjoyed a wide range of experiences seemed to do better than the very young, who were usually among the first to die. Some men were simply determined not to die in the camps, and such an attitude certainly helped, but not all of these men survived.

Most American prisoners agreed that Turkish POWs did better than the other U.N. soldiers. The Turks certainly appeared better organized. If something happened to one leader, another man immediately stepped up. The Turks, however, were professional soldiers, and most were captured after that first deadly winter when conditions had already begun to improve. Nevertheless, the majority of the American enlisted men admitted to chaos and disorganization, especially during those early months. The career officers did much better, as did the NCOs. Because they had chosen the military as a profession, they felt a sense of mission and belonging that most enlisted men did not.

The traditional American male belief in rugged individualism, that he is the captain of his soul, certainly made life tougher in the camps. Such men believed they always needed to be in control, but as prisoners they had to learn that no man is an island and that to help one another was certainly no weakness. For a determined Michael Cornwell, the keys to coping were one's home environment, an ability to adjust, and keeping busy:

I made up my mind they weren't going to kill me. If you didn't take that attitude, they'd leave you up there. I was a farm boy from Indiana where I was raised by my grandparents. I wasn't a pampered kid. I was a big tough kid who weighed 185 pounds. I was strong mentally and physically. City kids who had possibly been pampered by their parents did not do well. They didn't last long. They simply couldn't cope. Their mother wasn't there to look after them. . . .

After the Chinese took over, we got into a routine. We played cards that we made out of cardboard. We also played chess, basketball, and softball. We had a library; in fact, I was the librarian. The library was loaded with literature they wanted us to read. But there were lots of novels as well. I'm an avid reader so I didn't care what was there: Pearl Buck, James Fenimore Cooper, and Upton Sinclair. Charles Dickens, who, of course, wrote about the downtrodden, was really big. These books all came from the Chinese. We also got a weekly newspaper which was published in Peking. It was really slanted, to say the least. It contained no credible news of the war, and it always slammed the Americans for their alleged misconduct at P'anmunjŏm. We also got the *London Daily Worker* and the *New York Daily Worker*. They might have been four months old, but we got them.

You have to adjust to prison camp or you're finished. Hope is always there. You can't lose hope or you can't make it. Religion did not play a role with me. Unfortunately, I'm not a particularly religious person. I'm not an atheist, but religion played no role in my captivity. When

Akira Chikami, April 30, 1998

Robert Maclean, May 9, 1998

Robert Coury, July 1, 2001

In September 1950, more than fifty Americans and hundreds of South Korean "political prisoners" were executed in the so-called Taejŏn Massacre. In this photo, South Koreans are searching for relatives. *Life* Magazine, October 30, 1950

Newly captured American United Nations' soldiers. This photo appeared in the "United Nations POWs in Korea."

This propaganda shot from "United Nations POWs in Korea" suggested that the prisoners received good treatment in the camp hospitals. To those unfortunate prisoners who were forced to seek medical help, the caption, "Doctors and nurses wave farewell to three discharged patients—cured, happy and grateful" was a ludicrous insult.

This photo, which also appeared in the Chinese propaganda pamphlet "United Nations POWs in Korea," was captioned, "Extra rations of fruits, wine and other good things are issued for holidays and celebrations." In reality, few prisoners, other than those that were willing to cooperate with their captors, ever saw such items.

The Chinese allowed Frank "Pappy" Noel, who had been an Associated Press cameraman before he was captured, to take many of the photos which later appeared in the Chinese propaganda pamphlet, "United Nations POWs in Korea." This shot of a Catholic Church service in Camp Five was typical of those taken in an attempt to convince the world of the Chinese's "lenient policies." Photo courtesy of Jim Crombie.

The Chinese included this "pleasant and peaceful" shot of Camp Five on the Yalu River in their "United Nations POWs in Korea" booklet, but they failed to mention that hundreds of American bodies lay buried on the mountainside above the camp. Camp Five was the largest prison compound, containing approximately three-quarters of the American prisoners by 1953. Photo courtesy of Jim Crombie and the Andersonville National Historic Site.

The Death March

Carl V Cossin

Sketch of the Tiger Death March by former POW Carl V. Cossin. Photo courtesy of Andersonville Historic Site.

The Chinese and North Koreans made every attempt to drive a wedge between white and black prisoners. In this photo from "United Nations POWs in Korea," Clarence Adams (without cap) and three other black prisoners are shown with their Chinese guards. Adams was one of the twenty-one Americans who refused repatriation.

As further evidence of its "lenient" POW practices, the Chinese organized the Inter-Camp Olympics, which were held November 13–16, 1952, near Camps Five and Two in the North Korean town of Pyoktŏng. Some POWs refused to participate, but others welcomed the diversion and the chance to meet with prisoners from other camps. This photo of the opening ceremony appeared in "United Nations POWs in Korea."

guys were sitting around reading their Bibles, I was out hustling for something to eat.

For Robert Schaefer in Camp One, playing chess, reading, and a sense of humor were all-important:

A sense of humor helped. There was a guy, I can't remember his name now, I think he was from Cairo, Illinois, who had been a salesman and every day he told us a dirty joke we never heard before, and he did this for twenty-eight months. There was another guy from Missouri, I believe Bryant was his name. He had read all of the Zane Grey novels, and if we didn't have a book to read he would tell us one of those stories. He had every one of them memorized. He was also pretty damn rough at the chess board. He wanted to learn to play chess. Everyday he'd come over and bug me to teach him, so I did. Then one day he beat me, and I never beat him again.

African Americans faced unique challenges in the camps. Although President Truman had issued his desegregation order in 1948, the U.S. Army was slow to implement the president's policy, and most African-American troops continued to fight in segregated units as did the 24th Regiment's Buffalo Soldiers. The Chinese, of course, sought to exploit racial discrimination. They separated the black troops and made special efforts to persuade them to speak out against their country. Sgt. Jerry Morgan, who also served in World War II and Vietnam, rejected these heavy-handed attempts. For him, religion was much more important than anything the Chinese could offer. He also insisted that blacks supported one another better than did their white counterparts:

The Chinese asked us what kind of a life we lived in the United States and why were we over there fighting for the white man. They told us when we returned to the States we were going to have to do the same thing but that coming over to their side would mean an upgrading of our status. One time I made a comment and one the instructors heard it. I said, "Hobos and bums eating out of garbage cans back in the States live better than these Chinese." That wasn't smart at all [laughs]. They talked down to us. They talked against religion. The camp commander made the comment, "If you believe in God, why doesn't He come down here and save you?" We just mumbled under our breaths, "Don't worry, He'll be here." Every day we were looking for our troops to come over the hill. Every day we just tried to survive, hoping and praying we'd live to see the next day and that we'd soon be free.

The Chinese could not understand the black American. We were always laughing and talking and singing. The Chinese just couldn't comprehend that. We had them completely befuddled. We would be doing all that and right next to us would be a company of whites. They would be sitting around dejected, not laughing or talking. And there we were acting foolish. I say foolish in the eyes of the Chinese, but to us this was a means of survival. Back in the United States we were used to being down, and the only way for us to go was up.

Another thing was care. We didn't lose a man in my squad from the day of capture to Operation Big Switch—not a single person. There were ten of us. At one time one of our guys had given up, but we would not let him die. We made him get up, and we made him walk. We boiled water and forced him to drink it. He didn't want to eat, but we just kept pushing food into him until he had to swallow. Eventually, he ended up regaining his strength and came home and stayed in the service.

We looked out for each other more than did the Caucasians who were in the company next to us. You hear about esprit de corps, but when it gets down to the nitty-gritty, that's when it shows up. When it was a matter of life and death, we had to lean on one another. We had our private spiritual and religious prayer services within our own little platoon, and we did this without the Chinese even knowing it until they finally opened up and let us serve our Lord. We formed our own choirs and we had our own ministers. And we also used humor—all the time!

Before black prisoners were segregated from their white counterparts in the permanent camps, Robert Fletcher noticed that when sharing such abysmal conditions white and black prisoners often forgot there was such a thing as race:

It was amazing, but in prison camp we never looked at each other as black and white. We never heard people say, "Oh that's a white guy," or "That's a nigger or that's a black guy." You never heard those words because nobody had shit. And we depended on each other to make it. Elliott Sortillo was a white guy from Philadelphia. He was sixteen years old; I was seventeen. Shit, he and I had a lot in common. Those older guys he was with wished his ass was dead because he was a happy-go-lucky kid, and they had wives and kids, so they isolated him. Every evening he and I would talk about playing basketball and football and high school and girls. We'd just laugh and have a good time. I didn't know it, but at the time he was thinking about committing suicide. After we got back to the States, he got married, stayed in the service, and retired as a master sergeant. I go to the second reunion the ex-POWs had in Louisville, Kentucky, and somebody calls out, "Fletch." And I say, "Sortillo, how are you doing?" We grabbed and hugged each other. And his wife comes over and gives me a kiss and says, "I've been knowing you all my life and I thank you." I asked, "For what?" She says, "You saved my husband's life." I said, "Huh?" And Sortillo says, "Yeah, Fletch, I never told you. Before you and I started talking, I was thinking about committing suicide. Those guys didn't want me; they wouldn't talk to me; they thought I was too young."

Many prisoners credited their spiritual beliefs for their survival. Even for those who practiced no formal religion, faith and hope were all-important. Some men discovered religion only after they were captured, but Richard Bassett brought his God with him into service:

When I was captured, I had the New Testament in my fatigue pocket. It had been my daily habit to read it, and now I found myself reading more and more each day. I also was spending much of my time meditating on what I had just read. During my time as a prisoner, some of us would get together and study the scriptures, sing a few hymns, and pray. In those troubled times, it greatly helped to have faith in God and to believe that everything would be all right as long as we kept our faith. Maybe it had been the prayers of those who loved us back home that had preserved us in battle and were protecting us as prisoners. Prayer and religious fellowship brought me considerable comfort during my long months in captivity; in fact, I believe that the prayers of the folks back home and my faith in God played a tremendous role in my getting home.

There was no doubt in the mind of Billy Joe Harris that he needed the help of a higher being if he were going to survive:

Already while we were marching, I had come to the conclusion that none of us was going to make it. It was every dog for himself. I decided that if I was ever going to make it, a higher power was going to have something to do with it. Boy, I prayed. And I would say that's the reason I'm back. I still wonder why I made it when so many didn't. I was raised as just a country boy, and I was rough and tough and figured I could do about anything that anybody else could. But after I got over there and became a prisoner, I realized that if this old boy made it, somebody else was going to have to take a hand. I'm not saying that after I prayed things got better, because they didn't. It was some two years after I started praying before things began to get better.

Friendships could be all important. The men tried to talk and laugh together when someone got really down—and everyone did at one time or another. Jim Crombie was one who depended on a few good friends:

> I had a lot of help from my buddies. Some of these guys were just great. There were those few who would steal your food if you were sick and couldn't defend yourself or who would squeal to the Chinese if they thought you were doing something wrong. But if you had some real good friends, they helped you, and such friends certainly helped me survive captivity.

Harley Coon, however, warned that friendships could make one vulnerable, particularly if too many of these friends died. Coon also argues a prisoner had to guard against rumors and false hopes:

> I think loners might have done better in the camps, but I don't mean someone who had nothing to do with the other guys. I mean guys who kind of kept to themselves, yet were willing to help others. If you depended too much on others, or were too close to a friend or two, and then they died and you had to bury them, it had a very adverse effect on you.
>
> There were several factors that helped determine who would survive. I think those of us who had been overseas longer had an advantage because we were over the homesickness. I know some guys argue that the country boys did better than the city boys or vice versa, but I don't buy that. I was a country boy and a city boy both. I was born in Dayton, Ohio, but my dad used to sharecrop during the Depression on different farms. The main thing was that during the 1930s we had to do without so we didn't know what it was like to have anything. I think a lot of the guys who didn't survive were homesick and kind of startled by what happened. There were a lot of guys that got captured who had

never even fired a round because when the Chinese hit us in November of 1950, they went around us and hit the rear echelon. They got guys like radio operators, medical personnel, and truck drivers who had no experience facing the enemy. So it was more of a shock for them when they were captured.

It helped to be in good physical shape when you were captured. I had been playing football before I quit school and went in the military, and we really had a tough coach. I had all this physical conditioning, so when I went into basic training, I was probably in better shape than the drill instructor. We went on a thirty-mile forced march one day and it didn't bother me a bit. But the mental aspect also determined who made it. For example, rumors had a tremendous effect on some of the guys. They just lived on them. Somebody would say our forces were ten miles from us and that we were going to be liberated in the next two weeks. Then when that didn't happen these guys would keel over and die. To protect yourself, you had to make your mind almost a complete blank and block out anything these guys said that might give you false hopes.

Glenn Reynolds, who was from Kentucky, argued that the men from rural areas had the best chance to survive:

We found out that those who came from Appalachia—the coal mines and the timber and farming country—you could rely on. But those from the cities couldn't make it very long. Your physical endurance was also all important. If someone had never done anything physical, you could just write on the wall that he wasn't going to make it. We country boys believed you needed the constitution of a horse in order to survive.

Not surprisingly, Robert Blewitt, who grew up on the tough streets of Philadelphia, completely disagreed with Reynolds:

No, no, no. It was the farm boys, the good ole boys from Kentucky, that couldn't handle life as a prisoner. They could handle the easy, but not the tough. I always felt I was preparing for physical survival my entire life. When I was a kid, I would go into the wrong neighborhood, but I would know how to get out. The guys in these neighborhoods never caught me. I admit there were some things the country guys could do better, like knowing which weeds to eat. But we city kids knew we could always find somebody who could tell us whatever we needed to know.

Capt. Louis N. Rockwerk, a World War II veteran who rose through the ranks, argued that one could not generalize on which men had the best chance to survive. He also believed that battlefield courage did not always translate into prison camp survival:

I wasn't convinced that I was ever getting back home. In fact, I was pretty convinced that I wasn't. At the time, pride was the most important thing in my life. One of the officers who was with me during World War II was one of the first to go into the fetal position and cry for his mother. He was a spotless, spit-and-polish soldier. When he could see the enemy he could handle it and handle it heroically, but when he couldn't do anything about the situation, he broke down.

The toughest and best survivors were the young lieutenants that came out of the ranks, especially those who earned their commission during World War II. The ones that come out of West Point, no, and if they were ROTC, forget about them. They didn't compare to the officers who came up through the ranks.

It's a load of horse manure that country kids did any better than city kids. To begin with, the country kids never lived in the city, and they didn't know how tough it was there. And city kids didn't know a damn thing about survival in the wilderness or out in the open. So how could you measure? If they worked together, yes, because each gave his experiences to the other.

I can't honestly say I could predict who would do well and who wouldn't. Think about it. A real tough kid comes down with dysentery and is shitting in his pants all day long and killing fleas. Of course, this man's pride is gone. You couldn't hold it against him. It was nothing he could control. No, you couldn't fault him. This one Marine officer loved to talk, and the Chinese used this against him. Before long he was spouting the Chinese line. A B-36 Air Force pilot was another one that talked himself into fixes. They didn't know when to shut up. They had diarrhea of the mouth, and the Chinese knew that and used it against them.

What could we have done to better prepare our men for captivity? Teach them Americanism; teach them the values of our country. We are the only army that doesn't get seriously involved in teaching this to our troops. Oh, we gave lip service to all this, but usually someone was chosen out of the ranks who was totally unqualified. We should have had professionals teaching the men. Some who tried to teach the men were afraid what they said would sound like propaganda. But explaining why we fight and what it means to the country is not propaganda. It's part of our heritage. Remember, I'm talking about the period when most of us were first generation immigrants.[7]

Under the horrific and seemingly hopeless conditions in the camps, many men were unable to cope and simply gave up, while others did not. In American popular culture, whether in literary fiction or Hollywood movies, such differences can be easily explained by the courage and intestinal fortitude of larger-than-life heroes. John Wayne comes immediately to mind, but in reality, the Duke never saw a battlefield or the inside of a prisoner camp. Unlike fictional heroes, a man's physical appearance or exemplary courage did not guarantee survival. Then, too, men who had exhibited great bravery on the battlefield could act very differently when confronted by oppressive conditions in a POW camp. In the final analysis, to survive captivity one had to retain at least a semblance of sound health and a positive mental attitude. But even more important was a preponderance of good luck.

6

INJURIES, DISEASE, AND MEDICAL CARE

I want to make it perfectly clear that except for the POWs that were wounded at the time of capture, all the deaths in the Communist prison camps were caused directly or indirectly by starvation, exposure, torture, purposeful killing, and harassment by the enemy.
—Sidney Esensten, M.D. and Korean War POW

Many deaths [in the prison camps] were due to malnutrition and, of course, to disease. Although I was a physician, there was nothing that I could do since there was insufficient food and no medicine. All we could do was to eat whatever was available, from weeds to rats. Our job was simply to stay alive.
—Gene N. Lam, M.D. and Korean War POW[1]

According to a report filed shortly after repatriation by five U.S. Army physicians who were interned in prison camps in North Korea, "The health of all United Nations' prisoners was neglected throughout the period of captivity."[2] The doctors further added that the lack of medicine and health facilities resulted in the needless deaths of countless prisoners.

During the first month or two of captivity most deaths could be attributed to battlefield wounds for which there was little or no medicine to stave off deadly infections. A soldier's untreated wounds often meant he could not march, and those who fell out usually did not survive, as Jerry Morgan makes clear:

Yes, yes, that happened. If someone was wounded and lingered or got behind, the rest of us walked on, and we'd hear a shot. We didn't know what had happened, but we didn't see that person again. Mentally, we'd say to ourselves, "Well, they shot him." We knew it happened because the number of people on the march kept diminishing.

Almost every soldier captured during the bitterly cold winter of 1950–51 suffered from frostbite, and especially those captured during the retreat from the Chosin Reservoir. Those who were fortunate enough to have adequate footwear, extra socks, or who constantly rubbed their feet during the long marches to the north did better than the men described by Don Poirot:

> One of our prisoners had been in a bunch captured in that disaster at the Chosin Reservoir in November or December 1950. These poor guys lost toes and fingers to frostbite. One of them said that after his toes turned black he just snapped them off with his fingers. He lost all five toes on both feet. You don't realize how much walking depends on your toes to grip down when you take a step. As a result, this particular fellow had a funny wobbling gait when he walked.

Capt. Gene N. Lam was a battalion surgeon before he was captured on December 1, 1950. He estimates that only half of the approximately 1,200 2nd Division men who were captured with him at a Chinese roadblock near Kunu-ri survived. Lam believes that many of the individual deaths could have been prevented with better leadership, stronger discipline, an enhanced will to live, and a basic knowledge of how to protect and heal the body and mind, but he also insists that the underlying causes were malnutrition and the deliberately inhumane policies of the North Koreans and the Chinese. The year after he was liberated, Dr. Lam gave a speech on POW survival techniques at the Escape and Evasion School at Stead Air Force Base, Reno, Nevada, informing the young soldiers what drastic measures they might have to take if they were to encounter anything similar to what Lam and his fellow prisoners did in Korea:

> You may have injuries. You may be wounded, you may be burned. In case of an injury, if you can move, treat it and get going. Men in Korea gave up because they had a wound in their little finger—two or three drops of blood. They immediately ran to the first Chinaman they could find and said, "I'm bleeding to death, save my life." That's one extreme. At the other extreme were men who had broken bones, severe wounds, who amputated their own legs, whittled out a crutch and kept going. It can be done. But don't give up. A good example is a Navy helicopter pilot who bellied in on a mountaintop, and in doing so broke all the bones in both feet. He walked for fifteen days with no treatment. He cannot walk today, but he came out alive. Back injuries: men have broken their backs when they hit the ground. When they regained consciousness, they rolled around, found a stick or board,

strapped themselves to it, and got up and walked out. Men with open, sucking chest wounds stuck a handkerchief into that hole and kept on going. We had a man in our camp with a terrific chest wound; he stuffed it up, lived, and came out three years later. You may be burned: the book says wash it out and cover it with a sterile dressing. What are you going to wash it out with? Each man has his own supply of some of the most sterile water you'll ever find. It may have a few chemicals in it, but it's still sterile—and that's your own urine. It may seem rather rough to think of urinating into a wound, but it washes it out and sterilizes it. It won't hurt you and it may save your life. You may have a hemorrhage—and I'd like to make a plea here—if you are bleeding, do not put on a tourniquet. So many men have lost arms and legs because tourniquets have been put on. A tourniquet destroys tissue, gangrene sets in, and it is impossible to save it. Pressure will stop 99 percent off all bleeding—just constant, heavy pressure. Just stick your finger down in that wound and stop it—hold it—and in more than 99 percent of the cases, a tourniquet will not be necessary.[3]

On the marches, in the temporary camps, and even during the first months in the permanent camps, available water was badly contaminated. Sometimes the guards tried to warn the prisoners to boil their water, but often they did not. The result was often deadly, as Robert Fletcher found in Camp Five:

I think the most common disease was cholera from bad water. The well was just a pool. It was located below the farm fields that were fertilized with human body waste. The farmers would pour it on the fields and plow it in. When it rained, it would run down into our well. But we weren't even thinking about that. The Chinese kept telling us, "Cold water, no good, no good!" They boiled all their water before drinking it. We could not see it until we lost eighteen hundred people. This was also due in part to the lack of proper food. Dysentery was just rampant. I don't know a POW who didn't have dysentery. You'd just come back from the latrine and off you'd go again.

Even if a prisoner survived his long march, malnutrition, exhaustion, contaminated water, and insufficient protection from the elements made him especially susceptible to pneumonia or dysentery, which were the chief killers in the temporary camps and during the first months in the permanent camps. Most subsequent deaths were due to pellagra or beriberi. Former prisoner Dr. Sidney Esensten estimates that among the men taken prisoner between July 1950 and September 1951, "there was a minimum mortality of 75 percent," although, according to Esensten, "none of these men had illnesses that would have caused death had they been under normal conditions."[4]

On the long marches it was all but impossible for any of the captured physicians to do much for the men except to offer encouragement, but in the temporary camp at Sombakol, which the men called the Valley (see chapter four), Esensten and another American physician, Maj. Clarence L. Anderson, managed to set up a temporary hospital:

A few days after I got to Sombakol, the Chinese commander asked me if I wanted to care for the sick and wounded. Of course, I told him yes. At that time he brought in a Dr. Anderson who was captured with a group of Americans who were attacked on November 4. Until this time, he had not been allowed to care for the sick and wounded. They promised us a hospital, but it turned out to be two unheated buildings that were exactly the same as the Korean houses we lived in. Our sick and wounded consisted mostly of people who had been wounded during the firefights and brought north. Among those, we had seven cases of compound and infected fractures of legs or arms, many open bullet wounds, and one soldier who had a bullet go through his lung and out the other side. Fortunately, he lived. We also treated many for dysentery.

The hospital's equipment consisted of four hemostats, two of which clamped imperfectly, and two old-fashioned scalpels. When most of us took biology in school, we bought a little kit that had a solid blade with a handle—that's the kind of scalpel we had. We had two hook retractors, one bone clamp, and one old hand bone saw. We were also given a stethoscope. The ear pieces were like the hearing aids that fit into the ear with tubes that came down with a little bell on the end. We had to screw these into our ears. We had no bandages. The medications we had consisted of powders for diarrhea. One called tanalburnin and one called tannabarb, which were Japanese in origin. There were no aspirin, but there was a little methylate. The Korean doctor was supposed to keep the medicines, and Dr. Anderson and I were supposed to go up and down the valley every day visiting all the people to see who was sick. We were then to determine the illness, list the name of the patient and the medication we felt was required. We would add extra names to the list in the hope of getting more medicine. At night we would give this list to the Korean doctor, and he would dole out the medication to us. Some days we would get all that we asked for, and some days we would get none. It took twenty-four hours before we could institute treatment.

After Esensten reached Camp Five, which was a permanent camp, he noticed that because of extenuating circumstances the Americans prisoners did not do as well as did the British or Turks:

The British transferred people by regiments and the Turks by company. So when the British got captured they were with people with whom they had trained. And they were still together after they were liberated. So they took better care of each other because they knew one another and because they knew they would have to deal with each other after they got back to England. The same thing was true of the Turks. The Turks also had the advantage that the Chinese didn't have any people that spoke Turkish so they were left alone to take care of themselves. When a Turk or a British prisoner got sick and came to our hospital, they came with two or three helpers to take care of them. When our kids got sick, they had to take care of themselves, unless they were lucky enough to have been in the same unit for a while. Prisoners captured as a unit almost always did better than people who were captured as individuals.

Esensten also noticed that many of the prisoners simply gave up. "Face-the-Wall Syndrome," it was called in earlier wars, although some nationalities, World War II Germans, for example, did not attach the same stigma to this act as did Americans. Esensten also noticed various types of hysteria:

We saw people just willing themselves to death. But you have to understand, all were chronically sick with all kinds of ailments. Most were only eighteen or nineteen years old—just kids, who felt desperately alone with no support system. So when life got to be more miserable than they could handle, it was easier to die than to live in misery. They escaped by pulling themselves into a coma. When they could no longer cope, their bodies simply shut down to protect themselves; that's all it was. When you live like an animal, it doesn't take much urging to die. In that environment, it was easy to die, but it took guts to live.

As things got worse we begin to see hysteria, all kinds of hysteria, from visual, telescopic vision to inability to move hands and arms, to complete paralysis from neck down to coma. Some men were actually paralyzed except that they could move their eyes and they could talk. There wasn't much we could do for them, unless we could catch them early in their paralysis or before coma and get some buddies to get them out and walk them day and night and force feed them until they began to eat. But, we didn't do well with that kind of severe hysteria until, suddenly, one day I got called to see a young second lieutenant whom I knew. . . . I was so damn mad at him for allowing himself to get into this hysterical state that I just lost my temper. . . . I hit him in the jaw, and then I hit him two more times, and, by God, he woke up. I personally fed him, and he lived, only to die of starvation later on. From then on, anybody who got hysterical coma, or paralysis, got hit in the jaw three times. Now, I bet that's not the kind of medicine you learn in medical school but it was effective.

Gene Lam also witnessed "give-up-itis," but he believed that later critics of the Korean War prisoners corrupted the term because they seldom examined the appalling conditions that caused some prisoners to give up:

The term "give-up-itis" was a very common prisoner term. When a man seemed to lie down all the men said, "Ah, there's nothing wrong with him, he's just giving up." However . . . there was no such thing as "give-up-itis." The men were sick with some sort of disease, mental or physical, with which they could not cope; therefore, it seemed that the best thing he could do was lie down, pull something over his head, turn and face the wall and die. . . . [But] the use of this term and the ridicule attached to it by us and the other men of the camp seemed to have the desirable effect. The men would not listen to reason or to orders. However, if we ridiculed them enough, many of the men seemed to pull themselves off their deathbeds and walk.[5]

Lam denounced what passed for a hospital in Camp Five and some of the strange health procedures practiced by the Chinese:

Camp Five was a bombed out village on the banks of the Yalu River. There were four physicians from our division, one from the 1st Cavalry, and one from the 24th Division. I was assigned to the camp hospital, a Buddhist temple away from the village. The commissar gave us strict orders to "stop the dying." We suggested some food and medicine, but we were told that these items were being destroyed by our own Air Force. The hospital was just another place to die. My regimental surgeon died there, in my arms, shortly after arrival.

At Camp Five, we were to witness a "miracle of Soviet medicine," the chicken liver treatment. In about fifty men, pieces of chicken liver that had been soaked in a penicillin solution, were inserted in an incision between the ribs. This was to "prevent disease and death." At the same time these men were segregated and placed on a diet consisting of rice, meat, and eggs. Due to the better diet, none of them died although most of them sloughed the chicken livers. Our captors did give us some aspirin, a little sulfanilamide, and a few bandages, as well as a can of ether. Another doctor and I did some surgery until the ether ran out, primarily the amputation of frostbitten toes. It takes very little ether to anesthetize a starving man.

Another advance of Soviet medicine was presented to us: an inoculation "to prevent all disease." Only those who were sick were excused. Fortunately, I had beriberi and missed my shot. The first twenty men were inoculated using the same needle. Everyone protested and the whole procedure was stopped due to the lack of additional needles. All twenty later developed hepatitis but no one died.

About mid-May of 1951, we four remaining physicians were informed that it was "time to learn who to save, instead of how to save . . . " and our "education" began. From dawn until dark we were forced to undergo Communist indoctrination by English-speaking comrades. Marx, Engels, Lenin, and Stalin were our diet for the next ten months. We were the first American POWs who were forced to undergo so-called "brainwashing."

Conditions improved in July 1951 when preliminary peace talks were initiated. . . . The death rate began to fall with the advent of better food and as some medications became available. The POW physicians were not allowed to practice but we did wonders with hot water soaks for everything, from frostbitten toes to headache. By the end of summer and early fall, no further deaths occurred in our group, which consisted of 250–300 men.[6]

Don Poirot was one of many prisoners who suffered night blindness because of a lack of vitamin A in their diet:

During the winter, a lot of us came down with night blindness. According to some of the medics it was caused by a lack of a certain vitamin. It was really weird. In the dark if you looked straight out you couldn't see anything. It was just black. However, if you looked down at the ground in front of you, you could see from the top part of your vision. As soon as you looked up everything went black again. So many of us had night blindness that Joe Chink started experimenting. They claimed they had medication that could cure it. I was given a dose of medicine that was extremely bitter. It didn't help my night blindness but it sure kept me away from the Chinese medics. Someone told me later I had been given bile from the liver of a hog. We just rode it out until spring when we received the first green Chinese cabbage for a side dish with our food. One or two helpings seemed to take care of our night blindness.

No prisoner suffered more physical ailments than did Robert Jones, who was an eighteen-year-old enlisted man when the Chinese captured him on November 28, 1950. He was still suffering from his wounds and frostbite when he finally reached Camp Five. When be became incapacitated by beriberi, the Chinese decided to experiment on him by inserting chicken and pig livers under his skin. Jones ended up in the camp hospital where he was given up for dead:

> The Chinese mentioned that the Russians had come up with a new operation that might help us get better. They said this operation would make the swelling go down in my testicles. It was voluntary, so I volunteered. I had to take myself two miles up the road to another area, and they put me on this table. They had a bunch of men hold me down, and they operated on me. They put a big chunk of chicken liver in my side and stitched it up. I don't remember them using any anesthetic. Then I had to crawl back to the hospital. My condition didn't get any better. Eventually my side swelled up and burst. That chicken liver was supposed to draw the infection out of my body, and I was supposed to get better, but I didn't. So I volunteered for a second operation. I went through the same procedure, but this time I got about a half-pound of hog liver put in my side. I believe they actually thought this was going to help, but it didn't do any more than the chicken liver.
>
> I was being visited regularly by Father Emil Kapaun[7] who tried to cheer me up even though he had the same condition I had. His tes-

ticles were swollen to the size of a basketball or bigger, and he carried them around in a kind of basket. I hate to put it this way, but he had a basket full of balls. This went on for about six weeks, and they decided that I wasn't going to make it so I was moved to the hut in the rear where they put the dying.

There were eight or ten of us laid out on this mud floor. It was so cold back there that the ice on the walls must have been six inches thick. Every evening they would come in and move two or three right up to the opening to the outside. There wasn't even a door there. That was the last stop before they took you to the hill to be buried. The next morning the burial detail would come get them and drag them up the hill. I was back there about five days, which was long for that area. The fifth day they came around and put my dog tags in my mouth and moved me up beside the opening. I knew what they were doing, but I couldn't say nothing about it. The next morning they took me and two other guys up to the hill and threw us into this mass grave. I guess I was there two days when they brought another group of bodies up and threw them on top of me. But when they hit me, I moaned. The GIs who were on the burial detail were discussing whether I might be alive. They decided if I was, they would probably have to bring me back the next day. . . .

Tully Cox was a young soldier whose feet were so badly frostbitten on the march north that gangrene set in, and some of his fellow prisoners had to cut off his feet. When the gangrene returned, part of his legs had to be amputated. Fellow prisoner Roy Hardage describes Tully Cox's arrival in Camp One and his incredible courage. Cox miraculously survived his ordeal:

Tully Cox and some more guys arrived by truck in our camp. Believe me, they looked anything but human. We looked bad, but when we saw them, we felt like crying. They were all that was left of a group of POWs who had been kept down in some valley all winter. I told this one Chink interpreter if only the people in the States could see the way these men had been treated, what did he think would happen to his so-called volunteer troops in Korea. If just one picture could have been put in *Life* magazine. I really rubbed it in his face. I told him how did he ever expect any POW who saw this to believe the schooling where they bragged about humane treatment they were giving our prisoners. He finally got pissed off, said it was not true, and headed off to headquarters. You could always tell when you got the best of them; they would always say, "No, this is not true," or "You better correct your attitude."

We had just been issued some dried fish whose skin was as tough as an alligator's hide. A few of us gave the new men our fish, and they sat there beside the road and ate it like a bunch of hungry dogs. After seeing how starved they were, more and more of our men brought up their fish. I never will forget Tully Cox, a sixteen-year-old boy from Alabama[8] with both feet gone, hair like a shaggy lion, sitting there with that dried fish in his mouth.

In the early months of 1951, Tully Cox received some surgical medical treatment from the Communists. One of their so-called doctors came around to the squad where many wounded and dying Americans lay rotting away. Their toes and fingers would turn black from the cold and drop off or they would pull them off with their fingers, or sometimes when they tried to walk out in the snow to urinate they would stamp their feet on rocks and break off parts of their frozen feet because they either had no shoes or they could no longer get their feet in their boots because they were too swollen. This so-called doctor came around with a rusty hacksaw and cut the meat from Cox's legs, pulled the flesh back, and then started sawing on the big bones of his legs. It was about forty degrees below zero with no heat in the room, and the doctor used no drugs or anesthetics to deaden the pain. While he was sawing them off, Tully Cox raised up to watch and the "doc" couldn't stand it. He pushed him back and wouldn't let him watch. . . .

I think it was sometime in 1952 when a Chinese lady doctor came to our camp and operated on Tully's legs and cut more of them off and brought the meat down to cover the bones so they were no longer showing. Cox almost died during this process. This Chinese lady was well liked by all GIs because she did a lot to help them. She would have been the only Communist who wouldn't have been killed had we ever taken over our camp. When the rest of the Chinese began to notice her interest in saving POW lives instead of butchering them, she had to criticize herself to the camp officials who then sent her away. . . .

To be sent to the camp hospital was tantamount to a death sentence, and it surely would have been for Robert Schaefer had liberation come to Camp One a few weeks later:

The bad treatment eased up with the peace talks, but by then I was on my way downhill. I don't think I would have survived much longer. They had a so-called hospital. It was in a temple on a hill the Chinese had taken over. If you got sick they'd take you up to this hospital, but nobody ever came back from there. You simply died. In winter they'd roll the bodies down the hill and then in the spring finish burying them. I was in that hospital when we finally started exchanging prisoners. I just kept getting weaker and weaker, and I was pretty much scheduled to die because nobody ever came back from there. I was suffering from malnutrition and some kind of pleurisy for which I never really got any treatment. When we got back to our side, they started feeding us vitamins and good food and lots of rest. When I was captured I weighed about 220, about what I am now, but I didn't have any fat on me at all. When I got out, the first time I was able to weigh myself, which might have been after I got home, I was 146 pounds. But I'm sure I weighed a lot less than that in the prison camp.

No one knows how many prisoners died from disease and other causes. Dr. Esensten and his fellow doctors tried to keep a record, but the Chinese would not allow it:

The average ages of POWs was nineteen to twenty. We had seventeen-, eighteen-, and nineteen-year-old kids with us. When the boys died we tried to keep records of them by their name, rank, and serial number. The Chinese destroyed these records because we would put down the word starvation or malnutrition or pneumonia. The Chinese wouldn't accept this as the cause of death. They destroyed the records because the records would imply that they weren't taking care of our people.[9]

The lack of adequate health care and medicine, as well as the refusal of the North Korean and Chinese captors to allow captured American doctors fully to practice their skills, certainly contributed to the countless unnecessary deaths suffered by the Korean War POWs. This abysmal record also serves as further refutation to such postwar critics as Eugene Kinkead and William Mayer who blamed personal and societal shortcomings for the alarming prisoner death rate in Korea.

7

ESCAPE: MYTH AND REALITY

I had one friend who was in the same platoon I was before I got captured. He would try to escape at night during the marches. The Chinese would recapture him, feed him pretty good, and then catch him up again with the column. He did that several times, but then finally he just disappeared. Nobody ever knew what happened to him.

—Billy Joe Harris, Korean War POW

Escape? I won't say it was impossible, but I don't know of any who made it back from Camp Five to our lines. We had those that tried, but it was foolish. The Chinese made an example of them after they recaptured them. They would then try to make it tougher on the rest of us, but they couldn't punish us much more than taking away a little of that rice or millet or cracked corn they were feeding us.

—Jerry Morgan, Korean War POW

Americans have long been fascinated by stories of wartime prisoners who escaped. Over the years, countless novels, popular histories, and especially movies told and retold these tales. Most reduced captivity to a simple struggle between the forces of good and evil in which noble and courageous individuals fell into the clutches of unsavory and diabolical captors but survived their crucible to become even more exemplary human beings. Most such accounts have been long on adventure and heroics but short on substance and accuracy.

The old Revolutionary War adage, "Seldom have so few done so much for so many," clearly applies to the subject of POW escapes. Whatever the war, rarely has the number of escapees exceeded 1 or 2 percent of those incarcerated. For a variety of reasons, some of them very logically tied to self-preservation and a fear of reprisals, only the most daring and determined prisoners have attempted to escape and even fewer achieved success.[1] According to historian Robert Doyle's exemplary study of military escapes, "Many Americans chose to remain in captivity for various reasons. Most endured their hardships stoically; a few collaborated and decided to join their captors; some refused to break out even when given an opportunity, and some defied tremendous odds and escaped."[2]

Critics such as Eugene Kinkead and William E. Mayer cited Korean War prisoners' alleged unwillingness to escape as further proof of their singular lack of character, determination, and courage. In truth, however, the percentage of attempted escapes in Korea did not vary markedly from earlier wars. Successful escapes occurred from gathering points not far from the frontlines or during the subsequent marches. There were no successful escapes from the permanent camps along the Yalu River, although several men certainly tried. Men talked about escaping, and planning to do so was definitely good therapy, but an actual escape, especially from one of the permanent camps, was fraught with danger. Extreme distances and unforgiving weather, mountainous terrain, physical appearance, language barriers, and unpleasant consequences for both the escapee and those left behind discouraged all but the most resolute prisoners.

Predicting who might try to escape was difficult, although in American popular culture one can safely anticipate such heroes from the opening page or scene. Genuine escapees seldom looked or acted like such fictional counterparts as Steve McQueen, William Holden, Frank Sinatra, and Sylvester Stallone, all of whom played escaped prisoners in important World War II films.[3] For movie heroes, escape was part of a macho game in which culturally superior Americans always outwitted their plodding and inferior captors.

In truth, guilt was an important motivator for escapees who, if successful, could mitigate the opprobrium of having been captured. Others, who believed they were facing inevitable death, thought they had nothing to lose. Some men became claustrophobic when incarcerated, and simply had to break out. Finally, there were those like Rubin Townsend, who knew he had to get out to tell the story of those he had left behind:

> Those who say no one escaped are wrong. A lot of men did, even from the permanent camps, although none of them made it out alive. I was fortunate to have escaped early in the game. If I had gotten up to the Yalu River and a permanent camp, it would have been very difficult.
>
> I was so damn mad because of getting captured, but I can tell you anybody that's ever put on a uniform can get captured. I don't care if you're Superman or whoever, you can be captured. Some guys say, "Well, I'll never be captured." I say, "Hell, that's what I said too, but I got knocked silly."

I was MIA for 103 days, but it felt like 103 weeks. You do go into shock when you're first captured. Your freedom has been taken away from you, and that's the most precious thing you can have. I don't say everyone reacts the same way because people don't. I was immediately looking to get away, but you're at the mercy of the guards, and they would have shot you full of bullets if you even made a move.

I escaped while on one of the death marches after I was captured on February 11, 1951. Some people say these death marches didn't exist, but I saw what happened to our guys when they couldn't make it. If they fell by the side of the road, you'd hear "pop pop pop." I also saw guys get bayonetted. So I certainly knew what would happen to me if I fell out. I was damn lucky. I had my winter issue. Some guys didn't have boots, and they still had to march in that cold and snow, but they didn't last very long. I saw so many of our guys murdered—and I say murdered—because that's what it was on that march. I had nothing but fire in my eyes after I saw the first guy killed, and I was looking to escape anyway I could.

I jumped off a bridge the first time I escaped. It was February and really cold. There were two or three hundred of us that the Chinese had consolidated from various units. They were marching us north, and I paired up with two other guys. It was night and snowing like hell, and you could hardly see the person in front of you. When we crossed these railroad bridges, we noticed the guards would always go back to the rear. They sure as hell couldn't go along side of you because they'd fall off the bridge or somebody would have pushed them off. We were crossing this bridge, and I said to these two guys, "Now is our chance. If we don't do it now, we might not get another chance." So we jumped off that damn bridge. It was dark and snowing so hard you couldn't see five feet in front of you. I didn't know whether I was going to hit a tree, or boulder, or whatever, and that's a hell of a feeling. I was hoping I would hit snow and I did. I sank right down into it. Then I heard the other two guys land. We just stayed quiet, until we could hear nothing going over that bridge. Then we dug our way out and up into the mountains we went. Our adrenaline was flowing, and we were really moving. All kinds of things began to happen. I was getting cold, and then I realized, "Hey, my pants are freezing from all the wet and snow." We had to stop and rest because we got so tired. We found this old Korean hut way up in the mountains, and there were some old blankets somebody had abandoned for whatever reason. That hut saved our lives. Otherwise I think we would have died that first night.

We found some kimchi and rice. Apparently, somebody had got out of there fast because food was so precious in Korea. The next morning was fairly clear. We assessed that no one had been there for a long time because we would have seen footprints. We were able to start a fire with some flints we found. One of us kept watch. If someone came up that mountain, we would damn well see them and out the other way we would go.

After we recouped for several days, we stuffed our pockets full of food and started making our way back to our lines. We traveled only at night, and we used the stars to head us in the right direction. During the day we hid out, but we could check the sun to check which way was south. We would pinpoint a mountain or two that we wanted to move toward that night. After four or five days we ran out of the food we'd crammed in our pockets, and we made the mistake of going into what we thought was an abandoned hut. We found some food and were eating up a storm, but somebody had spotted us and apparently notified the Chinese. They completely surrounded the hut and cut loose with a number of rounds. As soon as we heard these rounds going through the hut, we hit the floor. We had no guns and I knew damn well what was probably coming next. At least I knew if I were them, I would have thrown in a hand grenade, which would have taken care of the whole thing. We figured we could wait in the hut and get killed or just surrender. So we found this old white coat, stuck it out the window, and surrendered. We had no choice.

This Chinese guy who spoke English told us to come out. We kept that white flag in front of us not really knowing if they were going to mow us down. They pushed and kicked us around a bit, and this guy asked us how we got there. We knew that if we told him we had escaped, they would have mowed us down right there so we told him we were in a big battle and got turned around and damned if we didn't go north instead of south and that we'd been hiding in the mountains because we didn't know any better. They bought it. Otherwise they would have killed us right there.

The Chinese put us in with another group of prisoners. We stayed with them for two or three weeks. The Chinese gave us a little bit better food and tried to indoctrinate us. They gave us some books we were supposed to read. Then they would ask us questions about what we'd read. We knew it was a bunch of bullshit, but we just sort of strung them along. We'd say, "Oh yeah, blah blah blah, this is what we read, and this is what we remember." Every now and then we would turn the tables and question what we were supposed to be reading. When we did that they really got mad. This Chinese major would scream and holler and get in our faces and say, "We're going to turn you over to the North Koreans, and they'll shoot you." All this kind of stuff went on for two or three weeks until I guess they had enough of us.

We were maybe forty miles behind the lines. I really don't know. Anyway, they finally got tired of us and got mad. They said, "We give you food and things to read, and all you do is tell us lies." I asked them, "Well, what would you do?" I got the shit kicked out of me a couple times. The Chinese turned us over to these North Koreans and they were tough. They were supposed to take us north, and they did. We were with these other Americans who were wounded and starving to death. Again, we saw things that really got us mad, but all we could do was live day by day. The three of us were lucky because we had been eating better during our escape, and we had had a couple of weeks of what I'd call fair food while the Chinese were trying to in-doctrinate us.

We started marching, and they were really rough on us. If we even blinked, they'd kick the shit out of us. They didn't like us too well because we were trying to resist. They had picked up some South Ko-reans, and we saw them taken away and we heard gun shots. They just killed them. We had heard from the South Koreans that they had shot some Americans, so we figured we were next. This one son of a bitch, who was really bad, bad, bad, had already stuck me in the ass with a bayonet, and he was just waiting for a chance to kill me. But they got careless.

They kept us guarded very closely, but there were two fellows named Bob and John with me in this little old room. I don't know their last names. They weren't from my unit. We made our plans because we figured we weren't going to survive. This nasty guard was guarding the front one night, and he leaned against the door and went to sleep. I had found a Korean sickle, and we also had a big old stone that was used to crush rice. There was another guard on the back door and he also went to sleep. I whispered to the other guys, "I think this is prob-ably our last chance." I'll be quite blunt: I reached out and grabbed this one guard by his hair and cut his goddamn throat. About the same time one of the other guys hit the other guard in the head with this big rock. We grabbed their guns and off we went. Now there was no turning back. They would have cut us to pieces and fed us to the dogs, especially after killing those guards.

We ambushed a three-man patrol and took a burp gun and food from them. Not long after that we got in a shoot-out with some Chinese at a bridge, and I lost track of the guys I was with. We had made a pact that we'd protect each other as much as we could, but if we got separated we had to go on our own. We didn't have any choice. We were knocking the hell out of them on this bridge with our burp guns because we had them in a cross fire. I was on one side and the other two guys were on the other side. We knocked out a number of Chinese, but I had just a few rounds of ammunition left in my burp gun. I hollered over and got no response from my guys so I figured they had taken off. I knew I sure as hell couldn't go across because I'd get shot to pieces. I had but one choice and I took it. I jumped off the bridge into the river. It was that or die. It was night, of course, and colder than hell. I paddled across as best I could. My boots filled up and the river started taking me down, but I made it to the other side. I was just barely able to crawl up the bank and head into the mountains. I was exhausted and by this time I had lost my burp gun. I walked and crawled until finally I got somewhere near the top of this mountain where I found a hole and crawled in. I poured the water out of my boots and wrung out my socks. Then I covered myself with some leaves and branches and went to sleep. I was totally exhausted. I woke up sometime the next afternoon. I was still damp, but I was able to work my way back to our frontlines. I never saw the other two guys again.[4]

Ray Baumbach, who earned Silver and Bronze Stars and three Purple Hearts in Korea, escaped three times while being marched north after he was captured in February 1951. His first two attempts were unsuccessful, but the third time he made it back to the U.N. lines where he fell upon his knees, kissed the soil, and promised God that he would one day repay Him—and he did, by devoting much of his subsequent life to a prison ministry. Baumbach credits early training and a mother's love for his determination to escape:

I've given a lot of thought to why I tried so hard to escape. I think being born and raised in a family of thirteen children and having an alcoholic father and a wonderful mother who had to raise us alone was a big part of it. We had to learn to survive even as kids; otherwise, we would have been separated and sent to homes. We leaned on each other, we ate what we got, and we didn't expect anything because there was nothing. I started my basic training for survival when I was five years old, learning how to find something to eat, and, because I was the smallest of my brothers, how to escape from them. I know all this helped when I escaped those three times in Korea. I also respected my mother so much that I just felt when I was in Korea that I had to get back for her sake. I didn't want her to go through any more hurt. When I was trying to get back to our lines, I could just picture her sitting at the kitchen table, drinking coffee, and waiting for me. Every time I saw her face, I would get up and begin moving. There were so many times I just wanted to sit down in the snow and give up. I was so sick and cold in those hills by myself that I just wanted to go to sleep and forget it. But her picture would come into my mind, and I would get up and start moving. After what my mother had done for us, I felt she had the right to see me come home.

The best time to escape was during the first few days after capture. Unfortunately, many new prisoners were disoriented, wounded, and in shock. Such was the case with Ray Baumbach, but after seeing some of his fellow prisoners murdered, he became convinced he would have to escape if he hoped to survive:

They marched us north, and all I did was walk along. At first, I didn't even know where I was, but after a couple of days, I had a pretty good idea what we were in for, and I knew that in my condition I wasn't going to make thirty miles a night to China or wherever they were taking us. I had shrapnel wounds in my shoulder from a mortar shell, and they roughed us up a bit when they first captured us. So I just kept looking for an opening. A short time later our jets came in and dropped napalm. The Chinese knew all about napalm, and when it hit, they and the rest of us scattered. That was the first time I escaped.

I took off with five other guys. Two of them were shot and killed immediately while we were escaping, and the other three died en route. They were all beat up, and they died with me in the hills, after maybe a week or a week and a half. We were heading south, just trying to follow the sound of our artillery. We traveled at night and just before daylight we would look for a village that had been burned out to try and find some rice or whatever else we could eat. Shortly after the last of the three died, I was recaptured. These Chinese jumped out from behind some shrubs, and I just put my hands up in the air because I had no weapons.

They took me to the closest group of POWs, and I joined them. They didn't really rough me up after recapturing me because I guess they didn't have time. They were in bad shape themselves, and all they wanted to do was get rid of us. The best way to do that was probably just let us die or to shoot us, but for some reason they did not.

We started marching, and once again our jets came in strafing because they saw movement. The Chinese normally kept us hidden during the day on the sides of hills and under trees, but our pilots must have seen some movement and, thinking we were Chinese, they strafed us. Four or five jets came down, and, once again, everybody scattered. This time there were three or four who took off with me, but, again, I was the only one to make it. I don't know why I was the one. This time I was out probably a couple of weeks. I just can't be sure about that. I was in a village, and they just walked in on me sitting there. I just raised my hands. I thought they were going to shoot me, and I was surprised when they didn't. Usually they wouldn't waste their time on just one guy. But again, I was fortunate because they must have known there was a group of POWs nearby.

I escaped the third time when we were marching and some artillery shells hit the group. We were in a makeshift camp where they had kept us for a day or two. I took off with one other guy who was shot up pretty good. He'd fall in and out of consciousness, and I had to practically carry him. We were walking alongside this road late at night. We knew we were close to our lines because we could see lights to the south. We figured it was our artillery firing and maybe some of our vehicles. So I said to the guy, "I'll help you, but we can't walk in this ditch anymore. We're going to have to get up on the road. That's our only chance of making it." We got up and started walking on the road, and somebody yelled, "Halt!" But I didn't know in what language. I thought, "Oh my God, the Chinese again." But the guy I was with said, "No, that's not Chinese. Just yell, 'American, American GI.' " And that's what I did. These were French troops. Their captain could speak English, and I said, "We're American GI POWs who have escaped." The first thing I did was bend down and kiss the ground, and the second thing I did was look up at the heavens. At the time, I knew nothing about God, had never fooled with him. But I said, "God, I want to let you know if you are a God, some day I will repay you for what you've done."

Homer Jurgens was a college student when the Army Reserves recalled him to active duty in October 1950. He was fighting with the 2nd Infantry Division when it was overrun by Chinese troops in what came to be called the May Massacre of 1951. Seven days after his capture, he escaped while being marched northward. Four days later he reached American lines:

I was very intent on escaping if it could possibly be done. I watched the guards' every movement. They would march us a while and then we would sit down to rest. On the night of the escape, the guards got up to move us out, but I just sat there with my head down between my legs. I felt they couldn't see me in the pitch dark. After I thought everybody had left, I started making my way from that scene. I hid during the day and moved at night, using the North Star, to work back south toward what I think was the Han River. I was also very careful where and how I moved, trying to make the least possible noise. Once I saw helicopters overhead, and I made a big sign with rocks: "Help," but nobody ever saw it or paid any attention to it. I hadn't had much to eat before I escaped, and while I was working my way back toward our lines I just grabbed anything I could find. I even ate a snake. I killed it with a rock, skinned it, and ate it raw. On one of those days during my escape, I came down from the mountain early, which I shouldn't have done, but I was thirsty and went down to this stream. I was sitting there scooping water when all of a sudden I heard this noise and looked up, and there was a Chinese patrol coming along. Boy, did I freeze. I stayed there a long time before I moved again. The Chinese had told us that if we escaped and were caught, they'd kill us, but I just give thanks to the mercy of God that I made it through and that I am still alive.

Melvin Shadduck was flying his eighty-first mission when he was shot down on April 21, 1951. He was injured and captured, but eventually escaped from a Chinese field hospital and returned to his lines. In spite of the passage of more than fifty years, for what he called security reasons, he was reluctant to tell his entire story:[5]

I'm telling you my story, but I shouldn't be talking about parts of it. Let's call this a sanitized story. I'm not telling you any lies, but there are certain little details that I have to leave out to protect people who might have helped me. I will say somebody fed me, but if their name became public it might be dangerous to their health. Then in the future somebody isn't going to help a downed pilot if they know the story is going to get out and they might be killed. There are also certain techniques that you use to fool the enemy that somebody might use again, but if it's published they're no good.

In the Air Force we weren't restricted to name, rank, and serial number. We could talk to our captors all day, as long as we didn't tell them any classified information. Giving only your name, rank, and serial number is all right, but it actually doesn't buy you what our leaders like to tell you it does. They say if you refuse to tell them anything more, they won't beat you, but that's bull.

I tried to shame this officer who was going to march me to this field hospital. I said, "Man, I am in no condition to walk. When we take Chinese prisoners, we fly them to a hospital. I know because I've done it."

He got real interested and said, "You personally flew Chinese prisoners to a hospital?"

I said, "That's right. They don't have to walk."

He said, "Well, if that's the case when you leave here you're not going to have to walk. We'll put you on a litter." And they did. They took me about twenty-five miles northeast that first night. This litter was like a rickshaw with bicycle wheels and a guy in front pulling it. Before we got to the destination the guy who was pulling became very friendly. I was shivering and shaking, and he even took his heavy coat off and laid it over me. But when we got to our destination, it was real steep and rocky, and he wanted to know if I could walk up with the rest of the prisoners. I walked up to a table, and this officer flew into a rage. He said, "You were carried here on a litter and you can walk!" So when we left that night I had to walk. By my estimate we covered twenty-five miles. When they are moving, they don't walk; it's more of a jog, with the guards prodding you with a bayonet if they thought you weren't moving fast enough.

They would also tell you, "Hurry up or we'll shoot you." Then they'd put a gun to the back of your head, but they'd fire right over it. When they did this, I jumped and they thought that was funny so it got to be a nice joke. After twenty or twenty-five miles, I was having more and more trouble walking. My leg was badly burned from my ankle to my knee, and when I stepped down on it, I began falling down. Finally, this one guard asked an officer if it was okay to put me on a litter again. This guy blew up. I don't know if it was the same guy that flew in a rage before, but he got so angry he beat me unconscious. They had to carry me the rest of the way. The guard told me later this officer was going to shoot me, but his commander stopped him.

The morning after this beating, the same commander looked me over. My head and back were bleeding, and this medic actually gave me some warm water and a rag to wash my head. The blood had combined with dirt where I laid on the ground, and it was all over the back of my head. That was the kindest thing that anybody did for me. The commander then ordered a couple of guards to take me to a nearby field hospital, and they did. There were four other Americans there and a Turk. It was from this field hospital that I escaped.

I was there about two and a half weeks. Our troops were moving north, and I could hear their artillery. I told myself, "Artillery only travels about twenty miles so I'm not that far from home." The other thing that made me escape was that one of the other American prisoners died. I was taking care of him, doing whatever I could. None of these guys could hardly walk more than a couple of steps. I was the only one who was mobile. When this one boy died, I buried him and rest of the guys just kind of fell apart. One of them said, "We're all going to die here." I told him, "No, you're not." That was what really triggered the escape.

I had a plan all laid out. That plan is still somewhat classified so I can't talk much about it, but I was going to get out and find help, and I did. I couldn't walk in a straight line, so it took me three nights and two days. The second night I did find some friendly Koreans who gave me something to eat, but mostly I was just going on adrenaline. I don't know if I should be talking about this or not, but I determined that they were friendly. If they hadn't been, one of them would have died, we'll put it that way. I was prepared to kill them with a rock I had. Anyway, I made it, and American tanks went in there and got those boys. That night we were all together in a hospital in Seoul.

Once the prisoners reached the permanent camps along the Yalu River, their chances for a successful escape were virtually nonexistent, although several men made every effort to do so. Interestingly, many of these camps had no fences or other man-made barriers; they had, however, something even more effective: the Yalu River and Manchuria to the north, and bleak, forbidding mountains in the other three directions. Camp Five was typical, as Harry Falck explains:

Two or three times a month someone would try to escape. I remember this one guy and three of his buddies were always trying to escape. They would pass the word down to us, "Hey, you're going to get some bread in your soup tonight. Save it. We're going to take off sometime." They wouldn't say when. So we saved it. They would come through and pick up what bread we could save for them and take off. Only one guy got caught and brought back. I don't know what happened to the other two. He was punished. Just before they got him back to camp, they tied him behind a jeep and then drove the jeep just fast enough that he had to trot. When he gave out and fell over, they dragged him the rest of the way so everybody could see him. Then they took him to the infirmary, and when he got well enough they turned him back to his group again.

Although there were no walls or fences, you couldn't really get very far. To begin with, they kept us so weak we became exhausted from any kind of effort. We also had beards, we couldn't speak the language, we were too tall, and we had a white complexion. The North Korean people knew if they got caught trying to help us, they'd get shot. The Chinese also paid them to tell on us.

Robert Schaefer, who was in Camp One, explains that even from a distance it was easy to distinguish an American from a Korean just by the way each walked:

There was one guy who tried to escape and he was a Nisei. If anybody could possibly have gotten away he should have. He could blend in with the population. But they brought him back in a couple of days and hung him by his thumbs. He had to be on his tiptoes or his thumbs would be pulled out of their sockets, and they left him that way for a couple of days. I don't think they would have been nice to any of us if we tried to escape, and I don't think there was any chance of a successful escape. You could spot any American by this height and the way he walked. By the same token, you could spot an Asian's walk from as far away as you could see him, just by the way he took his steps. An American had no chance out there.

Robert Fletcher, who was in Camp Five, also reveals why a successful escape was all but impossible, especially if one were black:

Nobody escaped from the permanent camps! Why? Number one, they wouldn't let you shave. Number two, the color of your skin. Koreans don't have heavy, bushy beards. They have just little old scraggly beards. If you escaped, all somebody had to see was the beard. They'd call the Chinese, and they'd hunt you down. Oh, we had guys who were gone two or three days, but they'd bring them back and say, "You can't escape because of the villagers." A dog would bark at night and the owner would contact the Chinese guards. They'd start searching the area, and finally they would find you. My platoon sergeant, Al Pough, tried to escape twice. The longest he was gone was a couple of days before they brought him back.

The Chinese would not always punish the individual who supposedly had done something wrong. The Communist way is to punish the person who is most liked. That punishes everybody. Oh, they were no fools. For example, this one guy tried to escape and killed a guard. The Chinese didn't bother the guy who did it; instead, they took this fellow who was liked by everybody and tied him on a tripod and threw cold water on him in thirty-five below weather. Every hour they went out and threw a bucket of water on him until he froze to death. The Chinese then pointed to the rest of us and said, "This could happen to you, and you, and you."

Although the military code of honor calls for prisoners of war to seize every opportunity to escape, conditions in Korea should have made it clear to even such unrelenting critics as Kinkead and Mayer why so few were able to do so. Unfortunately, such was not the case, and accusations of cowardice and "a lack of moral and characterological elements in war"[6] would continue to haunt the former prisoners long after they returned home from Korea.

8

INTERROGATION, PROPAGANDA, INDOCTRINATION, AND "BRAINWASHING"

Hell, everybody over there collaborated, if you want to call it that, even our bird colonel. When you are already on a starvation diet, name, rank, and serial number don't mean a damn thing. And the Code of Conduct didn't mean crap either. By the time they cut off your food for three or four days you forget all about that stuff.

—Jeff Q. Erwin, Korean War POW

You can't take a person who is starving and torture him and take away everything he has been accustomed to in life, and then tell him how much better off he would be with Communism.

—Harley Coon, Korean War POW

It was in Camp Three where they gave us the lectures and stuff. We would sit there and think about the beach in Atlantic City and girls in their bathing suits. At least, I know that's what I was thinking about.

—Robert Blewitt, Korean War POW

We have trained Americans to kill and then have no memory of having killed. . . . [Shaw's] brain has not only been washed, it has been dry-cleaned.

—Dr. Yen Lo, from the film *The Manchurian Candidate*

Did a disappointing number of American prisoners collaborate with the enemy? Fifty years after the beginning of the Korean War, historian Raymond Lech wrote, "The majority of the captive Americans did practically everything their North Korean and Chinese captors told them to do." Lech, who readily admits they did so because they feared death, credits the Communists' success to their deliberate policy of reducing their prisoners to a subhuman existence. "The enemy used a weapon that didn't cost a penny but achieved its purpose with remarkable efficiency: starvation. After they had cleaned the body of its meat, after they had living skeletons in their cages, they began to 'cleanse' the mind."[1]

The captors also attempted to sow dissension among their prisoners by first promising them that everyone would be treated equally and then ordering them to ignore rank. According to T. R. Fehrenbach, thus encouraged, many of the enlisted men shunned or disobeyed their officers, even calling them by their first names. Fehrenbach blamed this apparent erosion of discipline for many of the problems the GIs experienced in both the temporary and permanent camps:

> In this way, and in others, such as putting ranking POWs on the most degrading jobs, the Chinese broke what little discipline remained in the POW ranks. . . . Morale, among the captives, was already gone. Now the last shred of discipline went, and with it went many Americans' hope of surviving. There was no one to give the POWs direction, except the Chinese. Among the Americans, it could not be anything but dog eat dog, hooray for me, and to hell with you. . . . Men did not hold together, but came apart, dissolved into individuals, governed only by their individual consciences. And as fear, cold, sickness, and starvation deepened, conscience shallowed.[2]

Albert Biderman, who was generally much more sympathetic to the common soldier than was Fehrenbach, nevertheless agreed that segregating the officers had a deleterious effect on the enlisted men:

> Soldiers who have been trained to look for leadership exclusively from those who have higher rank will adapt poorly to circumstances in which all those of higher rank who show any signs of exercising authority are removed and punished.[3]

However, unlike Fehrenbach, Biderman argued that the U.S. Army's own rigid authoritarianism had produced passive soldiers who were unable or unwilling to challenge the enemy's heavy-handed supplications:

> Soldiers whose discipline is dependent upon the constant exercise of punitive sanctions by those in authority are likely to be disciplined subjects of whoever possesses the most powerful sanctions at the moment. . . . Those who are constantly told what their political, ideological, and religious views should be at home will not do well when they face change abroad.[4]

But the question remains: Did a disproportionate number of American prisoners actually embrace the pervasive propaganda of their captors, or were they grudgingly accommodating their tormentors because they thought doing so would enhance their chances for survival? After repatriation, the five physician/prisoners attempted to explain to the folks at home the extensive nature of the Communist program:

It is important to realize that every aspect of the daily life of the prisoner, from the moment of capture to the time of release, was part of the general plan of indoctrination. At the time of capture, each prisoner was given the general theme of indoctrination: "We are your friends. Your conditions of living are bad now, but we will work together to improve them. We will correct the errors in your thinking. Once you have learned the truth, we will send you back to your families."

The first necessary step was to break down the normal resistance to an alien ideology. This was accomplished by keeping the prisoners cold, hungry, and in a state of disorganized confusion until each person realized that resistance meant starvation and death. . . . After a few months of this treatment the resistance of the survivors had softened.

The second phase of indoctrination consisted of an intensive formal study program. For a period of approximately one year, most of the waking hours of the prisoners were spent in some form of supervised study. Food was gradually improved and more clothing was issued. It was made painfully clear to each prisoner that living conditions would be improved only so long as there was no resistance to the study program. The formal study program consisted of an endless repetition of two main themes; first, that the United States government is imperialistic, run by and for the wealthy few, and, second, that Communism reflects the aims and desires of all the people and is the only true democracy.[5]

Even before hunger, disease, and general mistreatment became their way of life, new prisoners usually faced interrogations. The Chinese and North Koreans understood that most POWs possessed little information of value, but they also understood interrogations could break down a prisoner's resistance, especially if they first introduced an element of terror, as was done with Ray Baumbach:

There were between seventy-five and a hundred of us prisoners when I was captured. This Chinese officer singled out fifteen of us and lined us up. He then shot every third man in the back of the head. I was standing right next to a man who was shot. I was just struck dumb. I couldn't think of anything. I just stood there figuring I might be next. The officer who did the shooting told us he had gone to Washington State University. He even said he had gone through Fort Lewis. After he shot these men, he said, "That is to let you know that if you step out of line, that's how many we're going to kill." They also shot men every night who couldn't make it. They just wouldn't fool with them. You could hear shots all night long.

Interrogators employed both physical and psychological methods if they suspected a prisoner was lying or trying to hide something. Before being captured, Glenn Reynolds had helped train South Korean artillery soldiers who called him captain, although he was actually a master sergeant. When some of these same South Koreans continued to do so after they were captured with Reynolds, the North Korean and Chinese interrogators wanted to know the truth:

The North Koreans gouged and poked me, trying to get me to admit that I was an officer. They finally just gave up and didn't say anything more about it. But then all that information was turned over to the Chinese when they sent us off to Camp Five, and they started in on me. "Oh, we understand that you're here on an espionage mission." I told them, "I don't even know how to spell espionage and what's more, I don't know what it is." They would talk and talk and then come back and say, "Yeah, you're an espionage agent, you're a spy, you're a reactionary to the People's Liberation Army. You're an imperialist dog." This went on back and forth for I guess a week. Then they got serious. They called me before a tribunal court.

I was not about to change my story: "I'm a corporal [Reynolds did not wear his sergeant stripes in battle], I drive a jeep, and I hold the mail." I stuck to that story to the bitter end. They beat me, and the psychological abuse they put me through was unreal. They'd send me back to my hut and just about the time I'd fall into a deep sleep, there would be this big old Mongolian guard dragging me by my feet, saying, "Come on. Let's go back to court." I have no idea how long I was there. They would fire their questions at me and make all these comments. Then they'd let me go back to my hut. In a few minutes the process would start all over again. The guys in my hut said this went on for five straight days, but I had lost all track of time. I didn't know where or who I was or what it was I was supposed to tell the truth about. But I did know enough not to change my story, and I didn't.

As a Korean American who had interrogated Communist prisoners before he himself was captured, Meung Ho Kim, who had also served four years in World War II, suffered brutal treatment at the hands of both the North Koreans and the Chinese:

When the North Koreans wanted something from you, they would give you a butt stroke with their rifle or punch or kick you. As a Korean American I knew the language, so they used me as an interpreter, and whenever they didn't like the answers, they always blamed me because I hadn't instructed the other prisoners correctly. I would then get worked over. I remember one time they stripped me naked and gave me a bamboo rod with a basket on each end. I had to fill the baskets with dirt and carry them back and forth for a couple of miles until I finally passed out.

The Chinese were different. They used a kind of psychological torture on me. I got in trouble with them in Camp Three because one of our prisoners told them I had worked for the 25th Division's chief of staff, which I had before I became an interrogator. The Chinese wanted to know all about this, so they put me in a hot room, and this officer, who had graduated from UCLA, took out his pistol, cocked it, and said, "If you don't tell me the truth, we might as well end things here." I figured it didn't make any difference whether I lied or not, I was going to end up the same way. A thousand little things go through your mind at a time like this, but I was young and aggressive and didn't give a damn. I'd gone through so much hell already that I said to myself, "What the hell, I can't get away so I might as well go." He pulled the trigger, and I heard the click. There was no bullet in the chamber.

Predictably, most captured prisoners knew very little, and if they were fortunate, their interrogations were mercifully brief or even nonexistent, as was the case with Roy Hardage:

Shortly after we were captured in late November 1950, we were marched to some kind of headquarters where we were asked name, rank, and serial number. We also filled out a registration card. Then the Chinks started in on us with their Communist propaganda. A North Korean officer came up to us and said, "Comrades, you have not been captured! You have been liberated!" I thought the war had ended and that our troops were fixing to take the place or that maybe our Airborne had landed. I looked all around but all I could see were North Koreans and Chinese. I knew something was cooking. Sure enough some of the men were called in for interrogation, but I was lucky. They didn't call me. This North Korean officer had a big smile on his face and was trying to be real friendly. He looked like a cat fixing to eat a canary. But his smile didn't fool any of us because we already knew what the North Koreans were like. The interrogations of the other guys must not have gone off like they figured because they began to get pissed and started jabbering.

Not surprisingly, after the massive bombings and strafing of the North Korean countryside, Chinese and North Korean interrogators were toughest on U.S. Air Force prisoners. They especially hoped to extract confessions of germ warfare.[6] Don Poirot felt sorry for the pilots who were shot down and then had to face brutal interrogation:

The increase in indoctrination classes was probably brought on by the capture of five young pilots who openly, according to Joe Chink, confessed to germ warfare. They admitted to everything under the sun, up to but not including the crucifixion of Christ. My heart went out to those poor guys. If you had something that the enemy wanted, he got it. I have often wondered what happened to those five. . . . When the Chinese were finished with them, they told everything they knew and some things they didn't know. I was always thankful that I was just an artilleryman. I didn't have anything they needed.

Bob Carman, who was shot down in his F-84 in late 1951, ended up in the notorious interrogation center outside of P'yŏngyang, which the prisoners called Pak's Palace:

We had this briefing officer who had told us, "If you ever get captured just tell them anything they want to know because they already know it." And he was right; they already did know a lot. They took me to a place called Pak's Palace, named after the guy in charge, and boy, they really did some debriefing on me. They would ask me questions I had no idea about. They wanted to know how many B-29s were on Okinawa, so I said, "Oh, a thousand." I had no idea what they wanted for an answer, but I figured the more the better. Well, they called me the dumbest first lieutenant they'd ever seen. I agreed and told them, "That's right I am."

First Lt. Jack Doerty was also a U.S. Air Force pilot, but he was captured in May 1951 while working on the ground as a forward air controller with a South Korean unit. Like Bob Carman, he ended up in Pak's Palace:

I was told by this North Korean pilot who I think had been shot in the butt and was grounded, "You're going to a very bad place." He was talking about Pak's Palace. There were about fifty people at Pak's Palace. Conditions were terrible. Everyone was sick. We were housed in a double-storied building. People would lose bladder and bowel control on the upper floor, and all that stuff would hit the people down below. A lot of people died there. It seemed like we buried one or two people every day. We were almost all officers, and, at least toward the end, mostly Air Force. They weren't trying to politicize us. I don't recall any attempts at so-called brainwashing. I think Major Pak's mission was to interrogate pilots, and that's what he did. The interrogations were all about our air fields, planes, and tactics. For example, they wanted to know how we would shoot down a MIG. We had an F-86 pilot, I think his name was Henderson, who explained to them how to shoot down a MIG. He took two pencils and did scrawls and turns all over a piece of paper. At the end, he drew a little airplane spinning down and told them, "That's a MIG."

Through their deliberate policy of exhausting interrogations, followed by general starvation and mistreatment, the Chinese carefully prepared their prisoners for the massive indoctrination programs that followed in the spring and summer of 1951. Lt. Col. John Dunn, who was a Tiger Death March survivor, explains the effect of such a policy:

Mass starvation is a state policy employed by the Communists to control people politically. By the use of harsh treatment, starvation, cold, accusations, and almost never-ending interrogations, they eventually break their prisoners down to the point where they come to the decision that the only way to survive is to show some outward form of collaboration.[7]

After witnessing the appalling effects of that deadly first winter, when more than half of their fellow prisoners died, the survivors were convinced there was little hope for their own future. Nor had they ever received any kind of training that might have helped prepare them for what was ahead. "We had no idea of what to expect," was a common complaint, and "We had no instructions on how to act as prisoners."[8]

Desperate, uninformed men are vulnerable, or so the Chinese hoped when just before Christmas 1950 they launched their first "educational" experiment with a group of 250 prisoners at Camp Ten, located just north of Kanggye. One of the Americans to endure this early attempt at what the U.S. media would later call "brainwashing"[9] was Roy Hardage:

The Chinese had already told us we were going to a school for a few weeks to learn about Communism, after which they would turn us loose. But they added that the backward students would be kept and given additional schooling. Backward students were those who kept their mouths shut, and good students were those who were willing to run down our government.

It was now Christmas time. Every morning a Chink came to our squad room, propped the door open, and made everyone sit up. We then had about two hours of discussion or schooling. I don't remember what the subjects were all about. All I know is he would preach Communism to us. I could hardly wait until he would leave so we could close the door to keep the cold wind out. On Christmas Day they put us in formation and marched us to this big barn. Every man had to attend. A few stayed behind, but I knew your best chance not to be murdered was to stay with the largest group. My legs were still hurting so somebody had to help me get to this building. It was only a barn with a dirt floor. We had to crowd in and sit down. If anything, it was colder than outside because it was also damp. On the walls were slogans like "Down with the Warmongers" or "You Were Duped by the Money Bags of Wall Street" or "You Are Cannon Fodder." I had never heard such terms as "Money Bags," "Cannon Fodder," or "Imperialists" before in my life. They also had "Merry Xmas" on the wall and a little Christmas tree was standing there. I had no idea what was going on until this Chinese started beating his chops, as we called it. He yakked and yakked in Chinese; then, this other Chink officer told us in English what he was saying.

I don't remember everything that was said because it was too cold to listen, but then some GIs got up and began running down Douglas MacArthur who was the best general ever to hit Korea. I then started paying attention to what was coming off. Someone said the president should be there fighting on the frontline and so forth. I didn't open my mouth. I just sat there surprised at what was being said. I got to thinking that maybe this was just to fool the Chinese in order to get turned loose. But one guy began talking in great detail about MacArthur's personal lifestyle. I knew that was uncalled for. This went on for quite some time. These guys were talking their heads off trying to be one of the good students and get turned loose. Most of them seemed to be educated and some had rank. Others were just plain dumb and were trying to talk about something they didn't know a damn thing about. The majority of us just sat there and listened, and the same ones kept getting up and yakking. Then the Chinks gave each of us three pieces of penny candy. It wasn't even a taste. But at the evening meal we got our first white rice with meat broth poured over it. Boy, this sure was good after eating sorghum seeds.

The Chinese began talking about the guys who never said anything during our study periods. They said that when a man didn't say anything, he was thinking negatively. This put a lot of us on the spot because I had only gone to eighth grade and did not even understand many of the questions they asked, much less anything about Communism. I knew that the U.S. government was against them and that was enough for me. As a soldier, my duty was to fight anyplace, anytime, and against anyone my government ordered me to fight, even if it were my mother and father.

The Chinese began making our squad leaders lead the discussions we were supposed to have in our rooms after the day's meetings. This was a lot better for us. Now we could stretch out and smoke a cabbage leaf cigarette without getting in trouble because we always had someone watching for the Chinks. We usually kept the door closed because of the cold, but we had peepholes to watch through. If we spotted a Chink who looked like he might understand English, we would immediately sit up like we were studying. We had some pretty intelligent guys in our two squads, and we would get together and answer the questions in a way so the Chinese wouldn't get too hostile, without, at the same time, running down our government. The answers were not what the Chinese had hoped for, and they often got pissed, but some of our guys could talk circles around any Chink, who would then get all bamboozled and jump up and leave. The Chinese said each man could express his true opinion, but if someone did, they accused him of interrupting the studies and insisted he change his attitude.

It is doubtful if the Chinese really expected to turn many prisoners into ardent Communists. They were, however, convinced they could sow dissension within the ranks and exploit the more cooperative men for propaganda purposes. As a result, they exerted tremendous pressure on the prisoners to write articles, make radio broadcasts, and sign petitions, all of which the Chinese hoped would convince the outside world that they sought peace rather than aggression. Roy Hardage was one of many prisoners in Camp Ten forced to sign a petition for peace:

About January 20, 1951, we had to go to something they called a Peace Rally. We were marched five or six miles to a small Korean village. We went in this building and sat down on logs on the floor. Finally, a Chinese got up and told us this was a peace movement. I didn't know what a peace movement was except that maybe they were getting ready to surrender their forces to the U.N. They had Gooks playing music and dancing. Then they passed around some hot water, gave us a drink, and each of us got four cigarettes. These were the first cigarettes we had gotten and some of the older smokers were really hurting. The Gooks had taken most everyone's cigarettes after we were captured. Everybody started smoking up a storm. Some smoked all four of theirs without stopping. Then the Chinese brought out what I think was called the Stockholm Peace Appeal. Several of our boys were supporting this appeal. I don't remember all that was said, but I do know the rest of us were so pissed off at a Sergeant Olson that we could have slit his throat.[10] There was a heck of a lot of commotion in the room; finally, the Communists laid the law down; they withdrew all their grins and make-believe friendliness and came right out and said that any man who failed to sign the Peace Appeal wouldn't return home. They also made it clear if we signed, we got chow; if we didn't, we would not and would never return to the States. We were in a fix. I just watched to see what the rest of the guys did, and I guess they were thinking the same thing because we all just sat there. Of course, Sergeant Olson and maybe a couple other cheese-eaters had their names already down. Finally, Major McGlahan, the ranking POW, stood up. Everything got very quiet. Usually, when a Chink or some other POW was talking, there was always a lot of noise, but now there was not a sound. He gave a real good speech and explained the situation to us. He argued it was best to go ahead and sign the appeal. Besides, we figured the people in the States would realize we were still soldiers and Americans. What they read to us didn't sound that bad, but when it was published a few months later, it included a lot of propaganda that we had never heard before. There were 279 of us who signed. A lot of men who were not at the rally because they were too sick also had to sign it. We really had no choice.

Their preliminary work completed, the Chinese closed down Camp Ten on March 1, 1951, and transferred Roy Hardage and 189 other prisoners to Camp Five. Another sixty prisoners were sent to a place called Peaceful Valley where they received additional "schooling." All were told they would soon be released, and nineteen of them actually were. The Chinese loaded up these nineteen with propaganda pamphlets calling for the immediate surrender of U.N. troops, which the freed prisoners promptly threw away after reaching their lines. The Chinese then used the remaining men to greet new prisoners and to instruct them on what they could expect from their captors' so-called leniency policies.

The apparent success of the Camp Ten training sessions undoubtedly encouraged the Chinese to launch their full-scale indoctrination programs in the permanent camps. Camp Five, which contained the majority of American prisoners, was singled out for massive efforts, but, as Jim Crombie recalls, relatively few men actually listened:

We had to go to the "re-education" classes. It wasn't very long before they knew who would cooperate and who wouldn't. I have to say only a handful really bought that crap. I don't know how even our so-called teachers could believe it. Many of them had been educated in the United States so how could they believe this garbage they were telling us?

Occasionally somebody would get a letter with a picture of a car. The Chinese would say that it just a cardboard cut out, with one of their family members standing in front of the cut out. So I couldn't understand how any of our guys could buy their line.

Robert Carman, who ended up in Camp Two after his interrogation in Pak's Palace, agrees that most of the men did not take their lessons very seriously:

They tried to propagandize us. They had books we were supposed to read and then write our opinions of these books. I don't know of anybody who really read them. We'd go into this big room and sit around. This fellow named Ralph Nardello would get up to read, but while he was reading, he was also announcing a baseball game. Of course, these Chinese guys understood English, but he was able to insert this baseball game in the text. This guy was phenomenal. Then we'd be sent back to our rooms where we were supposed to write our cognition of some author's writings. We'd write, "We don't believe this and this because this guy is a Communist and believes in Communism." We'd also write, "We need more rice, we need more chicken, we need more beef, and we need some clothes." Then we would turn it in, and that would be our cognition for the day.

Stateside critics who later accused the Korean War prisoners of collaboration or of having been "brainwashed" seldom defined their terms. Was simply listening to the lectures and participating in the discussions aiding and abetting the enemy? In the strictest sense, perhaps, but it had much more to do with survival, as Harley Coon, who would eventually serve as president of the Korean Ex-Prisoners of War Association, makes clear:

Somebody later wrote a book in which he accused most of us of collaborating.[11] I'd like to know what a collaborator is. What could we have really done? Almost everything was beyond our control, other than our own thoughts in our own minds. Was a collaborator someone who turned in other guys? Was he someone who was friendly with the guards and the instructors? Or was he someone who gave them information, although there was really no information we could give them? I'm never sure what these people mean by collaboration.

Brainwashing? I have never been accused of having a brain so it didn't bother me [laughing]. The Chinese in Camp Five would ask us who started the war, and I'd say, "the Russians." Then they'd really interrogate me. Sometimes I'd say, "What difference does it make? Who cares who started it? It's still going on, isn't it?" I also tried to use reverse psychology on them. If an instructor told me I had been duped and forced to fight, I would ask him, "What about the Chinese soldier who doesn't want to go off and fight, but has no choice?" The instructor couldn't answer that. Any time they would ask a question like that, I would pose the reverse question. Sometimes we would go along with them and sometimes we'd argue; it just depended on what our mood was at the time. We did find out that if we agreed with them, they would give us a little extra ration, but if we disagreed, they'd take it away, so we played games with them.

Enlisted man Michael Cornwell, who eventually rose through the ranks to become a lieutenant colonel, insists that although every man has a breaking point, his fellow prisoners in Korea conducted themselves as well as POWs in any other American war. Cornwell also denies there was any such thing as brainwashing:

Some people like to call it brainwashing. Well, it wasn't brainwashing. The Chinese liked to jump on the U.S. because we wouldn't allow them in the United Nations. They would also single out a given figure and attack the hell out of him. They weren't necessarily trying to convert us to Communism. Rather, they took the other approach: "We're going to show you what's the matter with your system." This went on every day for a long time. We'd have to sit around and discuss all this. You can imagine what those discussions were like [laughs]. We'd tell them, "All right, you've got all this literature. All we've got is our minds to come back at you. It's just a matter of our memories, and we don't think that's right." It wasn't brainwashing. It was just that they wanted to tell us what was so great about themselves and what was so bad about us. There was nothing subtle about it.

We had to give the Chinese something of our background. I think they had their reasons for that. One guy told them he and his parents were moss-gatherers, which was kind of comical. They gave us a test on germ warfare. I think most of us failed it. We knew the obvious answers, we just went the other way.

A guy by the name of William Mayer[12] wrote about the alleged misbehavior of the Korean War POWs, and there's not a POW who isn't thoroughly unhappy with what this guy wrote. I'd like to put Mayer in those camps for a while. According to him we were all collaborators, but that's just not true. I don't think Americans in any war have ever faced what we did. You look at the conditions, you look at what we didn't have. What would you expect?

Irv Langell was just as uncompromising toward his captors in Camp Three as he had been during the Tiger Death March. He especially enjoyed ridiculing the Chinese educators:

They say they brainwashed us. Whoever put that out doesn't know what he's talking about. The Koreans and the Chinese tried it. They would get their cadres out and lecture us about how great Communism was and how degraded we American warmongers were, and things like that. We were supposed to discuss what they were telling us. Well, I can tell you our conversations usually ended up on the subject of pussy, not Communism.

These educational sessions turned into interesting exchanges. You'd say to yourself, "Here we go again; let's see what they've got to say." Then you would just counteract what they said with all kinds of things. Some of the crap we'd say was barbaric. Oh, yeah, they'd threaten to take our food away if we didn't cooperate. They did in fact do it two or three times, but we just laughed at them.

The Chinese would say, "Tell us about your home life." Well, some of the goddamnest stories you ever heard in your life came out. Of course, we told them we all came from rich families, and we all had two or three cars. We'd just rattle on. We also had to write our auto-biographies. Most of these were just bare-face lies. Man, a lot of us wished our families had all the great things we told about. But these autobiographies would satisfy them, and they'd put the food back.

This one so-called educator was a little, old pansy guy, but we always referred to him as "her." In fact, we called him Lucia. Everybody would go up and pat him on the butt and say how cute he was. His dad owned a match company so he was wealthy, and he would tell us all this crap. We'd asked him if he ever got laid and nice things like that. We would get him so flustered he'd cut the session off. The next time he came around, we'd do the same thing.

Most of the prisoners mentally shut out the mandatory educational sessions. Charley Davis, who ended up in Camp Five after being captured by the Chinese, learned to appear interested, while not hearing a word that was said:

When they would start one of their propaganda sessions, I developed the ability just to turn off my mind. It took a while to be able to do this. You couldn't horse around and not appear to pay attention during these lectures because they'd rap you one. So I worked on my re-sponse, and eventually I could just stare them right in the eye and not hear a thing they said. I would just think about something else. But this became a bad habit that followed me home. Someone would be talking, and all of a sudden I'd be gone. My wife has often accused me of this very thing.

Billy Joe Harris described himself as just a tough, old, Missouri country boy, but he understood the Chinese indoctrination failures better than did many of the more sophisticated postwar critics who insisted the prisoners were easy marks for Communist propaganda. However, Harris did admit there were those few prisoners who would go along with their captors if it meant better treatment:

When we were first captured, they seemed to think that the tall guys were officers. What could I tell them about my outfit? They already knew more than I could tell them. Then, in the permanent camp they decided to make Communists out of us. I'm here to tell you when you come from a land of plenty and you go into a country like that where they can't even feed you enough to keep you alive, how in the world did they expect to cram Communism down your gullet. For Communism to work it's got to be a backward, underprivileged country. Communism is rotten to the core. But we had no choice. We had to sit there and listen to what they had to say. They'd come right in the room and read this stuff to you.

You'd just sit there and pretend to go along. But there were a few guys who became so weak, the Chinese could tempt them with something to eat in exchange for spying on their buddies. These were the Rats, and there were a few in my camp but not many. Some of these guys later got beaten up pretty badly, so they had to more or less stay in the protective custody of the Chinese.

Robert Fletcher, who had been captured while fighting with the all-black 24th Regiment, discovered there was also segregation in the prison camps, although for different reasons. The Chinese attempted to curry favor with African American prisoners, hoping to turn them against their homeland:

They segregated us by race in Camp Five in the spring of 1951, and I went into an all black unit. . . . Every morning an instructor would start roll call. Lin or one of the other English-speaking instructors would give us a little lecture for about a half hour or forty-five minutes. Then we'd break up into groups of ten or so for what they called study groups where we were supposed to discuss what we had just heard. The instructors would compare Communism to capitalism, starting back in the Stone Age with Lenin and Engles versus the Rockefellers and DuPonts. They would talk about when wars started none of the rich go but always the poor people. In the discussion groups we were supposed to discuss all this. The Chinese called me a reactionary because I'd say, "Let's look at the Second World War. I can talk about that because I was a young man. In Russia, which is a Communist country, who fought the fucking wars there? There was supposed to be no poor and no rich. But everybody was poor."

They'd say, "Yes, you see, that was a different matter."

And I'd say, "Yeah, it is always different when it's in your favor."

So they said, "You're not understanding what we're talking about. We need to punish you."

But I understood exactly they were talking about. They would say to me, "Everybody works." And I'd say, "You mean Chairman Mao gets out and works on the highways just like the peasants do?" And they would just look at me. So I'd ask, "Nobody serves him food? He cooks his own food?" Then they'd say, "You're a reactionary." I just could not play their games with them. So finally they had me up to headquarters and the commander was bitching and saying, "We should shoot you." I looked at him and said, "You know what you can do? Shoot me, fuck it." And I walked out of the building. He shouted, "We're not through talking." I just kept on going, figuring any minute the guard would shoot me. Later the guards would come by and point at me and say, "He's crazy; don't even bother him."

They had earlier told me that I did not have much education. Well, my platoon sergeant, Jerry Morgan, told me, "Fletch, don't let these people know what you know or you're in trouble." So when they first started asking about name, rank, and serial number, and how much education I had, I put down name, rank, and serial number, and sixth grade. They called me up to headquarters and said, "No, no, you have more than a sixth-grade education."

I said, "Well, if you say so I'll have whatever you want me to have, but in my country white people won't let me go to school."

That delighted them and they said, "Oh yes, yes!"

They were used to hearing tales about down South. So I said, "I had to quit to go to work. I had to do the mediocre jobs that white people didn't want to bother with such as cleaning toilets and sweeping the streets."

Again they said, "Oh yes, yes!" They never realized that I had almost finished high school.

The Chinese monitored the letters we wrote home, so I made a lot of mistakes. I'd spell "the" as "tha" and "that" as "tht." A lot of those letters made it home. Later I looked at those letters, and I laughed. They all are now in the University of Michigan archives.

They didn't play the race card so much during the interrogations as in the educational sessions. They would remind me that I had said, "You know white people will never let black people accomplish anything in the United States." So they'd tell me, "They're always going to control the money, control the jobs, make sure their friends will always have a job, and black people will just get so far. What you need to do is go back to your country and help start a revolution. Get the money out of their hands. Get the controls away from the warmongers." The Chinese did not like white people very much.

Although only a small minority of the prisoners ever took the Chinese propaganda and indoctrination techniques seriously, the people back home certainly did. Most prisoners quietly endured the "re-education" sessions, realizing that any overt display of their contempt was fraught with danger. Even the twenty-one Americans who declined repatriation paid more attention to their personal needs or resentments than they did to Communist ideology. But for the American public, caught in the throes of Cold War and McCarthy paranoia, the massive Chinese effort to indoctrinate and "brainwash" their captives became the indelible legacy of the Korean War POWs.

9

PROGRESSIVES, REACTIONARIES, AND THE TWENTY-ONE WHO CHOSE TO STAY

I still size people up as soon as I meet them. I listen to the way they talk, and I watch how they act and react. I want to see if they are real or pretending to be something they are not. I don't think I did this before I was a POW. In the camps you had to make sure someone wasn't going to get you in trouble over something you said.

—Charles Davis, Korean War POW

Ex-prisoners of Korea who collaborated with the Communists or who are under suspicion of collaboration fall into definite personality patterns: big dealers, play-it-coolers, introspectives, dupes, scared kids, praise-starved egotists.

—*Science Digest*, 1955

Progressives and Reactionaries stood at opposite ends of the behavioral spectrum, with each group including less than 10 percent of the prisoners. Progressives appeared to go along with the Communist line, either out of conviction or because they hoped for better treatment for themselves and sometimes for their fellow prisoners. Often classified with the Progressives were the Rats, but their sole motivation was to help themselves, usually at the expense of their fellow prisoners. They spied on other prisoners and willingly spread Communist propaganda, but not because they believed in the message. Reactionaries simply refused to cooperate with their captors and often tried to make life miserable for them. In a class of their own were the twenty-one Americans who, refusing repatriation, chose instead to live in the People's Republic of China. As has been the case in all wars, the vast majority of prisoners simply took the line of least resistance. According to Raymond Lech, "They did little or nothing to fight their captors and little or nothing to help them."[1] They passively sat through the lectures and discussions. They knew or cared little for politics, although the Chinese were able to coerce some of them into signing petitions and writing articles.

The Reactionaries were the only Korean War prisoners America recognized as heroes after their return home in 1953. In other wars, prisoners who escaped were singled out for public adulation; indeed, almost every movie or novel featured an escape. Although some Reactionaries did try to escape, they were singled out instead for their uncompromising opposition to their Communist captors. In truth, most of these men were as apolitical as were the vast majority of other prisoners. All Reactionaries exhibited uncommon courage, but only a few were able to articulate why they despised Communism. Many were impulsive, even rash, individuals who had frequently experienced trouble with their own military leaders before becoming prisoners. Typical was Wayman Simpson whose unruly and impetuous behavior resulted in the Chinese classifying him as a Reactionary. Clearly, Simpson marched to a different drummer than did most soldiers and prisoners; however, he insisted that the Rats were much more reprehensible than were the twenty-one prisoners who chose China over repatriation:

I was always in and out of trouble. I made corporal and sergeant six times during World War II. I got that from my grandmother Simpson's side of the family. My grandmother had a brother named Elliott, and my middle name was Elliott. The family said he was an ole Western outlaw. I visited him when he was ninety-one years old in Walla Walla, Washington. He still had his twin forty-fours hanging on the wall, loaded and oiled. He had two notches on the right gun. I knew what they were supposed to represent, but I wanted to hear him say it. He told me, "Well, in Abilene, Kansas, two yahoos tried to cheat me out of three and a half months trail-drive wages." That's all he said. I guess that's where I got my attitude.

Nobody knows where your breaking point is until you are put to the test. Some people can hardly stand anything. Other people can take everything and just keep on going. Then there are those who don't necessarily do big things but all the little things. There were twenty-one people who went to China, but the Rats we had in camp were worse than those twenty-one, and they caused us a lot more trouble. The twenty-one stood up and told the world, "We're going to China." The Rats were on the first boat back to the States. The Rats would tell the Chinese everything they saw or heard in return for a little candy or a cigarette or two. There weren't that many of them—certainly less than 1 percent—but we knew who they were. We finally kicked them out of our building, and the Chinese built them a lean-to by their headquarters building. We'd occasionally go over and tear the roof off their lean-to so they'd be out in the cold for a while. There was this one ole boy from Brinkley, Arkansas. He was a Rat from the word go. After we got back to the States, three of us heard he was in Hot Springs, Arkansas, so we went down there. We got this girl out of a nightclub and gave her fifty dollars just to coax him into a motel. When the door opened, I was standing behind it, and the other two guys were standing there in the dark. When he came in, I kicked the door shut and turned the light on. Have you ever heard a grown man cry and beg? We gave him what for and then just left him there. I don't know how he ever got home.

Bob Blewitt was also the kind of feisty individual who had been in trouble his entire life. When the Chinese tired of his stealing and sneaking out of camp (see chapter five), they transferred him to the Reactionary group in Camp Three. Soon he was again in trouble, this time for talking to a Progressive:

There were Progressives, informers, and opportunists in the camps. I had a history of raising hell with those guys that I thought were too friendly to the Chinese, and they had a book on me for that. During the march after I was captured, I bumped into this guy from Wilkes-Barre, Pennsylvania. About a year and a half later, I was coming back from a wood detail, and I ran into him down at the end of Camp Three where the Progressives lived. So I threw my log down and asked him what he had been doing and that it was good to see him. Then I went back to my area. That night I had just fallen asleep, when the Chinese came in and woke me up and took me out for questioning. They said, "Tell us what you did?" I hadn't done anything I could think of except that I never would fall out on time. They kept it up for about fifteen days. Every night they would come get me, so I couldn't get any sleep. During the day I would have to go out on wood details, but when I'd come back I'd lay down to sleep, and the Chinese would come and start again. They'd do this all night long. They made me stand against the wall with my hands down, my nose against the wall, and my eyes open. You know pretty soon your eyes are going to start to tear. If you blinked or moved, the guards would hit you with their rifle butts. One time this guy put a pistol to my head and said, "You always tell us the things we know. Now we want you to tell us the things we don't know. You write down everything you know." I figured it was too late in the game by then anyway. From the beginning I figured they were going to kill us, so I really made up all kinds of shit. I didn't put in any spacing or punctuation or anything. Then it finally dawned on me, and I told them, "I bumped into a guy coming back from wood detail that I had met on the march." I told them the whole story. They still weren't satisfied, so I had to stand against the wall again all that night, but that was the last time. They were sure I was harassing this Progressive, but then he must have told them that I hadn't. My friend may have been a Progressive but he was not a Rat. He told the truth and that ended the incident.

Robert Schaefer believes it was his hell-with-it attitude that landed him in the Reactionary squad in Camp One, but that attitude also helped him survive captivity:

I never thought I would make it, and that may be why I survived. I just lived from one day to the next. So it didn't bother me if they wanted to shoot me. At the time I would have been happy to have been shot, but I could never bring myself to self-destruction. I didn't want to be tortured, but if they wanted to shoot me, hell, why not? I really didn't think anybody was going to make it out alive.

I ended up in our company's Reactionary squad as soon as there was such a thing in Camp One. It was a sort of punishment, but we liked being together. It was a pride thing. The fence-straddlers would look up to us and want to be in our squad. We could count on each other, but you didn't want to get too close to anybody because that guy might die, and you'd already lost too many friends.

There were probably several things that got me put in the Reactionary squad. This one time, American planes bombed our camp, and the Chinese announced that we should all sign a protest. They showed us the document we were supposed to sign. They even named the town where our camp was located. We got word to the officers at the other end of the camp, and they agreed we should sign so we could get out the word on our location. After we signed, we discovered the Chinese took out the name of the town. After that, anytime they wanted me to sign anything, I willingly did so, but I signed former United States presidents instead of my name. I started with John Adams and worked my way through the presidents as far as I could remember [laughs]. Other guys picked similar names.

The Chinese divided us into discussion groups for their re-education sessions. They would present us with a problem, and we were supposed to discuss it. For example, once they asked us what could be done to enlighten the people in Indonesia. I said they ought to give each one a flashlight made in a capitalist country.

I also got in trouble with them over a photograph. When I went back in the service, I had a new Buick, and my wife had sent me a picture of it and our daughter who was born less than nine months after I left. This one Chinese guard said he knew what Buicks cost, and a private could not own a Buick, so I had to be lying to him, and that I was really an officer.

One of their punishments was to stand before the group and criticize yourself. Usually when I did that, I would talk rapidly and put in profanity about what I really thought of them, and I got away with it. Their interpreters couldn't understand English all that well, but I think maybe someone might have told them a time or two.

I often argued with them, but I always thought that I knew when to stop, and I guess I did because I never got into really deep trouble. One year they said they wanted our help harvesting crops. Our squad told them we couldn't do that because if we harvested crops that meant that able-bodied men could leave and go to the frontlines to fight. We just refused. Everybody else went to harvest crops but our squad went up the mountain to get firewood. The guards made us trot down the mountain with heavy logs, and they really made sure they were heavy ones. If we slowed down, they poked us with their bayonets or rifle butts. The next year when they wanted us to harvest crops, we did, but we tried to do more damage than good. It was probably sorghum grain. I told them that in Kentucky people didn't eat sorghum grain, but fed it to cattle. That didn't go over too well either. The Chinese were not kind to us, and our death rate pretty much proves that.

Lloyd Pate was only sixteen when he was captured on January 1, 1951. After the Chinese moved him from Camp Five to Camp Three, he became the leader of a Reactionary squad. His anti-Chinese activities eventually resulted in a one-year sentence at hard labor; yet, even he was forced to write a confession. Pate, who is a past president of the Korean POW Association, initially told his story in 1955 in a book appropriately entitled *Reactionary!*[2] Over the years, Pate has softened his views on some of the Progressives but certainly not on the Rats:

What turned me into a Reactionary? Just pride, I guess. Pride in my country and in being an American. The Chinese targeted us as Reactionaries because we argued against what they told us. I wasn't about to have them stand up there in those sessions and tell us what a rotten country we had. Out of my thirty-one and a half months as a POW, I'd say half were spent in one type of solitary or another. Sure, I knew there was a chance they might kill me, but I got to where I just didn't give a damn. One time an officer pointed an old Army forty-five revolver right between my eyes and cocked the hammer. What he didn't realize was I could look right up the chamber and see that his weapon was empty. So I called him a son-of-a-bitch and said, "Go ahead and shoot, you bastard." Maybe if I had seen a round in that cylinder, I might not have been so brave [laughs].

There is a difference between a Rat and a Progressive. We had Progressives who would never rat on another American, but they did go along with the Communist line. One of them was Jim Veneris. We called him the Greek, and I had a lot of conversations with him in Camp Three. As far as I know, he never ratted on a fellow prisoner. I think he was the only one of the twenty-one who really did believe in Communism, and that was because his parents had been Communists.

I would say that Progressives and Reactionaries each made up about 5 percent of the prisoners. The majority of the rest were just like Americans today. They just didn't want to get involved, but it was from this 90 percent that one found the informers or Rats. Probably only 5 or 10 percent of these men were actual informers. That leaves about 80 percent who just sat it out. If they could do something without getting into trouble, they would do it. They just weren't willing to stick their necks out.

A lot of the informers were what we called fence-sitters. They never participated in the discussions, but they were brown-nosers. They looked up to authority figures and always wanted a pat on the head. They had a weak character, and they were more dangerous than the Progressives who, for the most part, were not. The Progressives would stand up during the discussions and voice their opinions on how great Communism was. We knew who they were. Hell, their articles were posted on the bulletin boards. But we didn't always know who the Rats were.

The Chinese tried to condition us through the use of self-criticism. At first, we thought this was a joke. We'd say something like, "I criticize myself for not brushing my teeth." But this led to them insisting that we begin criticizing each other. I would then say, "Okay, I criticize Joe

Blow for not brushing his teeth." He'd then look at me and say the same thing. Hell, we didn't even have toothbrushes. To most of us it was just a joke to get them off our damn backs. We would never criticize a man because he was planning an escape or because of his political beliefs. But some men's character was such that they said, "Well, back in the States I reported to the teacher or the sergeant on rule infractions, and this is what they want me to do here." With such men, their collaboration just kept escalating.

There really wasn't one thing we did to get under the skin of our captors. It was anything we could think of, from openly disagreeing with them to repeatedly asking "why" to all of their statements as to the advantages of Communism over capitalism. If you have ever had a smart-ass student, you know how infuriating this can be.

I did write a seventeen-page confession in 1952. I had escaped and was brought back and put in solitary. In the meantime, the Chinese were pulling out the Reactionaries in my old squad, and torturing them. One was Vernon W. Clark, and they finally broke him down. He confessed to all our activities.[3] He named me as the leader and Donell Adams as second in command. Clark managed to get word to me through our pipeline, which was the latrine, on just what he had confessed. He apologized and said he just couldn't take any more.

At the same time I was being tortured. They first handcuffed my hands behind my back. They would take them off only when I ate or went to the latrine. They left them on at night, and it's painful as hell to sleep on a hard floor with your hands handcuffed behind you. I was limber enough, however, that I could just walk through them and get them in front of me, but they caught me. Then they put two pairs of handcuffs on me. I was able to walk the top pair down to my wrist and still walk through them, but they caught me the second time. Then they put three pairs on me, and they didn't take them off, even for eating or going to the latrine. They left those on for about two weeks. Next, the Chinese tortured me by suspending me from the ceiling with my arms tied behind me. It was because of this and knowing that Clark had already talked that I wrote the confession.

The Chinese believed that punishment had to be much worse for the instigator than for those who followed. So in my confession I put myself in the role of instigator to lessen the effect on everybody else. I think the court-martial took place in September 1952, but most of us had been in solitary since May or June. Adams and I each received a one-year sentence and the rest received less.

The Chinese actually gave up on mass indoctrinations about August 1952. I don't want to brag, but I would like to think it was because of the actions of the Reactionaries. By then, the Chinese decided to stop their political lectures and concentrate solely on the Progressives. They set up a special school for them in Camp Five for intensive training in Communism. But for the most part these were not the men who decided to stay behind. In fact, many of the most active Progressives came home.

Jeff Erwin, who was a battlefield-commissioned second lieutenant when captured at the end of November 1950, would later be court-martialed for allegedly collaborating with the enemy. Erwin claimed he had little choice after his Chinese captors threatened him with permanent exile in China and even death. The Chinese appointed Erwin to the Camp Five Peace Committee and later made him a delegate to the Central Peace Committee, which met in June 1951 at Camp Twelve outside of P'yŏngyang. Erwin insists that even his commanding officer understood his actions:

The Chinese generally found out who was not, what they called, "co-operating" with them. We had to read the American edition of the *Daily Worker,* and the squad leader had to sign out for every page of it so we couldn't use it as toilet paper or to patch holes in our building. Their propaganda attempts didn't work with anybody. We all thought it was a bunch of pure b.s., but we had to survive.

Every prison barracks signed a declaration addressed to the United Nations stating that the Americans had started the war and that it had to be stopped. They cut off our food until we all signed. We were fortunate to have a Marine bird colonel pilot named Guy Thrash who was a very smart man. He told us, "Gentlemen, this is no place or time to be a hero." The last time I saw him was in Hawaii in 1960. He was a major general then, and I think he retired as a four-star general. We thought the United States government would understand, but it didn't.

At his humiliating court-martial, Jeff Erwin was accused of making disloyal statements, leading discussions, signing petitions, and being a member of the Peace Committee. His defense attorney, however, successfully pleaded duress, and Erwin was found not guilty.[4]

For the folks back home, even more baffling than learning that some American prisoners had collaborated, was the news that a number of POWs had refused repatriation. The earliest reports listed twenty-three men who had chosen to remain with their Chinese captors, but on October 20, 1953, Cpl. Edward S. Dickenson of Crackers Neck, Virginia, belatedly requested repatriation. Then, on January 1, 1954, the United Nations facilitated the return of Cpl. Claude Batchelor of Kermit, Texas. That left twenty-one men, all of whom remained in China for various lengths of time.[5]

The U.S. media suggested a wide variety of reasons for their defection. In one article *U.S. News and World Report* argued most were Rats who feared retaliation. Later the editors concluded they were "lonely, bitter men who felt betrayed by their fellow Americans."[6] *Newsweek* found them to be "shifty-eyed and groveling" and suggested that half of them were homosexuals.[7] Other sources cited drug abuse, ignorance, criminality, atheism, a hatred of sports, poverty, and progressive education as reasons. In truth, it is difficult to generalize about these men.[8] Several had definitely cooperated with their captors, although their motives, as with so many other prisoners, were not always clear. Twenty were career soldiers; only one was a draftee. Their average age was just over twenty-three, although most had joined the Army at a very early age. The majority did come from broken, unhappy, and impoverished homes, but this was not unusual for the times. Several held grudges against American society or the Army. Three had attended college and one had graduated. Three others had finished high school. Most had regularly attended church in their youth. Three were married, but several others had fallen in love with Asian women. One had been in reform school and another in jail, but the others had not been in any serious trouble. As a group, they were little different than the more than 4,000 American prisoners who, with no hesitation, chose repatriation.

The single thing that separated the twenty-one from their fellow prisoners was their refusal to return to the United States. Cpl. Clarence Adams was an African American from Memphis, Tennessee, who bitterly denounced racism both in the Army and in his home city of Memphis. Sgt. Howard G. Adams was a decorated World War II veteran from Corsicana, Texas, who was working his way through college in 1950 when he decided to reenlist. Sgt. Albert C. Belhomme was born in Belgium but attended high school in Ashland, Pennsylvania. Belhomme, who spoke four languages, passed the examinations for officers candidates' school, but was not admitted because his naturalization papers were being held up. Pfc. Otho Bell was one of eleven children raised by a stepmother in Hillsboro, Mississippi. Dirt poor, Bell ran off to join the Army at seventeen. He was not a good soldier and was frequently AWOL. Sgt. Richard G. Corden of Providence, Rhode Island, was raised by a grandmother and attended mass regularly, but became a junior high dropout. He also spent time in reform school before enlisting in the Army in 1946. By all accounts he was a brilliant but unstable individual. He was also the leader of the twenty-one. At a Chinese-sponsored press conference on January 16, 1954, Corden called for "real democracy and racial equality" rather than "witch-hunts and McCarthyism." He also announced that all twenty-one planned to return home "when we can fight for world peace without being persecuted."[9] William A. Cowart grew up as an only child in a broken home in Monticello, Arkansas, and was only fifteen when he enlisted. Sgt. Rufus Elbert Douglas from San Angelo, Texas, had lost both parents by the age of eleven. After serving in World War II, he returned home to finish high school. He started college but then quit to rejoin the Army. Cpl. John Roedel Dunn of Baltimore had been active in the Episcopalian church, and his parents were corporate executives. He was a good student who had graduated in the top third of his class from Baltimore City College. Andrew Fortuna of Detroit had helped raise his two siblings because his mother was an alcoholic. He was a church-going Catholic who had fought in Europe during World War II. He had earned two Bronze Stars in Korea before being captured in 1950. Cpl. Lewis W. Griggs was from a solid, middle-class Baptist family in Jacksonville, Texas, and served as a medic in Korea. Pfc. Samuel David Hawkins, who enlisted at sixteen, was from a broken home in Oklahoma City, where his mother was a minister and a strict disciplinarian. Arlie Pate was from a long line of Baptist ministers in the poverty-stricken coal-mining town of Weaver, Illinois. Cpl. Scott L. Rush, from Marietta, Ohio, was raised in a middle-class Catholic family and was a high school graduate. After seeing a close friend killed in Korea, he declared "The war is useless." Cpl. Lowell D. Skinner was from Akron, Ohio, where he helped raise five siblings before dropping out of high school and joining the Army. Cpl. Larance V. Sullivan was an African American from a stable family in Omaha, Nebraska, where, after graduating from high school, he joined the Army. Pfc. Richard R. Tenneson from Alden, Michigan, had been a rebellious teenage runaway, who served a brief time in jail before enlisting in the Army. Cpl. James G. Veneris grew up in Vandergrift, Pennsylvania, the son of immigrant parents who had been Communists in Greece. Veneris would remain in China longer than any of the others. Sgt. Harold H. Webb from Fort Pierce, Florida, had lost both parents by the time he was eleven and was reportedly a loner. Cpl. William C. White, who enlisted at seventeen, was an African American from Plumerville, Arkansas, where he was raised by his grandparents. Cpl. Morris Wills was from an well-established farm family outside of Fort Ann, New

York, where he quit high school in his final year to enlist in the Army. After spending fourteen years in China, he returned to the United States and published a book in 1968 entitled *Turncoat: An American's 12 Years in Communist China.*[10] Finally, there was Cpl. Aaron Phillip Wilson from Urania, Louisiana, a devout Baptist who quit school in the eighth grade.

On January 25, 1954, Secretary of Defense Charles Wilson ordered that all twenty-one defectors be dishonorably discharged from the service. Normally, such an order could only come as a result of a court-martial, but, as Wilson explained, "You can't court-martial a man when he is not in your control."[11]

With the exception of James Veneris, who frequently travels back and forth between China and the U.S., none of the twenty-one remained in their new country. One died during his first year there. In July of 1955, William Cowart, Lewis Griggs, and Otho Bell became the first to return to the United States. They were immediately arrested and put in a stockade at Fort Baxter, San Francisco. Three months later a Federal court determined the Army had no jurisdiction over them, and they were released. Another eight had left China by 1958. By the end of 1966 only Howard Adams and James Veneris were still there, although three others had gone to Czechoslovakia, Poland, and Belgium respectively. The one British Marine who had defected also returned to England.[12] According to J. Robert Moskin, who helped write Morris Wills's *Turncoat,* "Under the chaos and harsh realities of life in China, the effects of Communist brainwashing wore off. Most of the American defectors found the regimentation, the conformity, and the puritanism unbearable."[13]

Although the twenty-one defectors have continued to live in military and popular infamy, many of their fellow prisoners have surprisingly not harbored any lasting animosity toward them. Michael Cornwell, who achieved the rank of lieutenant colonel in his post-Korea military career, remembers that Richard Corden was not only extremely intelligent but also a decent human being:

We had twenty-one who stayed. Richard Corden was the spokesman for the group, and he was my squad leader. He was not a bad sort of a guy. Could I have predicted he would stay? No. This guy was a super-intelligent person. I mean absolutely an intellectual. Corden could get more out the Chinese than any of us because he could be so diplomatic. But he did choose to stay. He went through four years of college over there and then came back. Of course, he doesn't attend our reunions. Strangely enough, I don't bear him any ill will. I thought he was a pretty good person. He just decided he didn't want to come home. He never talked about his politics, but he had a very weak family background: foster home, foster home, foster home. I think the Chinese offered him something he never had. Corden never did anybody any harm. He wasn't a Rat, and I knew him as well as anyone did in that prison camp. There were others who pulled some pretty slimy things, but not him. He was a high-strung sort of guy. I don't know what he did after he got back—maybe a college professor or something like that. He was just a super bright person.

Irv Langell also felt no individual enmity toward the twenty-one who chose to remain with the Chinese. In fact, he knew William Cowart quite well. Although he considered Cowart a "momma's boy," he agreed he was certainly no political ideologue:

You always hear about the ones that stayed. What were there, twenty-one of them? I think you have to look at their background. I only knew one, William Cowart, who was in my squad. Cowart was a good-looking young man, a woman-killer you might say, at least he thought of himself that way. He was very smart, but very immature and a follower. He was a momma's boy who had been given a lot of things in life. He had no self-confidence. That is the way I saw him, and I knew him probably better than most people. He thought he was trying to protect himself in order to survive. He was very easily led. I would sit there and shake my head: "Bill, what the hell is wrong with you?" He'd say, "I'm not doing anything wrong. I'm just getting some food." At the end, everybody was on his ass. They told him they were going to kill him for collaborating. Did he collaborate or didn't he? I don't know? It's all kind of vague now. I do know that when I came back I wasn't really pissed at him. I probably felt sorry for him.

James Dick also believes that most of the twenty-one were not political. Although he has forgotten most of their names, he mentions two he insists knew nothing about Communism:

I knew eleven of the twenty-one who stayed behind, but I couldn't name all of them now. I don't know why they stayed. As far as I know none of them collaborated with the enemy. Edward Dickenson was a big strong country boy from Virginia, but very uneducated in world affairs. Well, I wasn't that educated in world affairs then either. We were both too stupid to know anything about Communism. I had the belief when I went over to Korea if I could just get over there and kill Stalin this would settle everything. That's how stupid you are and the military likes stupid people. Anyway, Dickenson was the first to come back and, I think, they gave him five years.[14]

Claude Batchelor from Texas decided to stay, but then he changed his mind. He got twenty years when he came back. Batchelor was a nice guy who was always helping guys anyway he could. He was, I guess, a Progressive, but I never saw him do anything bad to anybody.[15]

Jim Crombie also had some positive things to say about Claude Batchelor:

Claude Batchelor was a fairly intelligent guy who apparently bought the Chinese line, but he also used his connections with the Chinese to help guys who were sick. He would get them aspirin and whatever else might help them.

Although Robert Fletcher did not agree with the decision of the three African Americans who chose to stay, as a fellow black he knew there were reasons for their decision that the mainstream press was not ready to examine:

There were three African Americans that stayed: Clarence Adams, William White, and Larance Sullivan. I knew them very well. All three were from the South. Adams and I slept in the same room; in fact, we slept head to toe with each other. We used to sit up at night and talk. Because I was born and raised in Michigan, I never understood the South, and I certainly never understood what blacks had to go through who lived there. Adams was from Memphis, Tennessee. He'd tell me, "I'm not going back to what I had to put up with." I told him, "Adams, I'm not going to put up with any bullshit either." I had never faced prejudice in the sense that he had—where you're walking down the street and a white person says, "Get off the street." I just couldn't fathom this in my mind. History books never told you anything about this in high school. By never living in the South, I never knew anything about it. Adams used to tell me, "Fletch, if you were born and raised down South, you'd be dead." I looked at him and said, "Maybe, but I wouldn't be by myself. Whoever came after me, some of them would go too." He said, "You just don't understand it do you?" I said, "No, I don't understand it and never will understand it."

When we were getting ready to be repatriated, I said, "Well, Adams, I'll see you down in Freedom Village." He said, "Yeah." Then I was in Freedom Village and I kept waiting for Adams because he and I had been very close. So I asked, "What happened to Adams?" Someone said, "They've detained him; the Chinese won't turn him lose." "What? For what reason?" And he said, "I don't know." Then we heard that twenty-one had actually decided to stay.

Adams stayed in China for about fifteen years, spoke Chinese fluently, and graduated from a university there. Then he decided he had enough. He found out there was no difference between Communism and capitalism. The powerful and rich few were still in control and always will be. If you have that, you're going to make it. If you don't, you're nothing. That's Communism or capitalism.

It was not only black prisoners who expressed a measure of empathy for Clarence Adams. Jim Crombie remembers an act of kindness Adams showed him after he arrived in Camp Five:

I have to say in Clarence's defense when I first arrived, and we were integrated then, he really helped me. He was a short, stocky, very personable guy. He really gave me a hand, asking what he could do to help.

Clarence Adams returned to Memphis in 1966 where he encountered open hostility on all fronts. Eventually, after things quieted down, he opened a string of Chinese restaurants with his Chinese wife. Adams died in December of 1999, but daughter Della Adams, who currently works for the Memphis Chamber of Commerce, tells her father's story with candor, wit, and a deep understanding of her father's motivation:

My father had several reasons why he chose not to come home. There were a lot of isolated incidents that just built on each other. His unit was an all-black artillery battalion, and when they saw white infantrymen retreating past them while they were moving toward the front, they wondered what was going on. At the time, they did not know the Chinese had come into the war. When he found out his battalion was providing cover for all those white infantrymen who were retreating, and knowing there was no way they could get out themselves, he realized they were being sacrificed. There's no other way to put it. I'm not a military person, but common sense tells you to move your big guns out first. That stayed with him. But they fought and they died. Right to the last, my father wanted to keep fighting. They were just a small, abandoned group at that point. The highest ranking sergeant said, "Look, I've got five kids at home in Texas, and I can't do this." So they laid down their guns. But they fought until it was hopeless to go on.

When he got into the prison camp he was astonished by all the racism that still existed. Two of his black buddies had to watch over him because several whites threatened to kill him.

Some people may call it brainwashing, but I don't think it was, nor did he. When someone points out something you already know, such as racism, is that brainwashing? He certainly had already experienced the racism of Memphis to which he knew he would have to return. He asked himself, "Why am I fighting for a country in which I have no rights, and when I go back, I'm still not going to have any rights?" So all these things—and others—made him decide to stay.

The Chinese promised him three things: 1) he would get an education as far as he wanted to go and was capable; 2) he would have a job; 3) he could get married if he could find somebody to marry him [laughs]. The Chinese made good on their promises, and he did find somebody to marry.

My father earned the equivalent of a master's degree in Chinese language. But it took him three years to grasp the language sufficiently to go on to his major courses. The Chinese had special classes just for the twenty-one to learn to speak and write the language.

When my father met my mother, she was a professor of Russian at Wuhan University. She never taught him, but they met through school activities. They married and I was their first child. I have a brother, but he was not born until we moved to Beijing because of my father's translating work for the Peking Foreign Press, which was a publishing house. . . .

We left China in 1966 some three months before the Cultural Revolution. In fact, that was one of the reasons why we left. My father had been spending a lot of time at the African embassies, and sometimes the Cuban embassy. The Chinese did not like this. They felt these embassies might be contaminated by Western ideas. Then the Chinese wouldn't allow my mother to work anymore. They doubled her salary, and paid her not to work. They feared she would influence young minds. First of all, she was from one of the feudal families and then she had married a Westerner. This was too much for those running the Cultural Revolution.

Because there was no American consulate in China, the British Consulate arranged our departure. We spent about a month in Hong Kong where the FBI and the CIA interrogated my father. I didn't know anything about this at the time. My father told me later. I just know that my father was escorted every day at eight o'clock in the morning from our hotel room and escorted back at the end of the day. He later told me it was a kind of psychological torture, even worse than the Chinese had ever done. Over and over again, they would ask the same things. They were trying to get him to confess that he was a traitor and had sold secrets. But if my father had any second thoughts about returning, it was too late. His African ambassadorial friends had offered him asylum in Ghana, and he did give that serious consideration, but he thought it was just time to go home.

His friends kept telling my father, "You don't want to go back to Memphis. You don't want to go anywhere in the South." When we arrived in San Francisco, he was contacted by UCLA and, I think, the University of Hawaii, and offered teaching positions. But he insisted he had to go home. They told him, "All right, go home and stay there for a while, but then accept a teaching position." I don't know why, but he wouldn't do it. Even after we had been back for a year, the schools were still writing him.

When we got to Memphis, there were death threats against us. The Ku Klux Klan and whoever else had organized a mob planned to meet us. We were supposed to arrive on an airplane, but we changed that after being told about the death threats. We ended up coming back a day early on a train. We just slipped into Memphis, so nobody knew we had arrived. My great uncles had arranged to get us secretly from the train station to the house. The next day the mob was out there, along with reporters, expecting us to arrive.

We had to have police guards at my grandmother's because we were still being threatened. This went on for a long time. We lived with my grandmother for, I think, two months. It was at least two months before we could even step outside. When we did go to the store, some people spit on us.

We were still living at my grandmother's house when my father was subpoenaed. I guess it was less than a month after we returned. He was called to Washington to testify before the House Committee on

Un-American Activities. The committee accused him of treason, and, of course, the punishment for that was pretty drastic. We still had a little money left and he told my mother, "If I don't come back, take the kids and go to Morris Wills in New York and try to find passage back to China."[16] I remember my mother crying. She didn't tell me what was going on. I knew he was gone for a week, and she was crying every day. It wasn't until later they told me what was going on. The Committee wanted him to get an attorney, but he refused. That was a smart move because any attorney would either have sold him out or worked a deal and got him to lie. He knew that if he was going to get off, it would be on his own. So he refused an attorney. The Committee members kept asking him all kinds of questions about what he had done: They asked if he had gone to China because the Chinese had coerced him.

He told them, "No, I did it on my own accord."

"You mean, you wanted to go?"

"Yes, I wanted to go."

HUAC also asked him about broadcasts he had made during the Vietnam War. Even though the armed forces had been desegregated, there was still racism and segregation, and the black troops were still being sacrificed. When he found out about this, he made broadcasts to the black soldiers. He told them, "If you are going to fight, you need to go home and fight for your own cause. You're being wasted for a cause that is not even yours."

When HUAC asked him if he had done this, he again replied that he had. His whole approach was, "Yes, I did it."

So then it came down to, "Why? What is wrong with you?"

He replied very simply, "Because I'm black."

The Committee responded, "What do you mean, 'Because I'm black'?"

He told them, "Every other race has the right to go wherever its members want. The white man has gone all over the world and done exactly what he wanted for his own benefit. Don't I have the right to do the same thing? I wanted to get an education, and I knew I wasn't going to get it here. I wanted to have a good job, and I wasn't going to get it here. So I chose to go to China to improve my life."

The Committee took a ten-minute recess and came back and said, "You are free to go." That was the end of it. Some FBI agents then took him out to dinner and a go-go bar.

Except in the American press, the entire issue of defections was a political defeat for the Chinese and their North Korean allies.[17] Shortly after the temporary cease-fire agreement of November 1951, tens of thousands of the U.N.-held Communist prisoners made it clear they would refuse repatriation to their respective homelands. After eighteen months of protracted and bitter negotiations and despite the tremendous pressure pro-Communist leaders put on their fellow prisoners at Koje-do Island and Pusan, only 90,000 of the 132,000 chose to return home. Whatever the measuring stick, the twenty-one Americans, one Briton, and 367 South Koreans pale by comparison.[18]

FREEDOM AND RECRIMINATION

Those Americans interviewing us after we were liberated never seemed to be that interested in our wounds or diseases. They really weren't interested in a damn thing except did we collaborate?

—Robert Jones, Korean War POW

When I came home there were no parades for me. There may have been for some of the POWs in certain towns. I don't know. And I was not issued any medals. The government didn't give a damn.

—James H. Dick, Korean War POW

Rumors abound in every prisoner of war camp. The most common rumor, and often the most devastating for the Korean War POWs, envisioned an imminent end to hostilities followed by a quick repatriation home. From the moment the first American soldiers were captured in July 1950, rumors circulated about their impending freedom, and they continued over the entire three years of their captivity. Unfortunately, for those men who put too much faith in such rumors, disappointment after disappointment often led to bitterness, depression, and even death.

Those prisoners captured early in the war had reason for hope when on October 9, 1950, the U.N. forces crossed the 38th Parallel and steadily pushed the North Korean forces north toward the Yalu River. General MacArthur's promise to have his men home by Christmas sounded wonderful to POWs who learned of the general's words from newly captured prisoners. But within weeks, the war took a devastating turn for the worse when tens of thousands of Chinese troops poured across the border and pushed the U.N. forces back to the South.

When it became increasingly obvious to both sides that there would be no quick, easy victory, they agreed to negotiate. The first truce talks began at Kaesŏng on July 10, 1951. Four and one half months later, on November 27, 1951, at P'anmunjŏm, the two sides agreed on the first cease-fire line, and shortly thereafter exchanged lists of prisoners. Rumors that the end of the war was once again imminent reached American prisoners. Unfor-

tunately, negotiations would lag on for another twenty months, and, ironically, the major sticking point was the issue of repatriation—not
concerning the handful of American prisoners who would choose China,
but of the thousands of North Korean and Chinese prisoners who refused
to return home.[1]

An April 1952 screening of U.N.-held prisoners indicated that not one
in five Communist POWs wanted to be repatriated.[2] When a second
U.N.-screening concluded that only 50 percent of the 140,000 military
and civilian internees wished to return to China and North Korea, the
Chinese insisted that at least 110,000 of their subjects be forced to return. The U.N. negotiators refused, and on April 25, 1952, the meetings
broke up.

By the summer of 1952, the adversaries had agreed on an armistice line
that changed little during the following year, but the issue of repatriation
continued to stall negotiations until 1953. Josef Stalin died on March 5,
1953, and three weeks later Chinese Foreign Minister Chou En-lai declared
that a neutral repatriation commission might now be acceptable. By 1953,
with death tolls continuing to climb, the U.N. leadership also wanted a
quick end to the war.

Operation Little Switch resulted in the first exchange of sick and
wounded prisoners at P'anmunjŏm between April 20–26, 1953.[3] The peace
talks were back on track, but South Korean President Syngman Rhee, who
adamantly opposed any compromise on repatriation, almost destroyed
them when on June 23, 1953, he ordered the release of 27,000 North
Korean prisoners who refused to be repatriated. In retaliation, the Communists again broke off negotiations. Finally, on July, 27, 1953, the two
sides agreed to an uneasy truce, and, beginning on September 4, the 4,000
surviving American prisoners walked through Freedom Village to become
free men.[4]

After so many disappointments, it was difficult for the prisoners to believe they were finally going home. Robert Fletcher explains how frustrating had been the many rumors of peace:

> When reading about the Korean War years later, I learned that the
> peace talks could have ended much earlier. The U.S. wanted voluntary
> repatriation, but the Chinese did not. We knew some of the details
> about the negotiations because our planes were getting shot down, and
> as these pilots came in or newer infantry people were captured, they
> would tell us, "Oh, we almost ended this sucker. We were at such and

such a point and the Chinese walked out." The Chinese would then tell us, "Oh, no, it was the Americans that walked out. They're the problem; they don't want you people back."

When it finally happened on July 27, 1953, it was to be a voluntary repatriation. The Chinese called us into formation and told us the war was over as of that day, and that we would be going home soon. Of course, everybody was very happy. The Chinese had allowed an AP reporter named Frank Noel to use his camera for propaganda reasons while he was a prisoner. The Chinese had screened his photographs and now they let some of them filter out to the press. These were always photos of someone enjoying himself, sitting around playing a guitar, or group singing. They were all propaganda. There was nothing of the atrocities. . . .

Richard Bassett describes his personal liberation and how anxious he was to climb onto the truck that would take him to Freedom Village:

Thus began the day I had been dreaming about for more than twenty-two months. I watched the first group load into the waiting trucks and waved goodbye. Another hour dragged by, and the second group loaded up, and once more I was there waving. The next hour seemed much longer. The trucks finally returned, and the Chinese motioned for our bunch to load up. As we rolled down the road to freedom, it seemed so unreal and unnatural to be spending my last few minutes as a prisoner of war. The truck finally stopped at a barricade. I waited nervously while the minutes ticked away. Finally, the barricade was rolled away, and we moved forward to the exchange point. The Chinese officer got out and was met by an American officer. Both had rosters in their hands, and one by one our names were called off. First the Chinese read my name; then the American did. I stepped down off the truck and was quickly escorted a few steps to an Army tent. As I walked across that line of freedom and entered the tent, another American officer shook my hand and said, "Welcome home, soldier." I was a free man, and my eyes filled with tears. At the other end of the tent another American officer handed me a brown manila envelope. I was then escorted to a waiting ambulance that transported me to this dreamworld called Freedom Village. It was too wonderful and emotional an experience ever to put into words.

Many things went through Billy Joe Harris's head when he learned he was about to become a free man after spending two and one half years in captivity.

They finally told us that the war was over and that we would be moved back south. That was another thing I had great trouble with. I knew the approximate size of Korea, and I knew that we weren't the only troops over there—that there were United Nations troops with us. So when I got captured on February 13, 1951, I thought six months at the longest. I figured either the Chinese would win it or we would. Six months was a long time. But then it went on for a year and then another year. I couldn't understand why it took so long. It doesn't take that long to win or lose a war.

I thought back on my first day in Camp Three after we had been marching for over three months with little or no food and without ever once washing. That first day I went down to this little creek to wash myself and my clothes. I looked in the water, and I saw a face. I looked around to see who it was; well, it was me. I couldn't even recognize myself. But when it was time for repatriation, I had regained some of my weight and was feeling much better. We had even made weights out of wood and had begun exercising. At my lowest I probably weighed about one hundred pounds.

They let the Red Cross come in the day we were moving out. They gave us some toilet articles. That was the first time we had seen the International Red Cross. Then they loaded us on trucks and moved us to a rail head and loaded us on a train—the cattle cars—and took us south. They had a holding area just on the north side of the 38th Parallel. They held us there and took so many of us each day in exchange for so many of theirs. I don't remember the exact date I was exchanged, but I do remember when my bunch crossed the Bridge of No Return, we threw away everything we had except our shorts. They ran us through a shower and gave us new clothes. They also offered us a cup of ice cream or a glass of milk. It was like a dream. We just couldn't believe we were free.

Jim Crombie also reflected back on his long months as a prisoner and how his religious faith had contributed to his survival:[5]

After twenty-eight months of captivity and all the rumors about the end of war, we finally received the news of the cease-fire. The electricity that went through the camp was awesome, and I immediately got down on my knees and thanked the Lord. He had protected me through all this in so many ways. Four or five times I could have been gone and that's the reason the words of the 91st Psalm meant so much to me.

> We live within the shadow of the Almighty sheltered by the God who is above all gods. This I declare that He alone is my refuge my place of safety. He is my God and I am trusting Him for He rescues you from every trap, protects you from the fatal plague. He will shield you with His wings. He will shelter you. His faithful promises are your armor. Now you don't need to be afraid of the dark anymore or fear the dangers of the day nor dread the plagues of darkness nor disasters in the morning.

I had never promised the Lord that I would do this or that. I never promised him I would go to seminary or that I would go to church four times a week. I always had the faith that I was going to get out of there. You always hear about foxhole Christians—people who say, "Oh Lord, if you get me out of here I'll do anything you want. I'll go to church every day. I'll go to seminary. I'll work for the Salvation Army." I didn't think I had to do that because I had faith that I would get out of there and get home. The most difficult part of my whole ordeal was not knowing what my parents were going through. I knew I was going to get out. I just have to tell you that faith was the key to my survival, and it has been an integral part of my life since then.

Charley Davis was also very happy to be free, but he also remembers that some prisoners were questioned in Freedom Village about their behavior in the prison camps:

> I never could figure out how our government had so much information when we got released. I remember when we were in Freedom Village they gave us a manila card that I still have. On it was "OK Chow." They told us that the press was in the next room and wanted to talk to some of us. This guy came up and looked at my card and said, "Okay, you can talk." He did the same thing with the next guy. How did they know that I was all right to talk to the press?

When he learned of the cease-fire, Glenn Reynolds worried about whether or not the Chinese would really release him and a group of fellow Reactionaries:

There were 222 of us who had been left in the last Reactionary group. On September 4 we were in the staging area about four or five miles north of P'anmunjŏm. That afternoon, they loaded us up on trucks and drove us out the front gate. But instead of turning south, where we should have been going, the trucks turned north. We quickly knew that we were heading toward China and not toward the 38th parallel. We decided they were planning to keep us so we planned to jump the guards. We realized that some of us would get killed, but we decided we had to risk it and take the vehicles and make a run for the 38th parallel. About thirty minutes later, the drivers pulled over to the side of the road and put us in a rice paddy. We knew something was going on. Then they put us back on the trucks and turned around and drove back to the staging area. The next morning they loaded us up again, but this time they headed south.

They eventually stopped, and we all got out and went through this gate. Then we had to strip off all our clothes and be deloused and washed. A fellow prisoner named Forrest Montgomery had a brother Roy with the United Nations' command. He was waiting for Forrest to come through, and he told us, "We almost lost you guys. Yesterday, the chief U.N. negotiator, General Harrison, asked the People's Liberation Army's chief negotiator when they were going to release the rest of their prisoners." When they denied having any, Harrison said, "You've got about six hundred up there. You keep them and we'll keep the thousands we've got." Harrison then got up and walked out. There were still thousands of Communist prisoners waiting to be repatriated to the north. That's the reason they stopped our trucks. So we got out of there by the skin of our teeth.

The exhilaration the men experienced in Freedom Village was tempered onboard the ship sailing home when they had to go through a series of interrogations, this time conducted by their own military personnel. Robert Fletcher, who had suffered through several Chinese and North Korean interrogations, became very upset about the tenor of the questions:

During the eleven days we spent on the ship coming home, I was asked all these questions about different people. I told the officers doing the

interrogating, "You know we were all in prison camps, and we all suffered the same goddamn thing. I didn't know anybody that got favors.
Not Clarence Adams, not William White, not Larance Sullivan [the
three African Americans who chose not to be repatriated]. If they got
sick, they didn't get any medicine—there wasn't any. So what are you
trying to get out of me? That some guys got better treatment? Better
treatment, bull." I told them, "The Chinese would call your ass up to
headquarters, and sometimes they wouldn't even speak to you. I was
called up there two or three times. They might give you a pack of
cigarettes and tell you to go back. That was so the rest of the guys
would see the cigarettes and say, 'Oh, oh, he must have told them
something.' When the guys saw you come back smoking a cigarette,
they figured you must have cooperated."

These American officers kept trying to trap us by repeating their
questions. One lieutenant would ask a bunch of questions. Then another one would come in and ask the same questions, just turned
around a bit. They finally decided, "Fletcher knows more than he's
said. If he stays in the service, we need to interrogate him more in-
tensely." So they classified me as a security risk. I didn't know about
this until years later when I got my records under the Freedom of
Information Act.

And it wasn't just me who was singled out for interrogation onboard
the ship coming home. I think we were all classified as Communists
until proven innocent. Of course, you have to remember, this all happened during the McCarthy era.

Jerry Morgan, who like Robert Fletcher was an African American, was
greatly disturbed that the black prisoners were not only interrogated but
also segregated on the ship coming home:

There were 328 of us on that troop ship coming back, both black and
white. But what really hurt me was that we blacks were segregated from
everybody else. We took physicals, and we were interrogated every day,
every day, every day. We went through that for eleven days on the
Nelson M. Walker. The interrogators primarily wanted to find out about
collaborators. Some doctors or technicians briefly inquired about our
health, but they showed only minimal concern.

In spite of his sterling record, both as a soldier and a prisoner, Michael
Cornwell also had to endure onboard interrogations:

You could call what happened on the ship coming home a debriefing or an interrogation, but it lasted all day long—some eight hours. I know they kept an eye on us. This was another unfortunate aspect of the war. There were allegations made by some people against others, often without any basis. Someone would be unhappy with somebody else so he would accuse him of collaborating with the enemy. The Army ran a bunch of investigations, but very few resulted in any kind of disciplinary action. But those debriefing us wanted us to inform on other prisoners—to say this guy did this and this guy did that. They wanted us to write up a bunch of allegations against people. There had been some pretty bad press about prisoner behavior, and the Army was responding to these allegations. I believe they flagged our records for seven years. I worked for a short time for the Joint Chiefs of Staff, but I had to take a lie detector test before I was allowed to do so. I also married an Army "brat" after my return from Korea. Her father was a West Point colonel. Of course, he had me investigated. Damn right he did. He was going to make damn sure his daughter wasn't marrying a pinko.

Harley Coon was another former prisoner who was uncomfortable with the onboard questioning, especially when asked about those who had died:

They asked you a question, and the best thing you could do was say, "I don't know." I went through eight hours a day of interrogations for fifteen days on the ship coming back. The worst thing for me was having to talk about the guys I knew who died over there. The interrogators had these lists, and they would ask, "Did you know this individual? Did you see him die? How did he die?" Those were the toughest for me. They also asked, "Did you see anybody tortured? Did you see any atrocities?" Everybody did, but we didn't say much about it because we didn't know exactly who was doing what.

They asked about the twenty-one who stayed behind and went to China. A strange question was, "Who was on the sanitation committee?" These guys were appointed by the Chinese to do this job. They had no choice in the matter, so I wondered what was wrong with that? They knew who some of these men were, but they weren't collaborators. I don't know what the purpose of the question was, but they were trying to find out everything. The one thing I knew for sure was when I got my report back, it said something to the effect I could have a security clearance because I was a very strong anti-Communist.

U.S. Army Captain Louis Rockwerk, who had served admirably in both World War II and Korea, had nothing but contempt for those interrogating him on board ship:

> Aboard the ship coming home a psychiatrist hands me a *Life* magazine with a picture of a young lady in a bra and panties. Of course, you can imagine my reaction. He asks, "What do you think about women?" I looked at him and laughed and said, "What in the goddamn hell do you mean, 'What do I think about women?' If I had one right now I would show you what I think about women." That was just ridiculous. Some psychiatrist or psychoanalyst wanted us to hold hands and then tell them, "It wasn't so bad." Most of us had spent years in prison camps, and we gave a damn about what had happened.

The interrogation of the former prisoners did not cease once they landed in the United States. Some men were hounded for years by military and government investigators. Charles "Pluto" Sherron was among a select number of returning prisoners sent to Fort Meade in the spring of 1954 for further interrogations. Sherron, who has no idea why he was singled out, was asked a wide range of questions, but most focused on suspected Progressives. Sherron was very cooperative, and the investigators invited him to pass on whatever he knew about his fellow prisoners. Years later Sherron acquired his file under the Freedom of Information Act. It contained some startling information, including hearsay comments others had made about Sherron himself, but the most exceptional observation was an interrogator noting that Sherron "did not clench his fists" when talking about Progressives. Nevertheless, after telling the investigators he agreed all Progressives should be punished, Sherron was cleared and able to finish his twenty-year hitch in the U.S. Army.[6]

Unlike Sherron, the feisty and irascible Irv Langell was not about to cooperate when representatives of his own government asked him insulting questions:

> The government pissed me off. We should have been flown back, but my group was put us on a slow boat, and we were interrogated every day. Nobody was concerned about our health, I can damn well guarantee you.
>
> After I re-upped in the service, I was sent to Germany. One day I got called up to the orderly room to report to the colonel. I wondered, "What the hell did I do now?" I was always in trouble. I used to walk

a fine line. I just did my own thing and I made it. The colonel told me that the CID [Counter-Intelligence Division] wanted to see me. The colonel also wanted to know what this was all about. I said, "I don't know." But I knew. The CID grilled me for a week about what had gone on. Every day they wanted me to talk about Bill Cowart and all these other things, but I wouldn't. I told them, "You are a bunch of sorry bastards." When they threatened me, I said, "What are you going to do? I hope you're not going to treat me as badly as the Chinese or the Koreans did because that didn't work either." They finally gave up on me. Afterward the colonel again wanted to know what it was all about. He was on my fanny for the rest of the time I was under his command, but I told him it was none of his goddamn business. He didn't like that, but that's exactly what I said.

James Dick was also cantankerous and uncooperative, especially when questioned by a psychiatrist on the ship, and he certainly didn't appreciate the FBI investigating him after he was safely back home:

On the ship coming back this CIC or CID Army major used to come down almost everyday and say, "Sergeant Dick, let's go up and have a talk." We would go up on deck, and we would talk and talk. He was a psychiatrist or a quack, I'm not sure which. One day he asked me, "You ever have sex with your mother?" So I said, "No, have you?"

After I got home, two FBI agents from Cincinnati used to come and harass me. I had just got a job in a steel plant working second shift, and they would show up early in the morning and interrogate me. I was smart and intelligent enough to ask, "Well, has somebody from the POW camps said something bad about me?" I didn't think anybody had. I hadn't done anything wrong, but you're under fear. I was newly married and under a lot of strain, and these guys would come and ask these questions. They tried to get me to rat against Claude Batchelor, but I told them, "You guys are no better than the Chinese. You condemn them for doing this, and now you're trying to get me to be a rat against Batchelor." The last time they talked to me I got so mad I said, "Now, if you two guys have something on me, you press charges, but I don't ever want to see you coming back here again." I should have asked them why they weren't over there fighting, but I was too young at the time. If it happened today, I would get my gun. You can't intimidate me now. I'm seventy years old.

According to Jim Crombie, it was not only the insinuating questions he resented but also the questions that were never asked, especially those that should have dealt with the mental and physical health of the returning prisoners:

> They did us a great disservice in that they did not make us sit down and tell them what was wrong with us when we came back. They could have started when we were on that ship for two weeks. Then we went to Fort Dix for a couple of days. All they asked was, "Are you feeling all right?"
>
> "Yeah, man, I feel great. I want to go home."
>
> "Well, okay. Is there anything else wrong with you?"
>
> "No, I'm fine. I feel good. I don't have any hurts, nothing." Then, in 1983 they called us in for a physical protocol, but that was thirty years after the fact. Then they asked, "Did you say anything about this when you got out?"
>
> "Hell no, I wanted to get out. I wanted to get home. I didn't want to take a chance on going to a hospital." I ended up in a hospital anyhow for about a year and a half. But I mean everybody was like that. All the guys were the same way.

Douglas Tanner found coming home to be a mixed blessing. He was, of course, delighted to be safely back, but he also faced the daunting challenge of telling a widow what had happened to her POW husband:

> I think the hardest job I had when I came back was telling the wife of one of the sergeants in my platoon that he had died—courageously shall we say? He wasn't really hurt badly during battle, but he did contract a cold, which developed into pneumonia, and we were carrying him on a stretcher most of the way on the march. With his tin can he'd grab anything that he thought was water and drink it. He died. I didn't tell his wife how he died. I just mentioned malnutrition and so forth in the camp. But he had given up. That's the whole thing.

Not even the indignities of the interrogations could diminish the excitement the former prisoners felt after finally arriving home. They had spent those dreary months in prison dreaming of the good times and the wonderful people they had left behind. Quite naturally, during their first weeks at home they were on an emotional high. They were free men and they celebrated. They drank too much, drove too fast, and played too hard as they tried to blot out their dreadful experiences. But the party had to end, and when they finally tried to resume a normal existence, most felt alone, depressed, and troubled by recurring flashbacks. Family and friends did not seem capable of understanding their anxieties or their inability to push their traumatic experiences out of their consciousness. Receiving no help or counseling, most had to make it on their own. Arguably, the more fortunate ones remained in the military where structure and discipline aided their transition. But for those who had to find their way in civilian life, the adjustment period became ever more difficult. In fact, for many of them it has lasted to the present day.

II

LEGACY

In their rememberings are their truths.

          —Studs Terkel, oral historian

As for his thirty-four months as a POW in Korea, my father took most of the memories to the grave with him. I think that it was all so horrible that he dared not even speak of it. . . . In 1990 someone asked to talk to him for an article. My father tried his best but shortly afterwards he had another heart attack. . . . I still think that talking about it upset him internally.

          —Sandra J. Merrill, daughter of Troy L. Reid,
a Korean War POW who died in 1996

You could be the most psychologically put together person that ever walked the face of the earth, but it is my belief that you could develop PTSD given enough stress.

          —Dr. Glenn P. Smith, clinical psychologist

When I came home everybody was happy and all excited to see me, and it lasted for two or three days.

          —Harley Coon, Korean War POW

Whatever the war, the vast majority of books and films about fictional POWs stop with liberation. However, for real prisoners incarceration remains with them for the rest of their lives. Too often these postwar years have been marred by painful, even crippling memories, social dysfunction, and physical and mental anguish.

Of the more than 150 former World War II and Korean War POWs I have interviewed, only a handful initially insisted they had suffered no long-term effects from their internment. All were officers who went on to successful military careers. One typical response was, "I don't know how to spell cope, psychoanalysis, or psychology." However, this same man kept a diary in which one day's entry dispassionately described three occurrences: what he ate, a fellow prisoner being shot and killed, and the arrival of spring, without drawing any qualitative differences. The wife of another officer who denied any repercussions refuted his claim by describing the nightmares he suffered anytime he spoke of his incarceration.

On the other hand, the former enlisted men readily admit they have been deeply scarred by their experiences in captivity. Many have suffered problems with alcohol, family abuse, holding a job, Post-Traumatic Stress Disorder (PTSD) and various physical infirmities. Most have spent years silently trying to excise painful flashbacks, and almost all agree that captivity was the central experience of their lives. Their legacy is wrapped up in their struggle to retain a sense of decency and self-worth in the face of what are often frightening and debilitating aftereffects. Indeed, theirs is the legacy of survival itself. Then, too, the Korean War prisoners suffer an additional indignity: the popular notion that a disproportionate number of them collaborated with the enemy.

There were no counseling sessions for the returning prisoners, but they could have cared less. All they wanted was to get back to America and their friends and loved ones. Their initial days home were indeed wonderful, but the euphoria quickly wore off, often to be replaced by feelings of emptiness, guilt, and anxiety. As lonely and neglected prisoners, they had quite naturally overly romanticized what they had left behind, but reality could never measure up to the sentimental fantasies that had kept them going during their long, dismal months in Korea.

Writing years later, Dr. Gene Lam, who remained in the Army after returning from captivity, noted the danger the newly freed prisoners were to themselves, as well as some of the long-term social and health effects they would suffer:

Shortly after repatriation, we suffered a fairly large number of accidents resulting in death, as well as several suicides. In the forty years since our captivity, some have, of course, died from heart disease, cancer and other diseases. Some men have residuals of beriberi, pellagra and deficiency disease manifested by neuritis and severe dermatitis. Several cases of severe optic atrophy occurred in camp and the survivors have not improved. Also, it seems to me that, as a group, the rate of divorce is unusually high.[1]

Over the past seven years Dr. Glenn P. Smith has worked as a clinical psychologist at the James A. Haley Veterans Hospital in Tampa, Florida, specializing in PTSD cases. He works with veterans and former prisoners from all recent wars, but he finds the former Korean War POWs to be unique:

> The Korean prisoners tend to feel a deep-seated resentment because of the labels that have been inappropriately ascribed to them—things like critics lumping them all together and calling them brainwashed and the whole thing about the forgotten war. . . .
>
> These men have been caught between two wars. On the one side there are the World War II veterans who were well received when they came home. They were credited with having done their duty and completing their task by winning the war. Of course, I don't want to minimize the individual traumas suffered by the World War II soldiers. At the other end of the spectrum are the Vietnam veterans who in many ways have been better able to verbalize something the Korean War guys secretly would like to do, which is to call attention to themselves and their plight. But the Korean War veterans were raised in a time when one didn't speak about what was going on underneath the surface. So they have trouble verbalizing their resentment.[2]

Peggy Himmelheber is a psychiatric nurse practitioner who over the past fourteen years has worked with former POWs at the Jacksonville, Florida, Veterans Administration Outpatient Clinic. She agrees that the road back has been particularly difficult for the Korean War POWs:

> The Korean prisoners are a different group than those from World War II. I think the biggest thing is the disservice that was done to them by our own government after they came home. There was such a big hullabaloo about how these individuals were lesser men than those from World War II, and that the country was in a shambles with no moral standards. Critics such as Kinkead and Mayer really put the blame on them, saying that they were less patriotic, more pampered, and had less stamina and integrity than previous POWs. They derided and blamed them for not being able to hold up, when in fact they held up just as well as did anybody else. They were certainly not pampered. Many had been in CCC [Civilian Conservation Corps] camps. I've treated a lot of men from the rural areas of the South, and some of them told me that they never had their own pair of shoes until they were inducted into the service.
>
> When they first returned home, almost to a man they drank too much, tried to kill themselves in one way or another, went through too

many women, and had too many motorcycle accidents. If someone could have interceded at that point, it would have helped. . . . The ones who did survive the first five or ten years—and probably 20 percent of them didn't—tend to seal over their past and get involved in something. They are usually very hard-headed. It's difficult to convince them that something is gray when they say it's black. That's what they hold on to. And that's why it's so difficult for them to raise children. When you raise children, you have to have some degree of flexibility, but they only learn that later because they have to maintain that rigidity to keep all this crap under wraps.[3]

Billy Joe Harris was typical of those returning prisoners who only years later realized there should have been some kind of debriefing or counseling before they returned to civilian life:

One thing I have against the government to this day was its lack of any kind of program to help us readjust to normal life. Of course, I didn't realize it at that time because all I wanted to do was get out and get home—and I did. They loaded us on a ship at Inch'ŏn and then gave us a lot of vitamins and food, but there was no debriefing or rehabilitating us. They didn't do anything.

I got a thirty-day convalescence leave and flew to Springfield, Missouri, to be with my mother who was sick. After that I reported to Fayetteville to get my discharge. That was it. I was just turned loose. It was really hard on me because I didn't even know how to act around other people.

We should have been counseled. I had a lot of trouble, and it continued until just a few years ago. It would usually happen when I got to talking about the war. I would just draw a blank about my experiences. I don't have it today, but I often did then, especially when I tried to talk to my own family or friends. I would be talking, and all of a sudden my mind would just go blank, and I wouldn't even know what I was talking about. So I didn't like to talk to them. I didn't know whether something was wrong with my mind, and it left me in a sad state. Not until years later did I find out that this was not all that unusual. I started going to the VA in Columbia, Missouri, and I started reading. I found out that it does happen to people like me. I also had a lot of flashbacks. I didn't only dream, I had nightmares. The Chinese and the Koreans were always in these nightmares, but they were on

American soil in places that I knew as a kid. These nightmares never took place over there—always here.

Although Ray Baumbach had only been a prisoner for a matter of weeks before he escaped, he nevertheless had a difficult time putting the experience behind him after returning to civilian life. He initially turned to alcohol and self-pity before eventually deciding he had a spiritual mission to help others:

After I got out of the service, it was fifteen years before I again realized that I owed my life to the Lord, and I've been in the prison ministry ever since. I think it took me so long to understand all this because I came from such a poor family that I wanted to be somebody. I had dreamed all my life of being a hero. In Korea I wanted to win the Medal of Honor. When I got back to the States, I had the Silver Star, the Bronze Star, and three Purple Hearts, and the whole town came out and put on a parade for me. Well, I got a big head and gave myself credit for what I had done. I thought for the rest of my life everyone was going to look up to me. Well, you know how long fame and honor lasts. Not long. Shortly after the parade I walked down the street and discovered I wasn't any different than anybody else. I had a terrible time accepting this. I thought, "It can't be over. This was supposed to last the rest of my life." I also began drinking when I came home. What I hated most in my turning to alcohol was this was exactly what my father had done.

Finally, one day I sat down and had a good talk with the Lord, and He straightened me out on who was really responsible for my survival. I finally understood the reason I had endured was that He had a plan. Since then I have turned my life around, and for more than thirty years I've been working for Him in the prison ministry. I can just look at those guys in prison and see myself, and because I was a former POW, I get their attention faster than anyone else. They see that I am not a phony, but someone who has also been a prisoner. We still have our problems—at least I know I do—but we just have to make up our minds that we can get through them.

I guess I'm also trying to pay the Lord back for those three hundred prisoners I had to watch being buried when I was captured. So far I have talked to at least three hundred men in prison who have turned their lives around. So I think what I am doing is substituting the men in prison for those American soldiers I saw buried in Korea. I guess I haven't yet completed my obligation because I'm still living and working.

Many of the returning men also needed medical attention. In Jim Crombie's case, debilitating physical problems made his psychological readjustment to civilian life even more difficult:

They did some psychological testing on us on the ship coming back. I guess we told them whatever we thought they might want to know. . . . After I was out a couple months, I found this girl, and I thought I was in love. We got engaged, then she broke it off. That was the first winter I was home. I was so despondent and depressed. I was building a stone wall for my mother and dad along their driveway, and I just couldn't finish it. I got pneumonia and pleurisy, and my family doctor said, "You're a sick puppy. We're going to put you in the VA hospital." I didn't think I was going to live anyhow, and I really didn't care if I did or not. So they stuck me into a TB hospital in Butler, Pennsylvania, and I stayed there for a year. I never did have a positive TB test, but I had pleurisy. They kept draining my lungs, and that was probably the best thing that could have happened. I was able to build my body back to where it should have been. I had time to lie there and think about where I was going and what I was going to do.

Glenn Reynolds was typical of many returning prisoners who kept everything locked up inside, but in his case he was ordered to do so:

When I was debriefed at Inch'ŏn before they put us on the boat home, they emphasized that under no circumstances was I to discuss my prisoner experiences with civilians. Three or four months after we got back, I was called in and interrogated by a bunch of CIC or CID guys about who did what, when, and where and about who was brainwashed. After that debriefing, they told me not to discuss this with anybody. I thought, "My God, they'll prosecute me if I do." So I just shut up and didn't talk to anybody. In my little community of Christmas, Florida, where I lived for twenty-one years, not a single soul knew I was an ex-prisoner of war.

Many of the returning men felt an emotional detachment, often accompanied by angry outbursts, which, as Harry Falck explains, were impossible to explain to loved ones:

When I first got out I was so hardened by my experiences with death it was pathetic. My wife would ask, "Why don't you ever cry?" I'd tell her, "Honey, I'm not faking. I could kill you and it would not bother me in the least." She'd say, "You couldn't; you're too easygoing of a guy." I'd say, "Please, don't trust me. Be my friend, but stay a little bit leery."

Over the years I've mellowed, but sometimes I get riled up and will tell a person who might have said something I didn't like, "Hey, look I'm leaving and I'll be back, but don't come and talk to me until that time because if I fly off the handle you're going to get hurt, and I'm going to regret it." Then I'll just walk off. If he starts following me, I will point my finger and say, "Now, I warned you." A few minutes later I come back and say, "All right, I'm sorry. Something just set me off, but I'm all right now."

Charley Davis repressed his emotions by keeping everything bottled up tightly inside:

Because I had seen so much death in Korea, I was immune when I got back to the States. When my mother died after I got back I don't think I ever shed a tear. It may have bothered me internally, but not externally.

I didn't really talk to my family after I got back home. My uncle was five years older than me, and we grew up together just like brothers. Maybe fifteen years after I got back, the two of us were talking one day and he told me, "I think you would have been better off if you would have talked about what happened to you when you first came back." I told him, "Yeah, you're probably right." But I didn't feel like I could make anybody understand what I had gone through. They might feel sorry for me, but I didn't think they could really understand. And I still don't think they can. Unless you were actually there, you can't know what it was like.

Many of the men also felt a sense of guilt. Homer Jurgens typically wondered why he had survived when so many of his buddies had not:

A big question in my mind has been, why me, and not somebody else? I'm no better than the other guys that died or were lost and never showed up. I just give thanks to the mercy of God that I made it through and am alive. I know the experience made me even more serious-minded about life, realizing that I had an opportunity that some of the other guys didn't have to survive and go on with my life and be a good citizen. I think it helped me in that regard.

Michael Cornwell, who insists he suffered no long-term debilitating effects from his incarceration, nevertheless was initially bothered by thoughts of a good friend he had lost in Korea:

I was able to pretty much shut out my experiences after I returned home. I had one real close friend whom I lost that bothered me for a while. I'd dream about him, but that eventually passed. I felt I didn't do enough for him, but I did all I could. He just couldn't keep his damn food down, and he died. His name was Whelan. He was from Boston. A hell of a nice kid. I had only met him in the prison camp. I felt pretty bad about that. Once in a while I have nightmares, but not often. I was never dysfunctional because of having been a POW. Never.

After the initial readjustment difficulties came the equally challenging long-term effects of incarceration. The term "Post-Traumatic Stress Disorder" did not appear in medical journals until the early 1980s, but these men certainly suffered its effects long before it had a clinical name. Often a specific event, such as a family tragedy, a problem at work, or the onset of retirement, would trigger PTSD. In Jim Crombie's case it was the Iranian hostage crisis:

My post-traumatic stress thing was real. It started with the American hostages in Iran. After the Iranians turned them loose and they began telling about their experiences, something just popped in me. I got downright despondent. I wasn't threatening suicide or anything like that, but I was really shook up, and my wife picked up on it. It brought back memories, and it started churning things around in my mind. I was also winding down my career. I was where I was going to be, and I wasn't going anywhere else. I talked to the shrink at the VA, and I overcame it. Of course, having a good wife and family helped immensely.

Glenn Reynolds agrees with Jim Crombie that something unexpected could precipitate an anxiety attack. "We talk a lot about that at our group meetings," says Reynolds. "The consensus is that something or other that we see or hear on television or somewhere else can trigger these attacks." Reynolds also explains that even when the men insist they are doing fine, there are signs that all is not well:

You look at every one of us and we appear to be healthy looking. But if you check with each of us, you would find we have two or three pantries filled with food. We have food hidden under the bed and everywhere. We keep checking the refrigerator to make sure the food supply is there. We were deprived so long that every time we go to the grocery store, we come home with too much.

I sometimes talk on the telephone with former POWs I haven't seen in quite a while. I'll ask them about their health. Every one of them will say, "Oh, I'm in good health. There's nothing wrong with me." Then in general conversation I'll ask them, "Well, do you still have nightmares about the prison camps?" They invariably say, "Oh, sure." And later you inject the question, "Do you ever wake up in the middle of the night in a cold, clammy sweat with your heart pounding?" And they say, "Oh, that happens to me quite often, but I'm fine." This is classic PTSD, but they just don't know they have a problem. They're trying to repress their feelings, and that's just going to make everything worse.

The prisoners themselves were not the only victims of the long-term effects of incarceration. Wives and children were also at risk, as psychiatric nurse Peggy Himmelheber explains:

The wives are a crusty bunch. It's unfortunate that we can't provide services to them as well. They are the strength of their men. They are the ones who snatched them up when they were drinking and screwing up too much and said, "Look, you've got a couple of kids. Now, you get your butt out and go to work." Sometimes it was wife number two or three who did this, but not always. I have men who have been married sixty years, and who are still married to the women who bore their children before they were captured. Those wives tolerated their husband's behavior and brought them through the hardest times. The ones who didn't tolerate it, left. But then the men found another one who would stand by them.

It is important to point out that these are not weak, beaten-down women. They tolerate the nightmares and the isolation, and they help their men watch their backs. They put up with all this, and in return they expect their husbands to be socially appropriate. Many of these men, with this support, are very good providers and become able to participate in some of the social activities that are important to their families.

It's the wives who get them to go to the POW reunions or to the clinics. I've had these tiny little women physically pushing these men into my office. They have a great deal of influence and they're subtle. They know when to exercise their influence and when to back off. . . .

The relationship between the father and the children varies a great deal. To a man they are all very proud of their children, but they are also awfully hard on them. They don't have great relationships with their children. I think there is respect, but not closeness. The men know they can survive alone because they had to in the camps. I think they miss that closeness, but they think, "Hey, I lived without it before, and I'm not going to violate my beliefs now." These men do much better with their grandchildren. Their kids have had a hard way to go.[4]

It was very common for the former prisoners to tell their wives little about their POW experiences. As a result, the wives often learned the details secondhand, or through a husband's offhand remark, as was the case with this wife:

Wife A:[5] He never mentioned anything about his POW experiences to me. I knew he had been a POW from things I had heard in town, but he just didn't talk about it. The first time he even mentioned anything about it was after we had been married four or five years and had moved out here on the farm. Another POW came to visit us, and those two men sat in our kitchen and talked and talked and talked. They were completely oblivious to anything else. I sat there and listened. I don't even think they knew I was there.

My husband really had a difficult time expressing himself to others. Maybe he was pleased that I finally knew. I don't know because it was very hard to communicate with him. One time we were driving home from a town about fifty miles away, and I was pregnant. I told him, "I need a Coke."

He said, "You'll have to wait a bit, but you do know you could wait until we got back to the farm. You'd live."

I told him, "Yes, probably I could wait, but I wouldn't be happy."

He said, "Oh, yes, you could make it. I made it for a long time without any water."

But that was truly the only time he ever held up his experiences to me. Before then he had never really said anything about his POW time. But, bless his heart, he did stop and buy that Coke for me.

Another wife learned some unexpected details about her husband's incarceration at a most inopportune moment—just as she was about to deliver their first child:

Wife B: I knew that my husband had been a POW in the Korean War, but that's all I knew. He never told me anything about it. I knew he had a shrapnel wound because I remember the first time we went swimming together he had a big hole in his back. I asked him, "Were you in an accident?" He said that was where he was wounded. That was about all he told me until I was in labor with our first child. During that first stage I was pretty miserable, so he decided to tell me everything about how tough he had it in Korea. I was probably drugged with whatever they gave you in those days so you didn't really care if you were in labor or not. The only thing I can remember saying to him was, "You have to be quiet. I'm getting sick."

This same wife discovered that she had to be careful not to upset her husband, especially when serving him dinner:

When we first got married we lived in a little apartment, and he would come home for lunch from his classes. This one day I had scooped out our dessert, and he acted very strange and angry.

I asked him, "What's the matter with you?"

He looked at me in total bewilderment and said, "You have one more cherry on your dessert than I do."

That just blew me away. In the forty-four years since then I've always been very careful when I've served our food to make sure he has more than I do, even if it is grits or something else I know he doesn't like.

This same wife remarked that control is an all-consuming issue with her husband, whether at work, while driving, or even in her kitchen:

He is very, very controlling, perhaps because in the prison camp he lost all control. He wants me to report to him everything I do. For example, on vacation he wants to approve or disapprove of everything I purchase.

He'll say, "But you don't need that."

And I'll say, "But I want it. I don't complain when you want something."

We wives have laughed about how our husbands hate all the other drivers on the road. I think this is one more controlling issue. They have zero tolerance for incompetence. I think that must be the most common characteristic of all of them. It's like, "Don't be such a wimp. Compared to what I went through you haven't experienced anything."

After my husband retired I became his total control person. In the office he had a lot of girls he told what to do and kept under his surveillance. Now, with the children also gone, I'm it. He's even reorganized my pantry. I can't find anything, but it's perfectly organized. I mean he never had time to really get me straightened out before so now he's reorganized my pantry and it's just wonderful. He also loves going to the grocery store. When he was a prisoner, he would dream of going to the store alone and picking out whatever he wanted. So now that's one of his delights, and he wants to carry the groceries into the house himself. I once said to him, "This makes you happy, doesn't it?"

He said, "Yeah, you know it does."

Another wife, who initially knew little about her husband's war experiences, discovered that going to POW reunions helped him open up:

Wife C: I knew my husband had been a POW, but he didn't talk much about it during our early years. Once the wife of a friend of ours asked him if he had killed anybody in the war. His answer was very evasive. In effect, he said, "I shot at people with a gun" or "I don't know what the gun did; it was the gun's fault." In other words, he blamed it on the gun rather than his having killed people. It wasn't until just a few years ago that he could even say, "Yes, I did kill people," but he is still very uncomfortable with the subject.

I think the turning point for him being willing to talk more openly occurred when we began going to the reunions. He would talk to the other guys, and it branched out from there. But there are still some things he really doesn't talk about.

When asked what advice this wife would give to other spouses of former POWs, she responded with complete candor:

> They have to expect not to get the kind of open love and support they had probably hoped for. I tell my husband, "You're a hard-ass son-of-a-bitch." And he answers me, "That's what I had to be to survive." We are both right. I also would tell these wives that they would not be able to expect the kind of fathering for their children that they might want, but on the other hand I'm making this sound all negative, perhaps because of the question. Certainly there are positive things. I'm not so masochistic that I hung in there for thirty-six years because I love being abused. Before we were ever married he said, "I will never strike you." At the time, that kind of struck me as strange because I was raised in a very close, loving family where I never even heard my parents argue, let alone any kind of physical abuse.
>
> But what has turned out actually to be a blessing for me was that when we were married I really didn't have a great deal of self-esteem. I wasn't a doormat, but I wasn't going to stand up all that much. So, in order to survive, I have become a much stronger person, which I think is generally good, but there are times when I'm afraid that I'm too harsh on other people, much like he is. . . .
>
> The wives I am close to are very open, and we do share things about our husbands. Then when I say something to him about one of his friends he will say, "Oh, he never told me that." It makes you wonder, "What do guys talk about besides the weather?" The wives are very open with each other and aren't afraid to show their emotions. We were in Washington, D.C., with another ex-POW couple, and we visited the women's monument, which I thought was just tremendous. The other wife was so taken by the experience that she left and sat down on a bench by herself. I let her sit a little bit, then I went over to see how she was doing. She just started to cry. She said, "I'm just so over-whelmed with emotion." We could do that kind of sharing, but the men can't.
>
> I have only seen my husband cry once in the almost forty years I have known him. This has really bothered me, and we have talked about it at times. I've asked him, "What would it take to make you cry?" Well, he didn't know. I asked him, "What if I died? Would you cry?" I do think that I am undoubtedly the most important person to him even though he can't express it very well. I know he is very much in love with me. But, he didn't know if he would cry then or not.

As Peggy Himmelheber suggested, many of these wives urgently pushed their husbands to seek the medical and compensatory aid to which they were certainly entitled. In this wife's case, the task was made more difficult because her husband insisted nothing was wrong with him:

Wife A: When we went to a reunion in Washington, D.C., maybe two years before my husband died, there was a lady named Lena Swanson who had made it her cause to know the ins and outs of the government bureaucracy. She had been interviewing a lot of the men who had never received any compensation. She came to the hotel, and one of the guys told my husband, "You ought to go see this lady." He said, "No, I'm fine. I've got a good life, and I don't need any money." Some of these other guys had been receiving compensation for years, but that didn't matter to him. But he did go down and talk to her. He told her, "I don't really have any problems, but these other guys talked me into coming down." She asked him to tell her about where he lived and about the farm. He did. Then she asked him, "Where are the windows in your house?" He looked at her like she was losing it. But he explained that all our windows in the kitchen, dining room, and living room looked out on the driveway. Then she asked, "You don't have any windows that look out on your neighbors, do you?"

He told her, "No, we don't need any on that side."

She said, "You're scared to death that someone is going to attack you, so that's why you don't have any windows."

My husband looked at her like, "Oh, you crazy broad."

When she later interviewed me separately, she said, "This is what these guys do." She was right. On the side of our house facing the neighbors, he had also planted privet hedges that were higher than the house. That was his safety. I don't know if he consciously realized this, but that was the way it was. We were out in the country where chances are you are not going to be hurt. These were all subconscious things, and she told me these were part of his trauma.

Other wives also noticed that their husbands were constantly on the alert for any unwelcome or unexpected intrusions:

Wife C: When my husband goes into a room of people, he likes to position himself in a strategic position for defense. He doesn't want to sit with his back to the door or somewhere where he could be easily cornered.

Wife B: When we go to church he always wants to sit in the back row. I'm sure you've heard from other former POWs how when they go into a restaurant, they sit so that they can have their back to the wall to see what's in front of them.

This wife not only encouraged her husband to go to the VA clinic, but actively supported him in his many battles with the hospital administrators. As she points out, no one knows more about a former prisoner's problems than the person who has to sleep next to him and endure his many nightmares:

Wife D: After the war, the VA Review Board didn't really believe what my husband was telling them, so I said, "You come and live with us, and you'll soon see there's no acting to the way he is." After all these years, I still hear him talking in his sleep. He'll be back in that POW camp. Maybe they've been sneaking out getting a potato or something. He'll say, "Hey, be quiet. They're coming. If they catch us, they'll shoot us." Many a night when he'd start that, I'd just slip out of bed and crawl, not walk, because I was afraid he'd wake up and hit me. If you wake him up suddenly, his good arm can knock you across the room. You don't yell at him when he wakes up. Just last night I thought he was choking, but when I tried to wake him up, he was ready for battle. I have to be very cautious because he's just as scared as I am. But he's much better now than he was before he began to talk openly about his experiences.

Seldom did the wives have the advantage of counseling for themselves; instead, they learned what war and incarceration had done to their husbands mostly from personal experience, from other wives or, in this case, from a book:

Wife C: What actually gave me a lot of understanding about all this was a book I read by Winnie Smith, who was a Vietnam War nurse. In the first half of her *An American Daughter Gone to War*, she describes her experiences in Vietnam, which, of course, were pretty horrible. But in the second half she tells what it was like for her when she came back to this country. She described these feelings that the guys don't talk about. She gave me a lot of insight into their lack of sensitivity. I could better understand when they say, "What are you belly-aching about? It's nothing compared to what I've been through."

According to the wives, most of the former prisoners have been very demanding of their children. Although they are usually very proud of them, they often have difficulty getting too close to them:

Wife C: As a family, we just accepted him the way he was. The way he would treat the kids would grieve me a lot, but I didn't have any great understanding of it at the time. I think as adults the children have grown to have an understanding of him. All of them have been to at least one of the POW conventions. And they've seen the documentary *The POW: Americans in Enemy Hands,* that he is in. That was an eye-opening experience. The film has been shown on national television a number of times, and it ran continuously in the POW museum in Andersonville. So this has helped the kids now as adults, but when they were growing up that understanding wasn't there.

Wife B: Food is very important to my husband, so he always insisted that the kids sit at the table until their plates were clean. I can remember one of our daughters feeding the dog peas one at a time so she could get her plate clean. Of course, I never told on her.

My husband made every effort to be a wonderful father, but he also wants to dominate the children. Our son will be thirty this year and he still likes to call him everyday. I've told him, "That's too much. You're not letting go." And when he was still working, he would call our daughters at least every other day. He's determined not to let go of the children. I have to say to him all the time, "Honey, back off, that's none of your business. If you care about something more than they do, you care too much." We've just had to deal with this, and we are still dealing with it. He has his little area of control and he won't let go.

Several of the wives made a special point of emphasizing positive things they found in their husbands:

Wife C: I really haven't said very much on the positive side, but my husband has been extremely loyal and hard working. I've never had any question about the stability of our marriage or of his caring for me. And I have always known, even with his physical problems, that he will immediately rise to my defense. If I were seriously in danger he would kill in a minute to protect me.

Loyalty is very important to these men. With him there is also this generosity of spirit. Again, it may not include emotions, but it certainly includes acts. I mean, look, he is not in good health and he is still running around the country on the VA advisory board, making a commitment to his fellow POWs. He'll make trips out of town and make long distance phone calls, all at our expense, but I never question this. Of course, this is great for his mental health.

Wife A: He was so happy to have a family and the farm, although there was almost an invisible fence around us all. No one whom my husband didn't want could be there. I don't really know how to explain it, and the kids and I were certainly never captive on the farm, but the farm really became his sheltered world. We had six children, and I think the farm and the kids brought him the most happiness in his life. He felt safe there, and I think he was very happy in our lives together.

Wife B: We've been married forty-four years, and my husband is a wonderful man. He has a fantastic sense of humor, is very intelligent, and he will give me anything I want, although only after arguing with me about it. His counselor seems to think that we have an incredible marriage, and I really do think that we do. I am committed to the man and he to me. And I do think that our religious faith has helped. Sometimes we would be arguing on the way to church, but we've always made it a rule to hold hands during certain parts of the service. When everybody else is praying we hold hands. Even if we're angry we hold hands. Those are silly little rules that help us in times of stress. Always when he came home from work, no matter what the stage of the dinner was, I turned the stove off, shooed the kids out of the room, closed the door, and we talked for fifteen or twenty minutes. He would unload his day and I mine. Then we had a happy evening.

We have a little rug in our laundry room that says it all: "There is a beautiful person who lives here."

Most husbands have great respect for their wives because, as Ray Baumbach explains, without their understanding and support, the men would not have made it:

Our wives are all-important to those of us in trouble. They're the ones that go though it every night. They're the ones who have to listen to the screaming and watch the tears and deterioration, and the depression. They see and feel it more than anybody. Without the wives being involved, you won't get the full story because we don't know the full story. For example, I don't know some of things I do in the middle of the night, but she certainly does.

Charley Davis credits his wife with getting him back on track when disturbing flashbacks resurfaced after his retirement:

After I retired my patience just left me, and I went into a depression and started eating and just sitting around doing nothing. When you lose your focus on working and providing for your family, all those old thoughts come back. My wife started making me get up and do something. It took me quite a while to come out of it and get back to being active. My wife really provided me with guidance. She has helped a lot, and I've heard other guys say the same thing. Without our wives there's no telling where we would be.

Clearly, there were several reasons why the men eventually became more willing to reveal their POW experiences. For many, going to the reunions had a salutary effect. For others, it was meeting an old buddy who had also been a prisoner. For some it was retirement because they now had time on their hands and the memories began to resurface. For Charley Davis it was going to his first reunion:

I guess I started talking to other people in 1983. I went to a Korean Ex-Prisoners of War Association reunion in Columbus, Ohio. My wife was going to go with me, but a friend of ours got sick and she had to take care of her. So I flew up there by myself. I thought, "When I get there I won't know anybody." Well, I checked in and put my luggage in my room. Then I went down to the lobby and looked at these guys. They were all so old. I walked around and didn't know anybody until finally this guy hollered, "Hey Davis!"

I thought, "Well, there's one that knows me, but I don't know him." So he told me his nickname, Long Jack, and I remembered him right off.

He said, "You see anybody in here you know?" When I told me I didn't, he said, "Come on, you know a lot of these guys." So he started putting a name on a face, and the resemblance came back real fast. Talking to those guys made me realize we were experiencing the same kinds of things. Before this, I thought I was an oddball. I had nightmares all the time but didn't remember them. My wife would tell me about them, but I still didn't remember a thing. That bothered me.

Hearing that some of other guys experienced the same thing made me feel a little better. I realized I wasn't crazy.

It took Glenn Reynolds forty-four years before he was willing to talk about his experiences, in part because the military had told him not to. All this changed after he attended a POW session in 1997 at his local VA hospital:

I didn't really open up about any of my experiences until September 1997. I'd get these newsletters about POW and cavalry reunions, but I wouldn't have anything to do with them. I didn't want to go there and be exposed to anyone and have them ask me questions. I just didn't want to face it. My wife finally said to me, "For years you've been getting these notices and you won't go. Let's go this year." I thought the only way to get her to shut up was to go to one. So we went to the POW/MIA Day at the James A. Haley VA Hospital in Tampa. Bob MacLean [see chapter one] was there and he asked me, "Have you been going to the VA for help?"

I said, "I go to the VA as little as I have to. For thirty-three years I didn't even go at all."

Then he said, "I've got a man here I want you to meet." He went out in the hallway and got Dr. Glenn Smith. We talked for a few minutes, but I didn't know who he was. He looked like a guy fresh out of high school. He said, "I'd like to invite you to join our group meetings."

"Meetings on what?" I asked.

Dr. Smith said, "A group of us get together and we talk about general things."

So I said, "Well, I'll try it."

I went down there the next week or so, but Bob wasn't there, and I got to thinking, "Man, I don't know what these guys are up to, but I don't like it." So I turned around and went back home. The next Friday I said to myself, "Well, I'll go back down and eyeball the situation again and see what's going on." I went down and got there early. At nine-thirty they have the American ex-POW support group. So I thought, "Shoot, I'll just go in there and sit down and listen to these guys." I didn't see or hear anything that was harmful. They weren't quizzing the guys or brow-beating them or putting them down or anything. I said, "Well, this is interesting." So I started going on a regular basis. But it was two or three weeks before I'd tell them anything about

244 / REMEMBERED PRISONERS OF A FORGOTTEN WAR

myself. They didn't push. They let everything happen at its own pace. Then Dr. Smith said, "The more you open up and bring this stuff out and talk about it, the easier you'll find it is to deal with it." I think I've only missed two meetings since then.

After I started going to these meetings, one of the guys asked me why I didn't have ex-POW tags on my car. I told him, "You're crazy. I don't want anybody coming up and asking me if I had been a prisoner of war." But I finally decided to do it. My wife drove the car down to the post office, and three or four people told her how surprised they were to discover that I had been a prisoner of war. In small communities everyone knows everything about one another, but not a single soul—even in my own family—knew about my having been a POW until my home county in Kentucky—Pulaski County—was doing a newspaper article on former veterans. So I sat down and wrote about a three-page list of all the things that had happened to me in the military. My daughter typed it up and mailed it out. My son said he had not known anything about his father for thirty-seven years. He didn't know I had been awarded ten Bronze Stars. The response to the news that I had been a POW was very positive. And that made me feel good.

Harley Coon decided to begin talking after listening to a professor's lecture on America's wars that ignored the Korean conflict:

After we returned home, we kept things pretty much bottled up. First there was the guilt of having been captured. There was no honor in becoming a prisoner. As a matter of fact, one senator said it's easier to give up than to fight; of course, he didn't know that after you have to surrender, the fight has just begun. There was also the guilt of burying your buddies over there, wondering why they died and you didn't. So when we came home, we wanted to put our lives back together. We all had obligations to take care of, and we didn't want to bring up such painful memories. We kept it all within ourselves. For maybe thirty years nobody knew I was a prisoner except my family, and I never talked to them about it.

Several years ago, I went to a program at one of the colleges. This history professor was talking about America's wars. He mentioned the Revolutionary War, the Civil War, World Wars I and II and then skipped to Vietnam. He didn't say a thing about Korea. I walked up to him afterward and said, "You know, you forgot one major conflict we've been in."

He asked, "Oh, which one is that?" When I said Korea, he said, "Oh, that was just a police action."

That irritated me. There was more suffering and a higher death rate in the Korean prison camps than in any other American war, including the Civil War.

As the surviving Korean War prisoners have grown older, their myriad physical ailments have predictably worsened. To a certain extent, this is due to the aging process itself, but, without question, their incarceration has played a dominant role in their worsening condition. Dr. Sidney Esensten, who himself continues to suffer repercussions from his time in captivity, describes chronic POW physical, social, and stress-related problems:

Most of the people who came back, and I am talking about the officers because I have seen more of them, had a divorce rate of about 65 percent during the first five years. About the same percentage also had problems with alcohol. I would suspect those statistics are about the same for the enlisted men.

We also suffered permanent physical damage from our time in captivity. I'd like to quote something from Veterans Administration material that compares men who are age forty-four to sixty-four among non-POW veterans and among ex-POWs. In heart disease, 9.7 percent of Americans in that age group would get heart trouble, 25 percent of returning POWs; cancer, 1.3 percent of the normal population, 13 percent among POWs; diabetes, 4.4 percent as compared to 9 percent; ulcers, 4.5 percent as compared to 35 percent; arthritis, 14.8 percent against 20 percent; cirrhosis of the liver caused by malnutrition, there were none in the normal population, but 35 percent of the POWs did. We are now beginning to see some of our POW friends dying of cancer of the liver due to their nutritional cirrhosis. Then, of course, there are irritable bowel problems. Irritable bowels or colitis are stress problems.

In spite of their physical and mental problems, many of the former prisoners tried for years to convince the Veterans' Administration that their long-term health problems could be traced back to their experiences in Korea. Then in 1982 Congress passed a POW bill that allowed the men to take a protocol physical examination to assess their condition. Like so many of the former prisoners, Robert Fletcher, who now works on health issues as a voluntary advocate for the Veterans Administration's National POW Advisory Committee, had initially wanted nothing to do with the VA:

As I got older my body started to deteriorate. I never went to the VA hospital because I didn't think I was allowed to. I thought the VA was for World War veterans. I was not a World War veteran. I was in a police action, and the VA says nothing about police actions. So I never went to the VA hospital until 1983 when I had that protocol exam. At the time, they told me as a former POW I was entitled to this. I asked, "Where in the hell did all this stuff come from?" In 1982 Congress passed POW Bill 9757. You had to have been a POW for thirty days to qualify for its benefits. At the time, I told them, "Nah, don't bother me. I got Blue Cross/Blue Shield. I don't need a handout from you people."

But I did make an appointment. I had become diabetic. I had thought diabetes was hereditary, but my doctor told me, "It doesn't have to be; food and stress can play a role. If you were under stress for a long period of time, you may not be immediately affected, but later your body can show signs of diabetes." Then I started having trouble with my knee. In 1987, the VA took X rays and decided to give me 10 percent disability. I told them, "You can keep your ten percent. I don't want any money. I just want to make sure it's on my record so if I need hospital care they won't make me pay the bill. Then my shoulders started bothering me, and by 1989 both knees were bad. Oh, man, I could hardly walk. The doctor told me, "Oh, yeah, you got arthritis really bad. We're going to have to replace your knees. You don't have any cartilage left in either one of them."

When I later went for a checkup at the Ann Arbor VA, I told the doctor, who also taught at the university, "I want you to sit down and listen to me clearly." You see, I was the patient telling the doctor. So we sat down and I said, "Doc, you can see by my records I'm a former prisoner of war. Do you understand what I went through?"

He said, "No."

I said, "Can I explain to you because maybe this has something to do with my physical makeup right now?"

He said, "Sure." So I told him.

He then said, "All your joints are bad. We know during your teen years that your body builds up your joints for old age, but now you have nothing in reserve, and you will never be able to restore them. If at the time they had put you on high doses of vitamins for about two years, you might have compensated and gained something. But we didn't know that back in the fifties."

So he wrote up a progress note and told me to take it to my service officer. I sent it in, but those guys said, "No, no, no; that doctor is speculating. He doesn't know what's happening." So we appealed to Washington. I had gotten on the advisory board in 1991, so I went to a guy there and talked to him. After he got a copy of my entire medical record, he told me that they had erred as far back as 1987. He said, "We're going to make this up." So they did and my disability became 100 percent.

Everybody but Congress says if anyone can verify he was a POW, he should get 100 percent disability. We've had four bills in front of Congress, but they say, "Oh, that's too much money." John McCain didn't support us, but he is rich. Once you've made it on your own you just don't look back.

I'm now with the VA POW Advisory Board in Washington, D.C. We're a two-fold organization. One part is medical and the other is what they call technical. The medical end is more important to us than anything else. We have found that there are twenty presumptive ill-nesses that POWs and only POWs can have. We helped establish those twenty. We also look at how former POWs are faring. As a rep, I'm in the field for three or four days at a time. Sometimes I just listen and get a feel for the guys and their complaints. Then I'll go back and say, "I'm hearing this from a lot of veterans. They are going to the VA hospitals, and they're being treated like this." And sometimes the big boys will say, "Well, we need to look into that."

Bill Ashworth, who is now confined to a wheelchair, becomes very emotional when discussing his frustrating battles with the VA:

I have a lot of vascular problems. That's why I'm in this wheelchair. In 1987 they did a bypass on my right leg. It didn't help. My left leg is paralyzed from a stroke so I can't walk at all. I also have the loss of use in one hand. So I have lost the use of three extremities.

I had never had a physical before I went into the service or before I got out. In the early 1980s I did go for a physical at the VA in Little Rock. They kept me there about a week. For about six weeks I didn't hear from them. Then I got a letter stating I was to receive 40 percent disability for PTSD, awarded retroactively. That amounted to sixty-three dollars and fifty cents a month. My health kept getting worse and worse, and I fought and fought with them. In 1986 I took the POW Protocol Physical. I spent less than fifteen minutes with two doctors in Oklahoma City before they turned me down for additional aid. One was a female doctor, and she just ran us through like we were a herd of cattle. There was also another psychiatrist up there who was just about as bad. He spent five minutes with one guy and told him he was finished with him. But the guy told him, "Well, I'm not through with you, and he refused to leave." The doctor had to call in security. They'd ask us about the president and what's the theory behind people living in glass houses not throwing rocks. They never asked us about our experiences.

I appealed and went to the regional office in Muskogee for a hearing. They asked me if I would be willing to go into the hospital for several days for an examination and evaluation. I told them I sure would. So on February 10, 1986, I went into the hospital in Oklahoma City. I got out eighteen days later. What helped me in Oklahoma City was a doctor who was a World War II veteran. He wrote me a very good letter, including describing my stroke and all my other problems. He wrote everything should be classified as service-connected. The regional office had written there was no reason why I wasn't gainfully employed. Finally, I got a letter in July of 1986 that raised my disability to 100 percent. But I want to emphasize, the VA didn't give me anything. I earned it.

Over the years Jack Browning has suffered excruciating pain from a wide range of physical problems:

Almost fifty years have passed, and the pain gets progressively worse. Many mornings I wake up hurting so bad I literally cry until I can get medication to ease the pain. The thing that most bothers me is eating salty foods. It doesn't take ten minutes until I start burning. Just as soon as it gets into the bloodstream I know it.

The POWs who spent long periods of time in captivity call what we have the Don't-Care Disease. It causes depression. You don't care if the world comes to an end. Depression without end. You have to force yourself to do everything. You no longer care about the interests you once had—or about much of anything else. You don't want to be around crowds of people. You find it hard to trust anyone you don't know really well. You find it hard to concentrate, and you feel irritable. Then there are the sleepless nights.

I awoke one night and couldn't move a muscle. There was no roof on our hut. I could see the sky clearly, and the stars were shining bright. It appeared we had been hit by a rocket from a fighter plane. My entire body was in a state of shock, or addled from concussion. Part of the side of the building was blown out and smoking. It was so vivid. I lay there several seconds; then I really woke up. Even though it was a nightmare that first occurred over forty years ago, it is still just as real today as it was then. These relentless nightmares come and go. They always start with a battle. I'm fighting as hard as I can, seemingly in slow motion, and I can never advance. I always get captured or shot. It seems if I don't wake up, my breath is being taken from me and I'll die. My wife has awakened me many times over the years while I'm in that state. I have struck her in my sleep, thinking I'm fighting North Koreans. I don't see how she has tolerated me for forty years.

There is no satisfactory way to end these stories, because the men themselves have seldom achieved closure. Some remain angry and bitter, especially about accusations of collaboration. Others are more introspective or simply endure as best they can. A few insist they are better men for the experience, although none wants to repeat any part of captivity. Then there are those like Meung H. Kim, who, shunning the outside world, withdrew first into the bottle, and then into himself:

I hardly saw a sober day in the service after I got back. I'd be right in front of the commanding officer with a bottle of whiskey, and I'd say, "Hey, have a drink with me." He would just look at me and shake his head and walk away. They wouldn't release me from the Army because I was a prisoner of war and maybe they kind of felt sorry for me. The problem was they were supposed to take care of me. After I got out, I drank a little bit more; then after fifteen years I just gave it up. I quit entirely because I couldn't take it anymore.

I did go to one or two POW reunions, but the guys irritated me. They would all talk about their experiences. Some of them made themselves look like heroes. That kind of bugged me because I know exactly what went on, so I vowed never to go back. I became a solitary man. I don't want to bother anybody. I just hide myself on my property.

James Dick is still so angry about his Korean War experiences that it affects his judgment in all kinds of situations:

> I asked myself, "Was this the America I fought for—the America I shed my blood for? I get so mad sometimes, and I can't give you the reasons, but I tell the person I'm talking to, "If I had to do it over I would turn my gun the other way." I'm all the time making such statements. For example, when some work has been done on my automobile, and the guy is trying to hold me up and I know it, I tell him, "Sir, I would rather be held up by a gun anytime than with a pencil. It takes guts with a gun; with a pencil, it doesn't any take guts."
>
> After I came back, I realized that some of the things they told me about the United States of America are true. Then, I was a young, completely brainwashed greenhorn, and you couldn't tell me anything because I thought, and I still think, that America is the greatest country on earth. But I have to be honest, I don't like my political system. When a man can be a draft-dodger and achieve what a lot of our draft-dodgers have achieved, and I'm not just talking about Clinton, I'm talking about Newt Gingrich, Dan Quayle, Pat Buchanan, Jack Kemp, and I don't know how many more that want the goodies of this country but who weren't ready to lay down their lives for it.

After returning home, Capt. Louis Rockwerk was reduced in rank for striking a superior officer who accused all Korean War POWs of being collaborators. Rockwerk admits he became terribly bitter and cynical about his Korean experiences until, much to his surprise, a few years ago he attended his first reunion, and several of his former soldiers presented him with a plaque in gratitude for what he had done to keep them alive both in battle and in the prison camps:

> What I resent most of all is that nobody, and I'm talking about the president of the United States, a former general, stood up and said, "Hey, these guys are American boys and they fought in Korea, and they fought the best they could. Yes, some of them were collaborators, but don't paint them all with that brush." Nobody said a thing. Nobody spoke in our defense.
>
> The only people concerned about the Korean War have been the veterans themselves and their families. All the rest don't care. They don't want to know what we went through. My experiences in Korea probably ruined my life. Instead of the happy-go-lucky young fellow I

was when I left for Korea, I guess I ended up somewhat of a grouch. I'm hard-headed. I'm telling you what my family tells me. We didn't break up. Oh no, we're a strong family and I'm glad for that.

I stayed in the military until 1963. Under other circumstances I would have stayed until I was a hundred years old. I retired as a major because I had earlier been reduced in rank for hitting a superior officer. He wanted to know why all of us prisoners were collaborators. If it weren't for the friends I had in the service, I wouldn't have been permitted to continue my career. Look, you don't, under any circumstance, strike a senior officer. I know I was wrong, and I know in the heat of the moment I lost my temper. It was very easy for me to lose my temper at that time. I don't blame the service for that. I deserve what I got, and I appreciate the fact that I wasn't totally bounced.

I was stunned when the men from our company honored me at a reunion several years ago. I thought, as their commanding officer, they had blamed me for everything. So I didn't go to the gatherings, but one of the medics in my company found me and prevailed upon me to attend. I said to myself, "Well, I've got to face up to it sooner or later." I told my wife, "Don't expect this to be a beautiful thing. They may not even want to talk to me." We went there and everything changed. If I had known how they felt forty years earlier, my life would have been very different.[6]

Irv Langell, who survived the Tiger Death March, acknowledges that his POW experience molded him in certain immutable ways:

Having been a prisoner made me the person I am today. After I came back I was always told that I was a hard taskmaster. I had very few friends. I was a loner. I'm still a loner except with my family and the few friends that I have around the country. When I have friends, I have real friends. They are right down the line. The rest of the people I could give a shit for. As soon as I meet somebody, I size them up. I ask myself, "Would he be alive today if he went through the same thing we did?"

I look back and I ask myself, "How in hell did we survive?" The winter of 1950 in Korea was one of the coldest in history. What did we have? Very little clothing. How did we live? We huddled and cuddled. We scraped by and when somebody died, his clothes were fair game. That's the way it was. Those were the facts of life. What you have in your head had a lot to do with it. I guess it kind of reminds me of today. From the neck up, I'm sixteen years old. From the neck down, forget it. The thoughts are still there and the mind is still willing, but the body has gone to hell. My body went to hell in Korea, but my mind was saying, "You can keep going; it's going to get better, it's going to get better."

Wayman Simpson, who was another Tiger survivor, remains angry with those who still insist the Korean War POWs were somehow lacking in character and courage:

It's a bunch of hooey that the Korean War POWs were somehow different from those in World War II. Sometimes I even run into this at our POW meetings. We've got two guys who were on the Bataan Death March. They think they are the only two guys in the world who ever did anything. I finally blew up and told them, "We got treated far worse than you people did, and our death toll was higher. I spent three years and eight months in World War II, most of them on the frontlines. Then five years later I went to Korea and got captured. You had it bad, I had it bad. Every prisoner had it bad. Some had it worse than others. Some had it longer than others. So why are you the only ones who really had it bad? You're crazy." They don't talk to me much anymore.

Rubin Townsend profanely agrees with Wayman Simpson that those who were not there forfeit their right to pass judgment on the Korean War POWs:

To those who are critical of how the prisoners acted, I say, "Bullshit! Get yourself in that position and see how strong you are." Seeing your fellow prisoners die and having to bury them in some little shallow grave was terrible. I know from talking to those who were prisoner a lot longer than I was that it was tougher than you can imagine. I never would condemn any prisoner unless he did something to hurt his fellow prisoners. That's where I draw the line.

On the other hand, there are those former prisoners, like Harley Coon, who insist they did manage to take something positive from the experience:

Being a POW is something I don't want to go through again, but it probably made a better person out of me. I learned to understand people and that things can be a whole lot worse than what they are. I know we all have to face challenges and problems in our lives. One of the biggest lessons I've learned is what freedom is really all about. We talk about freedom in school, but until you lose it you never really understand what it's all about. It's not just going to school or getting a job; it's that you are free to do with your life whatever you want. If you disagree with what the government does, you can stand up and say so without worrying about being executed.

Dr. Sidney Esensten also believes that in spite of the many physical and psychological challenges he and his fellow prisoners have had to endure, he came out of his experience a better man:

Personally, my problems have been stress, migraine headaches, and nightmares. I'm getting better now that I'm getting more mature [Laughs; he was seventy-five at the time]. I used to have a lot more problems than I do now, but I still have nightmares two or three times a week. Otherwise, I hate to say it, but I learned a lot in prison camp. The first thing I learned is that people do not survive in this world as individuals. The second thing is when I talk to other doctors or to my patients, I tell them that psychiatrists see people when they have gone over the edge psychologically and are then trying to get better. I have an advantage over them because I've dealt with people as they were going from normal to abnormal and then back to normal again. I can handle their stress problems because I tell them, "I've been there. I understand stress, I understand fear." This makes it a little easier for them to talk to me. They understand, "Gee, he's had the same problems."

Charley Davis also took some positive lessons from his time in captivity:

I learned a lot being a POW. Everything was not negative. It was an experience for which I would not take any money—nor would I take any money to be a POW again. I learned many things that I had taken for granted that I didn't have while I was a prisoner. I learned to appreciate the small things we have like lights, heat, and running water. When I came back I accepted these things as gifts more than as something that are just out there. I also learned to have patience because as a prisoner I couldn't get impatient. I wasn't going anywhere. I didn't know how long I was going to be there. I thought about it, but then after a while I just sort of put it out of my mind and said, "Well, I just have to take it day by day and see how it's going to go." I knew one day I would get out, but I didn't know when. I had to be very patient. Above all, I learned to respect freedom. You don't understand freedom until you lose yours.

Who should have the final word, but the former prisoners themselves? With this in mind, I have arbitrarily selected five final quotations that capture the essence of what it meant to have been a prisoner during and after the Korean War:

I've been accused of being paranoid, of seeing a Communist behind every bush. I often say I got my Ph.D. in Communism at the University of North Korea, starving to death on the banks of the beautiful Yalu River while overlooking the barren mountains of Manchuria. It was a three-year course.

—Jack Browning

We could have done better in terms of looking after each other, but I never saw mass collaboration. That's just a lot of baloney. But we were reduced to being nothing but bloody damn animals—or worse. Under those conditions, I don't think we did so badly.

—Michael Cornwell

If they could leave me the way I was before I went over to Korea, they could have all their disability money back.

—Robert Blewitt

Any prisoner of war who survived is a tremendous person. I don't care what war he was in or what camp or how long he was imprisoned. Every one of them is a top priority in my life.

—Jerry Morgan

Three of the men I knew better than anybody in the whole prison—Raymond Baylis, Louis Turner, and John L. Sullivan—all three of them are now dead. They were my three closest buddies. We used to play cards together. I guess I'm holding up the game. I visit them at Arlington, and that's where I'm going to end up one of these days.

—Robert Jones

POSTSCRIPT

It is an awesome responsibility to tell someone else's story. While interviewing a group of former Korean War POWs at the James A. Haley Veterans' Hospital in Tampa, Florida, I candidly told them, "Given our country's collective amnesia about the Korean War, I'm not sure how much interest there will be for this book. I hope people will read it, but I'm not at all sure they will." Bob MacLean, whose story begins chapter one, interrupted and said, "That's all right. We'll read it." I hope they do, and I hope they are not disappointed.

BILL J. ASHWORTH

Bill Ashworth, who was captured by the Chinese on November 26, 1950, has endured excruciating physical and emotional difficulties over the years. He has also suffered serious problems with alcoholism and antisocial behavior and is now confined to a wheelchair, where he only has full use of one hand. When talking about his experiences he continuously breaks down into convulsive sobs. Yet it took him and his fourth wife, who is a nurse, years before they could convince the Veterans Administration to classify him as fully disabled. Of his battle for benefits, Bill Ashworth says, "The VA didn't give me anything. I earned it. I think if some of those people in government ever walked a mile in our shoes, they might act differently."

RICHARD M. BASSETT

Richard Bassett is a deeply religious, retired high school history teacher who has been profoundly affected by his years of incarceration. Captured on October 6, 1951, after conditions had generally improved, Bassett managed to keep his New Testament with him after capture, but it was eventually confiscated when he began holding regular worship services among the POWs. He even preached at a Christmas service in Camp Five in 1952. While convalescing after his return from Korea, Bassett wrote down everything he could recall about his experiences, and he remembered even the smallest details. His memoir, *And The Wind Blew Cold*, is being published by Kent State University Press.

RAY BAUMBACH

Ray Baumbach, who earned a Silver and Bronze Star as well as three Purple Hearts in Korea, escaped three times while being marched north after he was captured in February 1951. The first two escapes were unsuccessful, but the third time he made it back to the U.N. lines, where he fell upon his knees, kissed the soil, and promised God that he would one day repay Him—and he has. Baumbach now works as a lay minister, talking in schools and to veterans' groups, but his main mission is to prison inmates where he tries to make them understand life can improve and that they can become better human beings. Growing up one of thirteen children with a supportive mother, an alcoholic father, and very little food helped Baumbach prepare for tough times, but nothing could erase the horrors of captivity. After repatriation, Baumbach had problems with alcohol and readjusting to civilian life before turning his life around with his decision to help others.

ROBERT BLEWITT

Bob Blewitt always rejected authority, whether in the fast and dangerous streets of West Philadelphia, in combat, or in an oppressive Communist prison camp. For Blewitt, life was an adventure to be attacked. Not surprisingly, his Chinese captors branded him a Reactionary. Blewitt was the kind of fearless soldier and prisoner that movie directors love, but he paid a price for his irrepressible actions. After his liberation, he could not understood why his own military diagnosed him as psychologically disturbed. In fact, he may still be in denial, although he now receives 100 percent disability, primarily for PTSD. Blewitt's fourth wife is now trying to write his life story.

JACK BROWNING

Jack Browning's background was typical of those who served as foot soldiers and became prisoners in Korea. He was born in hardscrabble Harlan County, Kentucky, where his father was a miner. Life was so difficult that when he was fifteen, his mother signed him off as seventeen so he could join the service. He was only seventeen when he was captured on July 8, 1950, six days after arriving in Korea, near the small town of Ch'ŏnan. Browning, who survived the Tiger Death March, later wrote an unpublished memoir of his experiences.

H. R. "BOB" CARMAN

Lt. Bob Carman, who worked as a test pilot after the war, flew F-84 jets in Korea. He was flying his forty-fifth mission when he was shot down and captured in late 1951. He was interrogated in the notorious Pak's Palace before being sent to Camp Two, where he and his fellow prisoners took a special delight in tormenting their guards and disrupting the system. Unlike most former prisoners, Carman insists he suffered no long-term effects from his Korean War experiences.

AKIRA CHIKAMI

A Nisei and former professional boxer who is still feisty, Akira Chikami served in both World War II and Korea. Sergeant Chikami used determination, humor, and an ability to put on his captors to survive his incarceration. He ended up in Camp Twelve near P'yŏngyang, which was a special re-education camp for prisoners the Chinese hoped would cooperate, but many of these men, including Chikami, did not, although they would be so accused after repatriation. Chikami himself was investigated for three years after he returned, before being cleared of allegations made by individuals he did not even know.

HARLEY COON

Harley Coon is a well organized, intelligent, and perceptive individual who has held executive positions in several veteran and ex-POW organizations. Based on his personal observations and research, Coon insists that more than 75 percent of those captured between early July and the end of December 1950 did not survive. Coon, who has spent considerable time and effort eliminating impostors from various veteran organizations, also warns that too many of the ex-POWs now consider themselves heroes, or, at the very least, Reactionaries.

MICHAEL C. CORNWELL

Michael Cornwell began as an enlisted man in Korea and ended up a lieutenant colonel after twenty years in the Army. Although Cornwell despised those prisoners who jeopardized the well-being of other prisoners, he bears no animosity toward several of the twenty-one Americans who chose to go to China rather than be repatriated. Although Cornwell admits that discipline was not always what it might have been, he maintains that American prisoners did not behave as badly as their critics have suggested. A very resilient and self-confident individual, Cornwell insists he suffered no aftereffects from his captivity, but also admits he would have killed himself rather than have been taken prisoner in Vietnam, where he also served.

ROBERT "BOB" COURY

Col. Bob Coury retired from the U.S. Air Force in 1974 after being one of the very few pilots to fly in World War II, Korea, and Vietnam. He also flew the Berlin Airlift. Coury was a twenty-nine-year-old captain flying an F-86 in Korea when he was shot down and captured on June 10, 1953, just a couple hundred yards short of his own lines. As a prisoner, Coury was not overtly mistreated, although he tried to escape at his first opportunity. Coury, who was extensively interrogated, readily admits that every man has his breaking point. In spite of the passage of more than fifty years, Coury, who tells his story with a detached objectivity, has almost total recall of the events surrounding his incarceration.

JIM CROMBIE

Jim Crombie, who was captured April 25, 1951, spent two difficult months marching north before ending up in Camp Five. Crombie, who practiced his religion even before going into battle, credits faith and good friends for his survival. After his liberation he spent a year in a TB hospital, before becoming a top corporate accountant. However, in 1980 during the Iranian hostage crisis, he admitted getting "very jumpy" and needing help when all his prison memories came flooding back.

PHILIP CROSBIE (CIVILIAN)

Father Philip Crosbie was a young Australian missionary priest in South Korea when he was captured during the first days of the war. He was one of the strongest of the civilians on the Tiger Death March, and he did much to help the others survive. While incarcerated in Ujang, he wrote down his experiences, but because he was unable to smuggle out his notes, he rewrote his story after his liberation in 1953. *March Till They Die* was published in Dublin, Ireland, by Browne & Nolan in 1955. An American edition was published the following year by Newman Press.

CHARLES DAVIS

When Charley Davis was captured on November 4, 1950, he fully expected the Chinese to kill him because earlier his unit had discovered executed American GIs. Then, shortly after his capture he saw three other prisoners led away, after which he heard shots. During the re-education sessions in Camp Five, Davis developed the ability to look at a person and not hear a word he was saying. After returning home he continued to show little or no emotion, even when faced with the death of a friend or loved one. Davis also refused to talk to anybody about his experiences until he attended his first reunion and his former prisoner buddies urged him to open up. Davis is presently a senior vice commander of the Greater Tampa Bay Chapter, American Ex-POWs.

PHILIP DEANE (CIVILIAN)

Philip Deane was the pen name for Gerassimos Svoronos-Gigantes. Born in Greece and educated in England, Deane was a war correspondent for the *London Observer* when captured. A Tiger Death March survivor, he later published two books about his experiences: *I Was a Captive in Korea* (New York: Norton, 1953) and *I Should Have Died* (Don Mills, Ontario: Longman Canada, 1976).

JAMES H. DICK

James H. Dick is a very perceptive but cynical individual who willingly speaks out on a wide variety of issues. He loves his country but is very angry with the government and politicians. He is especially bitter about the FBI harassing him for years after he returned to the States. Like so many of these survivors, he tends to be a loner. Dick amuses himself by circling the obituary names in the monthly *Ex-POW Bulletin,* noting that few of his fellow prisoners have made it to seventy years of age.

WALTER "JACK" DOERTY

Jack Doerty, who served in World War II, Korea, and Vietnam before retiring as a full-bird Air Force colonel, knows the role of chance in a prisoner's survival, and readily admits good fortune was on his side. However, he was also a very determined individual who twice attempted to escape, once while on a march and once from Camp Two. The second time he stayed out for five days before being recaptured. He was also interrogated in the notorious Pak's Palace outside of P'yŏngyang.

JEFF ERWIN

Jeff Erwin was a second lieutenant artillery officer when captured the day after Thanksgiving in 1950. Although he insists he hasn't suffered mentally, he is now on 100 percent physical disability. Erwin was one of those prisoners singled out for special indoctrination sessions. While in Camp Twelve he and others were coerced into signing a declaration addressed to the United Nations stating that the United States had started the war and that the U.N. should stop it. Erwin later testified that when their captors threatened to cut off their food unless they signed the declaration, his colonel told them, "Now is no time or place to be a hero." After repatriation the U.S. Army court-martialed Erwin for making statements disloyal to the United States, but he was found not guilty and returned to active duty.

SIDNEY ESENSTEN

Dr. Sidney Esensten worked as a medical doctor in the prison camps in Korea, and he continued to practice medicine until he retired in 1999 at age seventy-six. In the camps he faced the daunting challenge of keeping men alive without proper facilities and little or no medicine. Over the past fifteen years, Dr. Esensten has written extensively about his personal experiences and on "the chronic effects of POW life on former prisoners." In spite of his first-hand understanding of the POW experience, or perhaps because of it, Dr. Esensten admits that he still suffers nightmares three or four times a week.

WILBERT "SHORTY" ESTABROOK

After he retired from the U.S. Army in 1970, Wilbert "Shorty" Estabrook founded an organization called the Tiger Survivors, members of which include both the civilians and soldiers who were on the Tiger Death March. Estabrook also publishes a newsletter and organizes reunions that benefit not only the survivors, but also the families of those prisoners who lost their lives during or after the Tiger Death March. Without his resolute efforts much of this story would have been lost, and the survivors would not have the support system that now exists.

HARRY T. FALCK

A veteran of World War II and Korea, Harry Falck was a career soldier who in retirement has carefully tried to reconstruct his days as a prisoner. He has collected articles, books, maps, and photographs that he willingly shares. One of his most candid observations is how hardened he became to suffering and even death because of his experiences as a POW. While in Camps Three and Five, he tried to keep his sense of humor by baiting the guards, but nothing helped when he had to force-feed his fellow prisoners, or when he had to bury them when his efforts failed.

ROBERT FLETCHER

Robert Fletcher is an energetic, open, feisty, sixty-nine-year-old retired public service worker who now raises chickens on a farm outside of Ann Arbor. He is also a student of the Korean War. He fought with the all black 24th Regiment, originally known as the Buffalo Soldiers, whose members also had to fight against claims that in the heat of battle they had quit and run. As a POW, Fletcher was considered a Reactionary by his captors; yet, when he returned home the military labeled him a security risk, perhaps because he had considerable understanding for those prisoners who reacted less than heroically in the face of extreme hunger and hopeless conditions. Fletcher now volunteers his time on the VA's National POW Advisory Committee as an advocate for former POWs seeking recognition and compensation for what they have endured during and after incarceration. Fletcher also appears in a documentary entitled *P.O.W.: Americans in Enemy Hands: World War II, Korea, and Vietnam* (Arnold Shapiro Productions).

WILLIAM H. FUNCHESS

Lt. William H. Funchess spent 1,038 days in captivity. One of his remarkable achievements was to write down the names of some one hundred prisoners who had either died, been killed, or were missing. He then smuggled this list out of Camp Two in a fountain pen. In 1997, after his granddaughter and her classmates admitted they had never heard of the Korean War, he wrote a self-published, 135-page memoir of his experiences entitled *Korean P.O.W.: A Thousand Days of Torment*. About his book, parts of which appear in chapter four, Funchess writes, "I stayed with the truth and avoided exaggeration. I figured the truth about the Communist mistreatment of U.S. POWs was sufficiently horrible."

ROY H. HARDAGE

Oklahoma-born Roy Hardage was captured on November 29, 1950, by the Chinese near the Chosin Reservoir and spent time in Camps One and Three, before being released during Operation Big Switch on August 20, 1953. Military authorities suggested Hardage write down his POW experiences in October 1954 while he was convalescing in a military hospital. What he wrote certainly refutes the critics who blamed personal shortcomings for the POWs' physical problems, alleged collaboration, and high death rate. Perhaps because of his eighth-grade education and his earthy prose, military officials unfortunately paid little attention to his account. Hardage died in 1984, but his sister, Daisy Lawrence, sent along his memoir with the words, "I am grateful that someone remembers that there was a Korean War, and that it touched a lot of lives."

BILLY JOE HARRIS

Billy Joe Harris experienced the hard times of the Depression in rural Missouri. He describes himself as a "tough, old Missouri country boy." He thought he could handle whatever came along, but that was before he became a prisoner of war. By his own admission, what happened in Korea was more than he could handle by himself. After witnessing so much death and suffering, he credits a higher being with getting him through his crucible. Harris agrees that during tough times people normally do pull together, but his experiences in Korea far exceeded anything normal. With life hanging by a thread because of starvation and disease, Harris argues it became every man for himself, with good works having little to do with survival.

VALDER "VAL" JOHN

Val John's 24th Division was almost totally destroyed before he was captured during the first month of the war. He spent more than three months being marched northward, with stops in Seoul, where he received special attention because he was an American Indian, and P'yŏngyang. Conditions were appalling. Of the more than 370 prisoners who ended up with him in Seoul, the majority did not survive. They died in Seoul, on the march to P'yŏngyang, on the train to Sunch'ŏn, and in the Sunch'ŏn Tunnel Massacre. John survived the massacre because he pretended to be dead when the guards moved through the corpses, striking them with their rifle butts or poking them with bayonets. After his rescue, John spent eighteen months in Brooks Army Medical Center. Then, in 1954, he offered to return to Korea to help military authorities search for the bodies of those killed on the marches and in the Sunch'ŏn Tunnel Massacre. Nevertheless, John, like so many of his fellow prisoners, came under suspicion after he returned home, which certainly contributed to the difficulties he had adjusting to civilian life. He experienced problems with alcohol and social relationships before therapy sessions with former POWs and a successful second marriage turned his life around.

WAYNE JOHNSON

"Johnnie" Johnson was an eighteen-year-old infantryman when captured on July 6, 1950. As he was marched northward, he began keeping a list of names of those who died or were killed by their North Korean or Chinese captors. Amazingly, the U.S.

Army initially showed no interest in his list so he kept it to himself until 1989 when he attended his first ex-POW reunion. Eventually the Army did award Johnson the Silver Star, and in January of 1997 *Reader's Digest* published his story for the American people.

ROBERT JONES

Even by POW standards, Robert Jones's story is extraordinary. Suffering severe frostbite, the ravages of beriberi, and an infection from battlefield wounds, Jones was moved to the back room of Camp Five's so-called hospital, which was where the attendants put the dying. He was then thrown into a ditch where they buried the dead, but he miraculously survived. Jones was also operated on twice by his captors. The first time the doctors implanted a chicken liver; the second time a pig's liver, to absorb the poison in his body. Neither worked.

HOMER A. JURGENS

Homer Jurgens was a college student when the Army Reserves recalled him to active duty. He was fighting with the 2nd Infantry Division when they were overrun by Chinese troops in what came to be called the May Massacre of 1951. Seven days after his capture he escaped while being marched northward. Four days later he reached American lines.

MEUNG HO KIM

Meung Ho Kim is a Korean American from Hawaii who also served four years in World War II. Due to his ancestry, he was tortured by both the Chinese and the North Koreans. Because he spoke Korean, he could have possibly escaped during the marches, but he chose to stay and help the other wounded prisoners. Since his liberation Kim has led a troubled life. He remained in the Army but was constantly in trouble and even court-martialed. He became an alcoholic, endured two unsuccessful marriages, and suffered terrible flashbacks. He finally withdrew completely into himself. "I became a solitary man," he says. "I don't want to bother anybody. I just hide myself on my property."

GENE N. LAM

Capt. Gene Lam was the battalion surgeon for the 9th Infantry, 2nd Division. He arrived in Korea August 3, 1950, and was captured by the Chinese on December 1, 1950. He estimates that only about 50 percent of the approximately 1,200 2nd Division men who were captured at a Chinese roadblock near Kunu-ri survived. Lam believes that many individual deaths could have been prevented with better leadership, stronger discipline, an enhanced will to live, and a basic knowledge of how to protect and heal the body and mind when experiencing extremely adverse conditions. After repatriation, Lam remained in the service and wrote and lectured extensively about his experiences. He died on December 10, 1997, but his widow, June-Marie Lam, made available relevant letters, articles, and lectures.

IRV LANGELL

Irv Langell remains a tough, cantankerous, angry, but insightful Tiger Death March survivor who, in his words, doesn't "take any shit off of anybody." He was in and out of trouble in the service and was just as incorrigible as a prisoner. Langell had just turned nineteen when he was captured on July 11, 1950, only seven days after landing in Korea. He fought with the 24th Division, 21st Infantry, which faced overwhelming numbers at Choch'iwŏn. Langell believes the training his unit received in Japan was good, but he is sharply critical of the inadequate weapons he and his fellow soldiers had in combat.

ROBERT MACLEAN

Bob MacLean is a profane, witty, outspoken individual who spends much of his time as an unpaid volunteer at the Haley VA Hospital in Tampa, Florida, where he encourages former servicemen to come in for evaluation, counseling, and care. MacLean, who after fifty-one years finally was awarded the Purple Heart, also helps veterans apply for disability compensation. As a prisoner, MacLean so often annoyed his Chinese captors they assigned him to Squad Nine in Camp One, a special unit for incorrigible prisoners. After he beat up a guard, the Chinese sentenced MacLean to five years in solitary confinement. They also told him he would be sent to China to serve his sentence. MacLean, who is presently the commander of the Greater Tampa Bay Chapter, American Ex-POWs, has strong opinions on many subjects, and especially on the collective amnesia Americans have concerning the Korean War.

JERRY MORGAN

Jerry Morgan served in World War II, Korea, and Vietnam. After his capture on November 27, 1950, he ended up in Camps Four and Five. Morgan reports his ten-man squad did not lose a man from the day of capture to repatriation. He argues that his fellow African Americans were better able to withstand the rigors of imprisonment than their white counterparts because they worked harder at pulling together. Blacks were segregated in the permanent camps, as they were in the military in Korea and even on the ship coming home, although President Truman had ordered the military to desegregate in 1948. Morgan is presently commander of his local ex-POW chapter in Vero Beach, Florida, where he also does considerable volunteer work for church and school groups.

LLOYD W. PATE

Lloyd Pate was only sixteen when he was captured on January 1, 1951. After the Chinese moved him from Camp Five to Camp Three, he became the leader of a Reactionary squad. His various anti-Chinese activities resulted in a one-year sentence at hard labor. Two years after his repatriation, he told his story in *Reactionary!* (New York: Harper & Brothers, 1955). Pate is currently revising his story, which he plans to self-publish under the title *Reactionary, Revised 2000*. Pate served as president of the Korean POW Association in 1997 and 1998.

DON POIROT

Sergeant Don Poirot, who was captured by the Chinese on February 13, 1951, escaped during the march northward only to be recaptured and sent to Camps Five and Two. After his repatriation he spend twenty-one months in an Army hospital with tuberculosis. Over the years his health has steadily deteriorated, and when interviewed was suffering the effects of Parkinson's disease. A few years ago he wrote a memoir for his children, parts of which appear in his narrative.

GLENN REYNOLDS

Kentucky-born Glenn Reynolds is a superb, intelligent storyteller who is blessed with a near photographic memory. He also earned ten Bronze Stars during his nine months at the front before he was captured on May 14, 1951. He ended up in Camps Five and Two, where he came under suspicion when South Korean prisoners addressed him as "captain" because he had earlier served as an adviser to their unit. After he was liberated, American military authorities told him not to discuss his captivity with anyone. Reynolds told no one, not even his family, about his prison experiences until 1997, when he attended his first POW meeting at his local VA hospital.

LOUIS N. ROCKWERK

Uncompromising, opinionated, and cynical, Louis Rockwerk was captured on November 4, 1950. Then a U.S. Army captain, Rockwerk asserts that he worked hard to train his men to be soldiers, but he nevertheless took personal responsibility for the capture and deaths of his men when they were left exposed by what he considers incompetent field grade officers and their retreating troops. For years he felt guilty for not having done more to protect his men. Then, at a 24th Division reunion in the early nineties, his surviving men gave him a plaque in gratitude for what he had done to keep them from getting killed or wounded. Although he had served admirably in both World War II and Korea, Rockwerk was reduced in rank after hitting a superior officer when the latter asked him why all Korean War POWs were collaborators.

MELVIN D. ROOKSTOOL

Melvin Rookstool truly has a horrifying story. He was captured on July 27, 1950, during the early days of the war. Like many of these first prisoners, he spent months on the road as his North Korean captors slowly moved the POWs northward. While being kept temporarily in a police station in Taejon, a North Korean guard knocked Rookstool's eye out of its socket, and he carried it with him for sixty-three days. He also suffered numerous other wounds, both in battle and during his long march, before being shot and stabbed on October 30, 1950 at the Sunch'ŏn Tunnel Massacre. Miraculously, he was still alive when found the next day by American troops.

ROBERT T. SCHAEFER

Robert Schaefer, who is a retired Internal Revenue Service employee, has tried for years, without success, to get PTSD disability. Since his retirement, he has spent most of his time traveling in his Airstream trailer. A large, intelligent man with a good sense of humor, he does not appear to associate with other former POWs. His interview took place late in the day in his Airstream at a county fair grounds in Shelbyville, Kentucky.

As evening turned to night, he was so preoccupied with the telling of his story that he turned on no lights until I got up to go.

MELVIN J. SHADDUCK

Melvin Shadduck, who also flew in World War II, was shot down in a reconnaissance plane on April 21, 1951. It was his eighty-first mission, just nineteen short of finishing his tour. Although he was injured, he escaped from a Chinese field hospital and made his way back to his lines. He then helped direct tanks back to rescue three Americans and a Turk who were lying near death in that same hospital. Shadduck, who died some six months after being interviewed, admitted his experience as a POW totally affected his subsequent life but refused to say how it did so.

WAYMAN E. SIMPSON

Wayman Simpson, who had also been briefly held as a prisoner by the Japanese in World War II, was with Task Force Smith, which was the first American unit to engage the enemy in Korea. He survived the Task Force Smith disaster only to be captured a few days later on July 14, 1950, when the North Koreans completely overran the 63rd Field Artillery. Simpson also became a Tiger Death March survivor. Simpson has total recall, but some of his experiences defy credibility. Simpson, like many of the so-called Reactionaries, was in constant trouble with authorities both before and after he was captured. Simpson believes that mentally and physically he came through the war as well as anyone, but he has received 100 percent disability since 1994.

DOUGLAS A. TANNER

Sgt. Douglas Tanner, who also served in World War II, was captured on November 30, 1950, trying to break through to help Army and Marine soldiers trapped at the Chosin Reservoir. He ended up first in Camp One and then in Camp Four which was for NCOs. Twice he was sentenced to solitary confinement. Tanner, who stayed in the Army for twenty years, is now diabetic and arthritic and so nervous that he insists he has to keep busy or he drinks too much; unfortunately, he receives no disability payments.

RUBIN TOWNSEND

Rubin Townsend has a remarkable story, one that stretches the reader's credulity. He twice escaped after being captured in February of 1951, and the second time he was successful. Townsend is most emphatic on why he had to escape: "Somebody had to tell the stories of those atrocities." Townsend has instructed Air Force personnel on escape and evasion and has been active in ex-POW organizations. His story has appeared on the History Channel in a documentary entitled *Escape from a Living Hell.*

LARRY ZELLERS (CIVILIAN)

Although Larry Zellers had served in the Army Air Corps during World War II, he was a civilian teaching at a mission school in Kaesŏng, just a mile and a half below the 38th parallel, when the North Koreans invaded South Korea on June 25, 1950. Four days later he was a prisoner. After his liberation, he reenlisted in the Air Force as a chaplain and eventually obtained the rank of lieutenant colonel before retiring in 1975. In 1991, he published *In Enemy Hands: A Prisoner in North Korea* (University Press of Kentucky). Although he is now seventy-nine, Zellers's memory is total and precise. He is also fair-minded and philosophical. He does not hate his captors, although he witnessed truly horrifying and unnecessary tragedies on the Tiger Death March. Over the years Zellers has compiled a list of sixty of the approximately eighty civilian prisoners. According to his list, four of the eleven American civilians died during or shortly after the Tiger Death March. Nineteen civilians from other countries also lost their lives, as did seven South Korean political prisoners who disappeared into North Korea. Zellers has posted his list on the Internet: www.koreanwar.org/html/membership.html.

NOTES

ACKNOWLEDGMENTS

1   Richard Bassett's *And the Wind Blew Cold* is forthcoming from Kent State University Press.

PREFACE

1   Lewis H. Carlson, *We Were Each Other's Prisoners: An Oral History of World War II American and German Prisoners of War* (New York: Basic Books, 1997); with Norbert Haase, *Warten auf Freiheit: Deutsche und amerikanische Kriegsgefangene des Zweiten Weltkrieges Erzählen [Waiting for Freedom: An Oral History of World War II German and American Prisoners of War.]* (Berlin: Aufbau Verlag, 1996).

INTRODUCTION

1   "Tough Prisoners," *Time*, 21 September 1953, 28. Flanary was subsequently hounded by Federal investigative agencies and eventually committed suicide.

2   Robert Doyle, *Voices from Captivity: Interpreting the American POW Narrative* (Lawrence, Kan.: University Press of Kansas, 1994), 308.

3   H. H. Wubben, "American Prisoners of War in Korea: A Second Look at the 'Something New in History' Theme," *American Quarterly*, Spring 1970, 16.

4   W. L. White, *The Captives of Korea: An Unofficial White Paper on the Treatment of War Prisoners: Our Treatment of Theirs; Their Treatment of Ours* (New York: Scribner's, 1957), 265; T. R. Fehrenbach, *This Kind of War* (Washington, D.C.: Brassey's, 1998), 444.

5   Sidney Esensten, "Memories of Life as a POW 35 Years Later," *The Graybeards*, July/August 1997, 6.

6   Eugene Kinkead, "The Study of Something New in History," *New Yorker*, 26 October 1957, 154.

7   Philip Wylie, *Generation of Vipers* (New York: Rinehart, 1942), 199–208. Wylie returned to this theme in his *Sons and Daughters of Mom* (New York: Doubleday, 1971), 42, further arguing, "No woman on earth can ever represent or symbolize a male for her sons and daughters. But by psychologically courting her sons in that perverse delusion she emasculates all and makes many into homosexuals."

8   Edward Strecker, who was a consultant to the surgeons general of the Army and Navy during World War II, claimed that during the Second World War the U.S. Army was filled with "psychoneurotic" men who were weak, cowardly, and immature. According to Strecker, the military had rejected 1,825,000 recruits for service because of psychiatric disorders and had discharged another 600,000 for similar reasons. He also noted that another 500,000 men had attempted to evade

the draft. In total, "Almost 3,000,000 were either rejected or otherwise lost to the service for neuropsychiatric reasons out of 15,000,000, just under twenty percent." Strecker blamed the excessive and suffocating attention of "overprotective moms." Strecker initially published *Their Mothers' Sons* in 1942, but a new edition came out in 1951 (New York: J. B. Lippincott), 6, 23.

9 The Code of Conduct originated in Eisenhower's Executive Order 10631, which was released on August 17, 1955.

10 Kinkead, "The Study of Something New in History," 114. Kinkead later expanded this article into a book entitled, *In Every War But One* (New York: W. W. Norton, 1959).

11 Ibid. 154. Based in part on interviews conducted on repatriated POWs, the U.S. Army released its official report on the Korean POWs in 1955. The following year the Army issued a training pamphlet on prisoner behavior. Both reports were filled with contradictions; as a result, others, using these same materials, reached decidedly different conclusions than did Kinkead; see Wubben, "American Prisoners of War in Korea," 11. In contrast to the Army, the Air Force, Navy, and Marines did not publish derogatory information on their former POWs.

12 Wubben, 13.

13 Carlson, *We Were Each Other's Prisoners*, 12. Interview with Robert Engstrom.

14 Wubben, 14.

15 Kurt Vonnegut, who was himself a German-held POW during World War II, created just such a man in *Slaughterhouse Five*, the quintessential antihero, Billy Pilgrim. In the novel, a Harvard military history professor named Bertram Copeland Rumfoord derisively tells Billy, "I could carve a better man out of a banana." Kurt Vonnegut, *Slaughterhouse Five or The Children's Crusade* (New York: Dell, 1969), 184.

16 Maj. Clarence L. Anderson, Maj. Alexander M. Boysen, Capt. Sidney Esensten, Capt. Gene N. Lam, and Capt. William R. Shadish, "Medical Experiences in Communist POW Camps in Korea," *Journal of the American Medical Association*, 11 September 1954, 121.

17 Kinkead, "The Study of Something New in History," 114.

18 Ibid. According to Albert Biderman's *March to Calumny: The Story of American POWs in the Korean War* (New York: Macmillan, 1963), 156, the Chinese did take some 250 Army and 45 Marine POWs captured in early December 1951 at the Chosin Reservoir and Koto-Ri to an experimental indoctrination camp that the prisoners dubbed Peaceful Valley. Supposedly nineteen of these men were loaded with propaganda materials and released near the front in May 1951, but there is no evidence they ever conducted themselves as the Chinese hoped; see also, Harold H. Martin, "They Tried to Make Our Marines Love Stalin," *Saturday Evening Post*, 25 August 1951, 27, 107–10. After the war, Army psychiatrists and intelligence officers did examine all former prisoners, and by the spring of 1954 they targeted 215 cases for further investigation, 82 of which were then recommended for court-martial proceedings. Only fourteen of the men were eventually court-martialed, of whom eleven were convicted. Put another way, only 3/10th of 1 percent of the 4,428 surviving POWs were convicted of a collaborative or treasonous offense.

19 Ibid. 169.

20 An organization called Reality Zone offers a Mayer lecture entitled "Mind Control, the Ultimate Weapon" over the Internet; see www.reality.zone.com/audarvolfour.html.

21 Maj. William E. Mayer, "Why Did Many GI Captives Cave In?" *U.S. News and World Report*, 24 February 1956, 56.

22 Ibid. 57. Stung by postwar accusations of their mishandling of prisoners, the Chinese exploited Mayer's claim that personal weakness rather than harsh treatment explained the alleged misbehavior of American prisoners; see New China Press Agency, "No Ill Treatment of American Prisoners of War by the Korean and Chinese, American Army Doctor Maier (*sic*) Admits," 24 August 1956.

23 Ibid. 58.

24 Ibid. 60–65. Mayer later also blamed the Social Security Act and installment buying for further weakening the nation's moral fiber.

25 Kinkead, "The Study of Something New in History," 228–29.

26 Former prisoner Douglas A. Tanner suggests that one reason Turkish prisoners did better, at least in Camp Four, was the Chinese favored them over other nationalities, "perhaps because there was a Communist Party then in Turkey." Personal interview, April 26, 1998.

27 Wubben, 17. Wubben quotes noted military historian Gen. S.L.A. Marshall who informed a Senate subcommittee that the Turks were overrated: "The story about the Turks being perfect prisoners," said Marshall, "is a continuation of the fable that they were perfect soldiers in the line which was not true at all."

28 Betty Friedan, *The Feminine Mystique* (New York: W. W. Norton & Co., 1963), 286.

29 Ibid. 286.

30 "Why POWs Collaborate," *Science*, 11 May 1957, 301.

31 "Korean Puzzle: Americans Who Stay," *U.S. News and World Report*, 9 October 1953, 38–40.

32 "Inside Story Why Prisoners Balk at Coming Home," *U.S. News and World Report*, 25 December 1953, 24–25. Listed were Corp. C. V. Batchelor, Sgt. R. G. Gordon, and Pfc. Richard R. Tenneson, who wrote his mother, "I don't believe the U.S. authorities will allow you to speak to me. They are afraid. They have probably told you that I was forced, doped, brainwashed or some other horse manure that they use to slander and defile people like myself who will stand up for his own rights and the rights of men."

33 "The Sorriest Bunch," *Newsweek*, 8 February 1954, 40.

34 Harold Lavine, "Twenty-One GIs Who Chose Tyranny: Why They Left U.S. for Communism," *Commentary*, July 1954, 41–46.

35 "Is It a Crime to Crack Up?" *U.S. News and World Report*, 26 February 1954, 39–43.

36 "Reactionaries," *Time*, 7 September 1953, 32.

37 "Tough Prisoners," *Time*, 21 September 1953, 28.

38 The "hill" in the verse refers to where so many of the prisoners in the camp were buried; see William Brinkley, "Valley Forge GIs Tell of Their Brainwashing Ordeal," *Life*, 25 May 1953, 121.

39 Mainstream periodicals hailed General Dean's return with titles such as "Big Guy's Return" (*Newsweek*, 14 September 1953, 44); "America's Hero" (*Scholastic*

Nov. 18, 1953, 6); "Heroism of General Dean" (*Life*, 14 September 1953, 42); "Hero's Return" (*Time*, 14 September 1953, 33); and "Soldier's Soldier" (*Time*, 7 December 1953, 27). General Dean was the only Korean War POW to receive the Medal of Honor.

40   William L. Worden, *General Dean's Story* (New York: Viking Press, 1954), 3.

41   Ibid. 131.

42   Ibid. 163–66.

43   In a strange twist of fate, director John Frankenheimer drove Robert Kennedy to the California hotel where he was assassinated in 1968. *The Manchurian Candidate* was rereleased in theaters in 1987 and is now available on video.

44   Greil Marcus, *The Dustbin of History* (Cambridge: Harvard University Press, 1995), 195.

45   Quoted in *Halliwell's Film and Video Guide*, 1999, 511.

46   For an analysis of these films, see Lewis H. Carlson, "*The Manchurian Candidate* and Other Korean War POW Films," an unpublished paper delivered at the National Association of Popular Culture in New Orleans, April 20, 2000.

47   The original 1963 edition was published by Macmillan. Brassey's published the 1998 edition and changed the subtitle to *The Classic Korean War History*.

48   Fehrenbach also blames the weakening of Army discipline on the 1945 Doolittle Board, which was charged with examining inequities and the class/caste system in the Army, as well as "the domestic leaders of the Democratic Party [who] were totally unfit by training and inclination for playing roles in foreign affairs." Fehrenbach, 23, 27.

49   Ibid. 66, 84.

50   The draft was responsible for only 15 percent of the POWs. It was overwhelmingly the regular Army and reservists who did the early fighting and became the first prisoners to die in such large numbers. Whatever the alleged social decay and inadequacies of post-World War II society, these men had not certainly been exposed to them. Many of those who did come from more privileged backgrounds, and had enjoyed the "pampered childhoods" that Kinkead, Mayer, and Fehrenbach so deplored, were able to avoid the draft through college deferments.

51   Fehrenbach, 317.

52   Fehrenbach, 320.

53   According to Albert Biderman, *March to Calumny: The Story of the American POWs in the Korean War* (New York: Macmillan, 1963), 159, the British had about the same range of collaboration versus resistance as did the American prisoners. The major difference was that after the war England chose not make this an issue.

54   Fehrenbach, 376.

55   Fehrenbach, 378.

56   White, 265.

57   Ibid. 87.

58   Ibid. 330.

59   Biderman, 1, 5–6, 101, 188. Biderman argues that most academics did not want to produce scholarly rebuttals to charges they considered unscholarly.

60   Ibid. 75.

61   For accounts of successful escapes, see Clay Blair's *Beyond Courage* (New York: David McKay, 1955); Ward Millar's *Valley of the Shadow* (New York: David McKay, 1955), which is an account of his own escape; and the narratives of Ray Baumbach, Homer Jurgens, Melvin Shadduck, and Rubin Townsend, all of whom were interviewed for this book.

62   Quoted in Biderman, 72.

63   Biderman, 135.

64   Wubben, 11.

65   In addition to Biderman's *March to Calumny*, see Walter Hermes, *United States Army in the Korean War: Truce Tent and Fighting Front* (Washington, D.C.: U.S. Government Printing Office, 1966); S.L.A. Marshall, *Pork Chop Hill: The American Fighting Man in Korea* (Nashville: Battery Press, 1986); and *The River and the Gauntlet* (Westport, CT.: Greenwood Press, 1953, 1970); David Rees, *Korea: The Limited War* (New York: St. Martin's Press, 1964) and *The Korean War: History and Tactics* (New York: Crescent Books, 1984); and Russell Weigley, *History of the U.S. Army* (New York: Macmillan, 1967).

66   Quoted in Wubben, 19.

67   In addition to Fehrenbach's *This Kind of War*, see Anthony Bouscaren, *A Guide to Anti-Communist Action* (Chicago: H. Regnery, 1958); Robert Leckie, *Conflict: The History of the Korean War, 1950–1953* (New York: Putnam, 1962) and *March to Glory* (Cleveland: World Publishing, 1960); Harry Middleton, *Compact History of the Korean War* (New York: Hawthorn Books, 1965); and Max Rafferty, *Suffer Little Children* (New York: Devin Adair, 1962) and *What They Are Doing to Your Children* (New York: New American Library, 1964).

68   David Hackworth, "Code for U.S. POWs Must Be Reaffirmed," *Austin American-Statesman*, syndicated column, 20 January 1995.

69   Ibid.

70   Ibid.

71   For almost fifty years the Defense Department used the figure of 54,246 for Korean War battle deaths. Then, in the year 2000, it revised the figure downward to 36,940, blaming the earlier, higher figure on a clerical error that included all noncombat deaths worldwide; see *Time* magazine, 4 June 2000. *Newsweek*, 19 June 2000, also citing Department of Defense figures, puts the number of known deaths at 33,686, with 8,100 MIAs. This lower fatality figure likely does not include noncombat deaths in Korea.

I: THREE PRISONERS OF WAR

1   Lt. Col. Harry Fleming was the spokesman for the American prisoners in Camp Twelve. North Korean Colonel Dong Suk Kim administered this small camp for the sole objective of exploiting his prisoners for propaganda purposes. Kim clearly threatened Fleming, who responded, "I will give my soul in hell to get every man out of here alive." After Fleming's return to the States, military authorities arrested, incarcerated, and court-martialed him for collaborating with the enemy and on September 12, 1957 dismissed him from the service without pay or allowances. For a comprehensive and generally sympathetic account of

Fleming, his career, and his court-martial, see Raymond B. Lech, *Broken Soldiers* (Urbana: University of Illinois Press, 2000), 117, 243–45, 268–69.

2   A U.S. Army court-martial found Lt. Col. Paul Liles guilty of aiding the enemy but gave him the comparatively light sentence of a twenty-four-month suspension in rank and a reprimand. See Lech, *Broken Soldiers*, 275.

2: "LET THEM MARCH TILL THEY DIE"—THE TIGER DEATH MARCH AND BEYOND

1   The term "POWs" or "GIs" refers to military prisoners, as opposed to captured noncombatants or civilian prisoners. Depending on the source, the number of POWs at the start of the Death March varies between 756 and 758 and the number of noncombatants between 74 and 87. This confusion occurs in part because there were also several South Korean political prisoners on the Tiger Death March. The 87 figure comes from Tiger survivor Larry Zellers who has spent years compiling biographical sketches of the civilians. For a website listing of Zeller's names, see www.koreanwar.org/html/membership.html.

2   Wayne Johnson, who was one of the survivors, and whose story appears in this chapter, kept a secret list of those who died on the Tiger Death March, but often the victims on the many other marches simply fell by the wayside or were pushed off the mountain trails into the canyons below, becoming anonymous statistics among the Korean War's 8,177 MIAs.

3   Approximately 600–700 of the 10,000 Bataan prisoners died on the actual march. As was to be the case with those on the Tiger Death March, many more died after the march because of their weakened condition, the ongoing mistreatment, and the lack of proper food and medicine.

4   Biderman, *March to Calumny*, 115, 118.

5   When a former prisoner's words are the result of a personal interview, I do not source them; however, I have noted any quotations from published sources.

6   Actually, Task Force Smith landed in Korea on July 1, 1950, but did not go into battle until July 5, when Americans suffered their first casualties.

7   Two hundred men normally made up a company, although the first companies sent into Korea were seldom at full strength.

8   The word "Amerikanski" is, of course, neither Korean nor Chinese. However, many of the North Korean officers had been trained in the U.S.S.R. where they might have heard the term.

9   Dr. Eugene N. Lam, who himself was a POW in Korea, agreed that putting urine in a wound when there was no other way to sterilize the infection was a wise thing to do (see chapter six).

10   Larry Zellers, *In Enemy Hands: A Prisoner in North Korea* (Lexington, KY.: University Press of Kentucky, 1991), 59. This and all subsequent noted quotations from Zellers's book are reprinted from *In Enemy Hands*, Zellers, copyright (c) 1991, by permission of the University Press of Kentucky. Non-noted Zeller quotations in this chapter are from a July 14, 1998, interview conducted by the author.

11   Philip Deane, *I Was a Captive in Korea* (New York: W. W. Norton, 1953), 88–89. This and all other Deane quotations in this chapter are reprinted with his permission.

12   Father Philip Crosbie, *March till They Die* (Dublin: Browne & Nolan, Ltd, 1955), 87. This and all other Crosbie quotations in this chapter are reprinted with his permission.

13   Zellers, 61.

14   Captured with Zellers in Kaesŏng were four American missionaries: Nell Dyer, Helen Rosser, Bertha Smith, and Kris Jensen, as well as Dr. Ernst Kisch, an Austrian physician who worked at the mission hospital.

15   Zellers, 27, 30, 32.

16   Crosbie, 42–43.

17   Ibid. 136.

18   Zellers, 84.

19   Ibid. 139.

20   Crosbie, 139–40.

21   Shorty Estabrook believes the Tiger was also in charge of the Sunch'ŏn Tunnel Massacre. Val John, who was one of the few survivors of the massacre, verifies this as well (see chapter three).

22   Gen. William F. Dean was taken prisoner during the first days of the war when his jeep made a wrong turn in Taejon. During his three years of captivity, General Dean did not see another American except for his fleeting glance of the POWs in Manpo; *General Dean's Story*, 187.

23   The fifth paragraph of Zeller's description of the first day is from his *In Enemy Hands*, 87.

24   Deane, 111.

25   Ibid. 111–12.

26   Zellers's description of Lieutenant Thornton's execution comes mostly from his *In Enemy Hands*, 89–92, although he also described the execution in his personal interview.

27   Crosbie, 143.

28   Father Crosbie estimates that the prisoners covered approximately twenty miles on days two and three, but there was no accurate way of estimating distances.

29   Zellers, 94, 98–99.

30   Crosbie, 145.

31   Ibid. 147.

32   Zellers, 103–104.

33   Crosbie, 148.

34   Zellers, 106.

35   Ibid. 108.

36   Crosbie, 156–57.

37   Ibid. 156.

38   Deane, 116.

39   Zellers, 113.

40   Ibid. 113.

41   Crosbie, 162.

42   Deane, 116. Shorty Estabrook puts the actual death count during the nine days of the Tiger Death March at eighty-nine.

43   Zellers, 126.

44   Ibid. 127.

45 Deane, 149–50.

46 Ibid. 116.

47 Zellers, 130–31.

48 Ibid. 152.

49 Ibid. 155.

50 Ibid. 156.

51 Ibid. 202.

52 Ibid. 208. After their stop in P'yŏngyang, the civilians traveled by train to Antung on the northwest border of North Korea where, on April 30, 1953, they were turned over to Soviet officials, who then shipped them across China to the U.S.S.R. and on to Germany and finally to the U.S.

53 Malcolm McConnell, "Johnson's List," *Reader's Digest,* January 1997, 49–55.

54 The Tiger Survivors Reunion is now held in conjunction with the annual Korean War Ex-POW Association's Reunion for all former Korean War POWs.

55 http://tigersurvivors.org/johnson.html

3: THE SUNCH'ŎN TUNNEL MASSACRE

1 A special U.S. Senate report entitled *Korean War Atrocities*, Senate Report 848 (83d Congress, 2d Session, Jan. 7, 1954) lists several mass killings of American prisoners. This report was forwarded to the United Nations with a request for further investigations.

2 Fehrenbach, 116.

3 *San Antonio News*, November 13, 1953, 1.

4 The actual number of those shot at the Sunch'ŏn Massacre differs in several accounts. Survivor James W. Yeager puts the number killed at more than 180, with 23 survivors; see Mike Blair, "Reds Slaughtered American Prisoners," *Spotlight*, 8 December 1950, 3. Other sources, including survivor Val John, whose story appears in this chapter and who took his statistics from accounts in contemporary periodicals, put the number killed at approximately eighty and the survivors at twenty-one; see *Time*, 30 October 1950, 36. Senate Report 848, 11 January 1954, concludes that "one hundred and thirty-eight American soldiers lost their lives in this atrocity; 68 were murdered at the tunnel, 7 died of malnutrition while in the tunnel, and the remainder died of pneumonia, dysentery, and malnutrition on the horror trip from P'yŏngyang." In truth, no accurate count could be kept of the those who died during the long march northward, during the temporary stops at Seoul and P'yŏngyang, and even while on the train heading for the Sunch'ŏn tunnel. Further complicating the numbers is the fact that several survivors died shortly after their rescue.

5 Thirty years after the fact, survivor James W. Yeager recalled that one of the North Koreans had told him the train was taking the prisoners to Manchuria to work in the mines, although at the time China had not officially entered the war. The two survivors whose stories appear in this chapter knew nothing about this possibility, although they, like many of the other prisoners, had heard stories of POWs being taken to Manchuria; see Blair, "Reds Slaughtered American Prisoners," 3.

6 General Allen appeared before the Senate Subcommittee on Korean War Atrocities on January 7, 1954; Senate Report 848, "Korean War Atrocities."

4: DEATH VALLEY AND THE TEMPORARY CAMPS

1   Part of the confusion of names stems from the fact the Japanese established
    several mining camps during World War II that were then abandoned in 1945.
    However, many of the buildings survived, and the Chinese and North Koreans
    used them for housing U.N. prisoners. For example, Conley Clarke, who arrived
    at what he called the Mining Camp on July 4, 1951, describes a power generating
    plant located at the base of the mountain, along with towers and cables that
    indicated some mining was still going on. Clarke located the camp two days
    march east of the North Korean capital of P'yŏngyang, some thirty or forty miles
    south of the Imjin River. However, the Imjin River runs north and south and is
    almost entirely south of the 38th Parallel; see Conley Clarke, *Journey Through
    Shadow: 839 Days in Hell: A POW's Survival in North Korea* (Charlotte, N.C.: Her-
    itage Printers, 1988), 123–89.

2   Stan Sommers, ed., *The Korean Story*, published for the National Medical Research
    Committee of American Ex-Prisoners of War, 1981.

3   Dr. Lam, who died in 1997, wrote paragraphs one and three in a letter to Ms.
    Joy Winstead, the Director of Communications, the Medical Society of Virginia
    on January 30, 1994, which was later published as "Another War—Same Hard-
    ships," *Virginia Medical Quarterly* (April/May/June, 1994), 112. Paragraph two was
    from a draft Dr. Lam wrote for a report he and four other physicians (Maj.
    Clarence L. Anderson, Maj. Alexander M. Boysen, Capt. Sidney Esensten, and
    Capt. William Shadish) later published in the *Journal of the American Medical As-
    sociation*, September 11, 1954. Copies of all the above were made available by
    June-Marie Lam, along with many other papers of her late husband's.

4   Audiotaped lecture Dr. Lam gave in 1954 at the Escape and Evasion School at
    Stead Air Force Base, Reno, Nevada. Made available by June-Marie Lam.

5   Lech, 39.

6   David Polk, *Ex-Prisoners of the Korean War* (Paducah, KY.: Turner Publishing, 1993),
    29.

7   Lam, audiotaped lecture.

8   Fehrenbach, 234–36, 317–18, tells the story of Charles B. Schlichter.

9   Ibid. 319.

10 Sommers, 3.

11 Fehrenbach, 321. Fehrenbach writes that the Chinese closed down Death Valley
    on March 21, 1951. If true, they soon reopened it for a new group of U.N.
    prisoners.

12 Some of Esensten's comments are from a personal interview and some from a
    speech he gave on November 21, 1985, at Fairview Riverside Hospital where he
    had been chief of staff. This speech was later published as "Memories of Life as
    a POW 35 Years Later," *The Graybeards*, July/August, 1997; September–December,
    1997.

13 Lech, 42–43. Esensten disagrees with Lech. He argues that Liles did little to help
    him and a Major McCabe care for the men; nor does he even remember Flem-
    ing; interview with author, March 6, 2001.

14 Quoted in Lech, 46.

15 According to his later court-martial transcript, Liles was so ill while in the Valley that he had to delegate much of his authority to Fleming; see Lech, *Broken Soldiers*, 46.

16 William Funchess, *Korea POW: 1000 Days of Torment* (self-published, 1997), 20.

17 During the march the Chinese released four of the prisoners as "proof of their Lenient Policy." Lieutenant Funchess asked all four to contact his wife and tell her he was alive and a prisoner. At first, military authorities ordered the four not to contact the families of any POWs, but in February of 1951, largely because of the persistence of Funchess's wife Sybil who had seen a Chinese propaganda story about the release, the military relented and gave her the names and addresses of the four freed enlisted men. See Funchess, 36.

18 Funchess, 40–42.

19 Lech, 50.

20 Don Poirot's comments are from both a personal interview and an unpublished account he wrote in the early 1990s for his children.

21 According to Lech, thirty-three of the Bean Camp survivors died of carbon-monoxide poisoning after boarding a train in Sinanju that then backed into a blocked tunnel with its engine running. *Broken Soldiers*, 61.

22 Prisoners passed through several other camps besides those described in this chapter. Pak's Palace was a notorious interrogation center near P'yŏngyang, as was Pike's Peak. The Caves was a mysterious place located northeast of P'yŏngyang where the North Koreans sent South Korean and U.N. prisoners it especially wanted to punish. According to Raymond Lech, the Caves, or Camp Nine as it was officially known, was "a place of horror" from which few survived. Lech 129. There may well have been other temporary holding areas where the Chinese and North Koreans briefly held prisoners before sending them on to permanent camps.

5: LIFE IN THE PERMANENT CAMPS

1 Initially, the North Koreans and the Chinese co-administered several of the permanent camps, but by the middle of 1951 the Chinese were solely in charge.

2 In 1951, the United Nations military command released a map entitled *Where Reds Hold Allied Prisoners*, which located and numbered eleven permanent camps. Unfortunately, as with the temporary camps, there is considerable confusion about these camps and their location due to misspellings and changing numbers.

3 Lech, 66, 70. Lech paints a particularly dismal picture of Camp Five where the men "lost on average 40 percent of their normal body weight in early 1951" and "half . . . died within the first twenty weeks of the camp's opening."

4 Roy Hardage died in 1984, but his sister, Daisy Lawrence, made available an unpublished memoir he wrote in October 1954 while he was convalescing in a military hospital.

5 Deane, 121–22.

6 Esensten, 7.

7 Almost to a man, the enlisted men, and even some of the NCOs, admitted they were ill-equipped to defend their country and its values when the Chinese attacked the United States and its institutions during their propaganda sessions.

6: INJURIES, DISEASE, AND MEDICAL CARE

1 Letter from Dr. Gene N. Lam to Chris Mosley, February 18, 1995. Made available by Mrs. June-Marie Lam.

2 Maj. Clarence L. Anderson, Maj. Alexander M. Boysen, Capt. Sidney Esensten, Capt. Gene N. Lam, and Capt. William R. Shadish, "Medical Experiences in Communist POW Camps in Korea," first read at the 103rd Annual Meeting of the American Medical Association, San Francisco, June 24, 1954, and later published in the *Journal of the American Medical Association*, September 11, 1954, 120–22.

3 Dr. Lam's widow, June-Marie Lam, made available an audiotape of this lecture her husband gave in 1954.

4 Esensten, 6. Dr. Esensten's subsequent comments in this chapter come both from a personal interview and this article.

5 From a draft Dr. Lam prepared that would later be incorporated in the report the five former prisoner-physicians published in the *Journal of the American Medical Association*, September 11, 1954. Made available by Mrs. June-Marie Lam.

6 Letter Dr. Lam wrote to Ms. Joy Winstead, Director of Communications, the Medical Society of Virginia, January 30, 1994, and made available by his widow, June-Marie Lam.

7 Several survivors have praised the unselfish efforts of Chaplain Emil Kapaun in comforting his fellow prisoners. Father Kapaun died in Camp Five on May 23, 1951. There is now an effort to canonize Father Kapaun; see William L. Maher, *A Shepherd in Combat Boots: Chaplain Emil Kapaun of the 1st Cavalry Division* (Shippensburg, PA. Burd Street Press, 1997).

8 Robert MacLean, who also reported the Tully Cox story, thought Cox was originally from Arkansas.

9 Dr. Gene Lam, however, was able to smuggle out a list containing more than 300 names which was then used to notify the next of kin. Someone in the camp had split a military script dollar into two pieces, onto which another man wrote down the names of the deceased before giving the bill to Dr. Lam. Mrs. June-Marie Lam still has this list.

7: ESCAPE: MYTH AND REALITY

1 Between 1 and 2 percent of German-held Allied prisoners attempted an escape; the percentage was even lower among those held by the Japanese.

2 Robert Doyle, *A Prisoner's Duty: Great Escapes in U.S. Military History* (Annapolis: Naval Institute Press, 1997), x–xi.

3 With the exception of *King Rat* (1965) and *Slaughterhouse Five* (1975), every significant World War II POW film featured a heroic escape: e.g., William Holden in *Bridge on the River Kwai* (1957), Steve McQueen in *The Great Escape* (1963), Frank Sinatra in *Von Ryan's Express* (1965), and Sylvester Stallone in *Victory* (1981). Of course, Stallone also played a former POW who had once escaped in *Rambo* (1985). On the other hand, Hollywood's Korean War POW films dealt with collaboration and brainwashing rather than escape.

4   After Rubin Townsend got back to his lines, he was able to describe a Chinese weapons cache on an island in a river that American bombers subsequently destroyed. In 2000, Townsend told his story on the History Channel in a documentary entitled *Escape from a Living Hell.* Military authorities also interviewed and videotaped Townsend and used his story to teach escape and evasion tactics.

5   After repatriation, U.S. military authorities ordered some prisoners, and especially those who had escaped, not to talk about their experiences. After the passage of so many years, most of these former prisoners are now willing to talk, but not Melvin Shadduck, who died less that six months after this interview.

6   Mayer, "Why Did Many GI Captives Cave In?" 60–65.

8: INTERROGATION, PROPAGANDA, INDOCTRINATION, AND "BRAINWASHING"

1   Lech, 3.

2   Fehrenbach, 318–19.

3   Biderman, 181.

4   Ibid. The Chinese and North Korean prisoners were even better examples of Biderman's conclusions. After being exposed to extensive U.N. indoctrination sessions, at least half of the 140,000 taken prisoner insisted they did not want to return to their Communist homelands.

5   "Medical Experiences in Communist POW Camps in Korea," *The Martin Journal,* published by Martin Army Hospital, Fort Benning, Georgia, and made available by Mrs. June-Marie Lam.

6   Historian T. R. Fehrenbach suggests that when the spread of typhus, carried across the Yalu by invading Chinese troops, spread to the civilian population, the Chinese saw an opportunity to blame this on the U.S. Air Force; Fehrenbach, 318. According to Raymond Lech, 160, "Thirty-six men admitted to either planning or participating in the (germ warfare) program." However, unlike the Army, the Air Force did not attempt to punish its men for alleged collaboration.

7   Quoted in Lech, 73.

8   Biderman, 181.

9   No Korean POW ever heard the term "brainwashing" until after returning to the United States.

10   Master Sgt. William Olson was a former boxer and seventeen-year Army veteran who had landed at Omaha Beach on D-Day. According to Raymond Lech, the Chinese coerced Olson into becoming a spokesman for their so-called "Lenient Policy." He thus became a *gong-so-yen,* or staff member, and wore a regular Chinese Army uniform. While in Camp Ten, he also wrote a confession, which, among other things, stated, "Our hands are stained with blood, the blood of an innocent people. I am ashamed of this. We were told by the capitalists and imperialists of our government that we were to fight to preserve peace in the Pacific. Instead we brought ruin, death, and destruction to a peace-loving people. We destroyed their homes and caused them untold misery and unhappiness." At his court-martial Olson was found guilty of making speeches for the enemy and sentenced to two years at hard labor. See Lech, 83–87, 269–70 and 295–96.

11   Coon is undoubtedly referring to *In Every War But One* in which author Eugene Kinkead insisted that one in three American prisoners had collaborated; see Introduction, 4.

12   For a discussion of William Mayer's views on the Korean War POWs, see Introduction, 7–8.

9: PROGRESSIVES, REACTIONARIES, AND THE TWENTY-ONE WHO CHOSE TO STAY

1   Lech, 4.

2   Lloyd W. Pate, as told to B. J. Cutler, *Reactionary!* (New York: Harper & Brothers, 1955). Pate is currently revising his story, which he plans to self-publish. His new title is *Reactionary, Revised 2000.*

3   In his 1955 autobiography, Pate says his Reactionary Squad worked diligently and quite successfully to thwart the Chinese indoctrination attempts. He explains, "Our main weapon was to appeal to the men themselves. Pride of country, pride of family, faith in God. This usually did the trick." Sometimes, however, Pate and his fellow Reactionaries resorted to physical measures to convince their fellow prisoners they should not cooperate with their captors: "We beat up a couple of dozen men, maybe a little more," said Pate, *Reactionary!*, 97.

4   In 1954, the U.S. Army court-martialed fourteen former POWs for alleged misbehavior and collaboration with the enemy. Erwin and two others were the only ones found not guilty. For a description of Jeff Erwin's court-martial proceedings, see Lech, 249–52, 264.

5   In addition to the twenty-one Americans, one Briton and 367 South Koreans chose not to return home.

6   "Korean Puzzle: Americans Who Stay," *U.S. News and World Report,* 9 October, 1953, 38; "Inside Story Why Prisoners Balk at Coming Home," *U.S. News and World Report,* 25 December 1953, 24–25.

7   "The Sorriest Bunch," *Newsweek,* 8 February 1954, 40.

8   An article entitled "Twenty-One Who Chose Tyranny: Why They Left U.S. for Communism," *Commentary* (July 1954), 41–46, provided brief sketches of some of the men, as did *Newsweek* in "Case Histories of Those 21: What Their Lives Show" (18 January 1954), 52–53. Like the mainstream articles, Virginia Pasley's *21 Stayed: The Story of American GI's Who Chose Communist China—Who They Were and Why They Stayed* (New York: Farrar, Strauss and Cudahay, 1955), often oversimplifies and distorts the background of the twenty-one.

9   Quoted in "The Sorriest Bunch," 40.

10 Morris R. Wills, *Turncoat: An American's 12 Years in Communist China; the Story of Morris R. Wills as Told to J. Robert Moskin* (Englewood Cliffs, N.J.: Prentice-Hall, 1968). According to Moskin, Wills chose to stay because "The fear of being left [in the prison camp] to rot, the despair of ever getting out, the lack of preparation to meet Communist indoctrination—all left a vacuum that the Communists filled," 5.

11 Quoted in Lech, 259.

12 Wills, 13; Lech, 259–60.

13 Wills, 13.

14 Edward Dickenson, who had only a sixth-grade education, was the first of the twenty-three to change his mind. On October 20, 1953, while waiting in the neutral zone, he walked over to an Indian official and announced he wanted to go home. He was also the first to be tried for collaboration. His trial corresponded to the army/McCarthy hearings in April 1954. Dickenson served three years of a ten-year sentence. See Lech, 210–11, 266.

15 Claude Batchelor was among the twenty-three who initially refused repatriation, but he changed his mind in Freedom Village, supposedly at the insistence of his Japanese-born wife. After returning home he was court-martialed and sentenced to life imprisonment. One month later, his sentence was reduced to twenty years, four and one-half of which he actually served. See Lech, 267–68.

16 Morris Wills returned from China in 1965, one year before Adams.

17 Raymond Lech disagrees over which side won the propaganda campaign: "The shooting war may have ended in a draw," he argues, "but that was not the case in the propaganda war, which the enemy won hands down." In addition to the twenty-one who defected, Lech concludes that at least 20 percent of the returning Progressives "remained active in the movement for which they had studied for three long, hard years. . . . By October 1953 hundreds of soldiers and former soldiers were back in the United States with 'missions' inspired and controlled by the Peking government." Although the Chinese certainly hoped their indoctrination programs would bear fruit back in the U.S., this sounds more like the plot of *The Manchurian Candidate* than it does reality. Lech offers no evidence of such "missions," and certainly none of the men I interviewed or historians of the period suggest such activities; Lech, 185, 193–94.

18 For a discussion of the prisoner repatriation issue, see Fehrenbach, 383, 415, 440, 450.

10: FREEDOM AND RECRIMINATION

1 The cease-fire line established by the two sides on November 27, 1951 would change little over the ensuing twenty months of negotiations. In the meantime, thousands of American and other U.N. soldiers would lose their lives at such places as Old Baldy, Arrowhead, White Horse Mountain, Pork Chop Hill, and countless other hills known only by impersonal numbers.

2 Many of the Chinese prisoners insisted they had fought for Chiang Kai-shek and had been impressed into Mao's armies after the 1949 defeat of the Chinese Nationalists.

3 According to T. R. Fehrenbach, 444, many of the Americans released "were not hardship cases but . . . 'collaborators' whom the Communists expected to give a favorable picture of their captivity on return."

4 Rumors still persist about Korean War prisoners who remain MIAs. Fehrenbach, 450, for example, argues that after Operation Big Switch the Communists retained 3,404 POWs including 944 Americans.

5 In addition to a personal interview, Jim Crombie sent me an audiotape of a talk he made at his church on July 7, 1995, parts of which are incorporated in this passage.

6   Charles "Pluto" Sherron was in very poor physical shape when I interviewed him in June 1998. Suffering from a heart condition and emphysema, he was attached to an oxygen tank. He was also very confused about much of what had happened to him in Korea, but he did show me the file the U.S. Army had compiled on him.

II: LEGACY

1   Lam, "Another War—Same Hardships," 114.
2   Interview with author, August 12, 1998.
3   Interview with author, October 14, 2000.
4   Interview with author, October 14, 2000.
5   I have included the stories of four wives who, because of the very personal and often revealing nature of their comments, remain nameless. Two are career professionals and two are housewives. Two are first wives, one is a second wife, and the other is a fourth wife.
6   Charley Davis describes the ceremony honoring Captain Rockwerk: "We presented him with a plaque in St. Augustine, Florida, at the division reunion. That was the first time any of us had seen him since we got back. The plaque stated how much we appreciated what he had done for us in Korea, both in battle and after we were captured, before the officers were segregated from the enlisted men in the camps. He just broke down and cried because he said he'd felt guilty all these years. He believed he hadn't done enough for us. But you always feel that way. You always think back to what you could have done differently."

SELECTED BIBLIOGRAPHY

BOOKS

Adam-Smith, Patsy. *Prisoners of War, from Gallipoli to Korea*. Victoria, Australia: Viking, 1992.

Alexander, Bevin. *Korea, the First War We Lost*. New York: Hippocrene Books, 1986.

American Red Cross. *Report of the Red Cross Team Operations in Korea*. Washington, D.C.: American Red Cross, 1953.

Appleman, Roy. *South to the Naktong, North to the Yalu*. Washington, D.C.: Center of Military History, U.S. Army, 1986.

Atkinson, James David. *The Edge of War*. Chicago: H. Regnery, 1960.

Biderman, Albert D. *Communist Techniques of Coercive Interrogation*. Lackland Air Force Base, Tex.: U.S. Air Force, 1956.

———— *March to Calumny: The Story of the American POWs in the Korean War*. New York: Macmillan, 1963.

Biskind, Peter. *Seeing Is Believing: How Hollywood Taught Us to Stop Worrying and Love the Fifties*. New York: Pantheon Books, 1983.

Blair, Clay. *Beyond Courage*. New York: David McKay, 1955.

———— *The Forgotten War: America in Korea, 1950–1953*. New York: Times Books, 1987.

Blanchard, Carroll H., Jr. *Korean War Bibliography and Maps of Korea*. Albany: Korean Conflict Research Foundation, 1964.

Bouscaren, Anthony. *A Guide to Anti-Communist Action*. Chicago: H. Regnery, 1958.

Bradbury, William C., Samuel M. Meyers, and Albert D. Biderman, eds. *Mass Behavior in Battle and Captivity: The Communist Soldier in the Korean War*. Chicago: University of Chicago Press, 1968.

Breuer, William. *Shadow Warriors: The Covert War in Korea*. New York: John Wiley & Sons, 1996.

Brode, Douglas. *The Films of the Fifties: "Sunset Boulevard" to "On the Beach"*. Secaucus, N.J.: Citadel Press, 1976.

Brune, Lester H., ed. *The Korean War: Handbook of the Literature and Research*. Westport, CT.: Greenwood Press, 1996.

Bussey, Charles M. *Firefight at Yechon: Courage and Racism in the Korean War*. Washington, D.C.: Brassey's, 1991.

Chinnery, Philip. *Korean Atrocity! Forgotten War Crimes, 1950–1953*. Annapolis: Naval Institute Press, 2001.

Cole, Paul M. *POW MIA Issues*. Santa Monica: Rand, 1994.

Cunningham, Cyril. *No Mercy, No Leniency*. London: Leo Cooper, 2000.

Downey, Andrew. *The Films of the Fifties: The American State of Mind.* New York: Morrow, 1973.

Doyle, Robert. *A Prisoner's Duty: Great Escapes in U.S. Military History.* Annapolis: Naval Institute Press, 1997.

——— *Voices from Captivity: Interpreting the American POW Narrative.* Lawrence, KN: University Press of Kansas, 1994.

Edwards, Paul M. *A Guide to Films on the Korean War.* Westport, CT.: Greenwood, 1997.

——— *To Acknowledge a War: The Korean War in American Memory.* Westport, CT.: Greenwood, 2000.

Enock, Kenneth. *Statements by Two Captured U.S. Air Force Officers on Their Participation in Germ Warfare in Korea.* Peking: Chinese People's Committee for World Peace, 1952.

Evanhoe, Edward. *Dark Moon: Eighth Army Special Operations in the Korean War.* Annapolis: Naval Institute Press, 1995.

Fehrenbach, T. R. *This Kind of War: The Classic Korean War History.* Washington, D.C.: Brassey's 1998.

Foot, Rosemary J. *A Substitute for Victory: The Politics of Peacemaking at the Korean Armistice Talks.* Ithaca, N.Y.: Cornell University Press, 1990.

——— *The Wrong War: American Policy and the Dimensions of the Korean Conflict, 1950–1953.* Ithaca, N.Y.: Cornell University Press, 1985.

George, Alexander L. *The Chinese Communist Army in Action: The Korean War and Its Aftermath.* New York: Columbia University Press, 1967.

Giangreco, D. M. *War in Korea, 1950–1953.* Novato, CA.: Presidio, 2001.

Goldstein, Donald M. and Harry J. Maihafer. *The Korean War: The Story and Photographs.* Washington, D.C.: Brassey's, 2000.

Goulden, Joseph C. *Korea: The Untold Story of the War.* New York: Times Books, 1982.

Halliday, Jon, and Bruce Cummings. *Korea: The Unknown War.* New York: Pantheon, 1988.

Hansen, Kenneth. *Heroes Behind Barbed Wire.* Princeton: Van Nostrand, 1957.

Harris, Elliot. *The "Un-American" Weapon.* New York: M. W. Lads, 1967.

Hastings, Max. *The Korean War.* New York: Simon and Schuster, 1987.

Henderson, Gregory. *Korea: The Politics of the Vortex.* Cambridge: Harvard University Press, 1968.

Hermes, Walter. *United States Army in the Korean War: Truce Tent and Fighting Front.* Washington, D.C.: U.S. Government Printing Office, 1966.

Hoare, James E. and Susan Pares. *Conflict in Korean: An Encyclopedia.* Santa Barbara: Clio Press, 1999.

Hunter, Edward. *Brainwashing: From Pavlov to Powers.* New York: Bookmailer, 1960.

——— *Brainwashing: The Story of the Men Who Defied It.* New York: Pyramid, 1958.

——— *Brainwashing in Red China: The Calculated Destruction of Men's Minds.* New York: Vanguard, 1953.

Jolidon, Lawrence. *Last Seen Alive: The Search for Missing POWs from the Korean War.* Rochester, N.Y.: Ink-Slinger Press, 1995.

Kagan, Norman. *The War Film.* New York: Pyramid Publications, 1974.

Karsten, Peter. "American POWs in Korea and the Citizen Soldier." In *The Military in America: From the Colonial Era to the Present.* New York: Free Press, 1980.

Kaufman, Burton I. *Korean War: Challenges in Crisis, Credibility, and Command.* Philadelphia: Temple University Press, 1986.

Kinkead, Eugene. *In Every War But One.* New York: Norton, 1959.

―――― *Why They Collaborated.* New York: Longmans, 1959.

Lech, Raymond B. *Broken Soldiers: American Prisoners of War in North Korea.* Urbana, IL.: University of Illinois Press, 2000.

Leckie, Robert. *Conflict: The History of the Korean War, 1950–1953.* New York: Putnam, 1962.

―――― *March to Glory.* Cleveland: World Publishing, 1960.

MacDonald, James A. *The Problems of U.S. Marine Corps Prisoners of War in Korea.* Washington, D.C.: U.S. Marine Corps History and Museums Division, 1988.

Marshall, S.L.A. *Military History of the Korean War.* New York: F. Watts, 1963.

―――― *The River and the Gauntlet: Defeat of the Eighth Army by the Chinese Communist Forces, November 1950, in the Battle of the Chongchon River, Korea.* Westport, CT.: Greenwood Press, 1953, 1970.

Matray, James I., ed. *Historical Dictionary of the Korean War.* New York: Greenwood Press, 1991.

Mayo, Mike. *War Movies.* Detroit: Visible Ink Press, 1999.

Meyers, Samuel N. and Albert D. Biderman, eds. *Mass Behavior in Battle and Captivity.* Chicago: University of Chicago Press, 1968.

Page, William Frank. *Health of Former Prisoners of War: Results from the Medical Examination Survey of Former Prisoners of War of World War II and the Korean Conflict.* Washington, D.C.: National Academy Press, 1992.

Paschall, Rod. *Witness to War, Korea.* New York: Berkley Publishing, 1995.

Pasley, Virginia. *21 Stayed: The Story of American GI's Who Chose Communist China—Who They Were and Why They Stayed.* New York: Farrar, Strauss and Cudahay, 1955.

Pease, Stephen E. *Psywar: Psychological Warfare in Korea, 1950–1953.* Harrisburg, PA.: Stackpole Books, 1992.

Pincher, Chapman. *Traitors.* New York: Penguin Books, 1988.

Polk, David. *Ex-Prisoners of the Korean War.* Paducah, KY.: Turner Publishing, 1993.

Quirk, Lawrence J. *The Great War Films.* New York: Carol Publishing, 1994.

Rees, David. *Korea: The Limited War.* New York: St. Martin's Press, 1964.

―――― *The Korean War: History and Tactics.* New York: Crescent Books, 1984.

Ridgeway, Matthew. *The Korean War.* New York: Doubleday, 1967.

Sanders, James D., Mark A. Sauter, and R. Cort Kirkwood. *Soldiers of Misfortune: Washington's Secret Betrayal of American POWs in the Soviet Union.* Washington, D.C.: National Press Books, 1992.

Sandler, Stanley, ed. *The Korean War: An Encyclopedia (Military History of the United States),* vol. 4. New York: Garland, 1995.

Sayre, Nora. *Running Time: Films of the Cold War.* New York: Dial Press, 1982.

Shall Brothers Be. Peking: Foreign Languages Press, 1952.

Shinn, Bill. *The Forgotten War Remembered, Korea: 1950–1953.* Elizabeth, N.J.: Hollym International, 1986.

Sommers, Stan. *The Korean Story.* Marshfield, WI.: American Ex-Prisoners of War National Medical Research Committee, 1981.

Stang, Alan. *The Prisoners: Why Does America Abandon Her Own?* Belmont, MA.: American Opinion, 1970.

Suid, Lawrence H. *Guts and Glory: Great American War Movies*. Reading, MA.: Addison-Wesley Publishing Co., 1978.

Toland, John. *In Mortal Combat: Korea, 1950–1953*. New York: William Morrow, 1991.

Toplin, Robert Brent. *History by Hollywood: The Use and Abuse of the American Past*. Urbana, IL.: University of Illinois Press, 1996.

———, ed. *Hollywood as Mirror: Changing Views of "Outsiders" and "Enemies" in American Movies*. Westport, CT.: Greenwood Press, 1993.

Tucker, Spencer C., ed. *Encyclopedia of the Korean War: A Political Social, and Military History*. Santa Barbara: Clio Press, 2000.

Vetter, Harold J. *Mutiny on Koje Island*. Rutland. VT.: Charles E. Tuttle, 1965.

Wakin, Edward. *Black Fighting Men in U.S. History*. New York: Lothrop, Lee and Shepard, 1971.

Watson, Peter. *War on the Mind*. New York: Basic Books, 1978.

Weigley, Russell. *History of the U.S. Army*. New York: Macmillan, 1967.

Weintraub, Stanley. *War in the Wards: Korea's Unknown Battle in a Prisoner-of-War Hospital Camp*. San Rafael: Presidio, 1976.

Wetta, Frank J. and Stephen J. Curley. *Celluloid Wars: A Guide to Film and the American Experience of War*. Westport, CT.: Greenwood Press, 1992.

White, William L. *The Captives of Korea: An Unofficial White Paper on the Treatment of War Prisoners: Our Treatment of Theirs; Their Treatment of Ours*. New York: Scribner's 1957.

Whiting, Allen S. *China Crosses the Yalu*. Stanford: Stanford University Press, 1960.

CAPTIVITY NARRATIVES: AMERICAN

Brown, Wallace L. *The Endless Hours: My Two and a Half Years as a Prisoner of War of the Chinese Communists*. New York: Norton, 1961.

Clarke, Conley. *Journey Through Shadow: 839 Days in Hell: A POW's Survival in North Korea*. Charlotte, N.C.: Heritage Printers, 1988.

Condron, Andrew M., Richard Cordon, and Larance V. Sullivan, eds. *Thinking Soldiers*. Peking: New World, 1955.

Dean, William Frishe, as told to William L. Worden. *General Dean's Story*. New York: Viking Press, 1954.

Funchess, William A. *Korea POW: 1000 Days of Torment*. Self-published, 1997.

Hunter, Edward. *Brainwashing: The Stories of the Men Who Defied It*. New York: Pyramid, 1956.

Knox, Donald. *The Korean War—Pusan to Chosin: An Oral History*. New York: Harcourt Brace Jovanovich, 1985.

——— *The Korean War: Uncertain Victory: An Oral History*. New York: Harcourt Brace Jovanovich, 1988.

Lane, Raymond A. *Ambassador in Chains: The Life of Bishop Patrick James Byrne (1888–1950), Apostolic Delegate to the Republic of Korea*. New York: P. J. Kennedy, 1955.

Maher, William L. *A Shepherd in Combat Boots: Chaplain Emil Kapaun of the 1st Cavalry Division*. Shippensburg, PA.: Burd Street Press, 1997.

Mahurin, Walker M. *Honest John*. New York: Putnam, 1962.

Millar, Ward M. *Valley of the Shadow*. New York: D. McKay, 1955.

Pate, Lloyd W., as told to B. J. Cutler. *Reactionary!* New York: Harper & Brothers, 1955.

Snyder, Don J. *Soldier's Disgrace: Ronald Alley Died Trying to Clear His Name.* Dublin, N.H.: Yankee Books, 1987.

Spiller, Henry. *American POWs in Korea: Sixteen Personal Accounts.* Jefferson, N.C.: McFarland, 1998.

Thorton, John W. *Believed to Be Alive.* Middlebury, VT.: Eriksson, 1981.

Tomedi, Rudy. *No Bugles, No Drums: An Oral History of the Korean War.* New York: John Wiley, 1993.

Voelkel, Harold. *Behind Barbed Wire in Korea.* Grand Rapids, Mich.: Zondervan, 1953.

Wills, Morris R., *Turncoat: An American's 12 Years in Communist China; the Story of Morris R. Wills as told to J. Robert Moskin.* Englewood Cliffs, N.J.: Prentice-Hall, 1968.

Zellers, Larry. *In Enemy Hands: A Prisoner in North Korea.* Lexington, KY.: University Press of Kentucky, 1991.

KOREAN WAR POW NARRATIVES: BRITISH, AUSTRALIAN, CANADIAN, AND OTHERS

Brumbaugh, Thoburn T. *My Marks and Scars I Carry: The Story of Ernst Kisch.* New York: Friendship Press, 1969.

Crosbie, Father Philip. *March till They Die.* Westminster, MD.: Newman Press, 1956.

Davies, S. J. *In Spite of Dungeons: The Experiences as a Prisoner of War in North Korea of the Chaplain to the First Battalion, the Gloucestershire Regiment.* London: Hodder and Stoughton, 1954.

Deane, Philip. *I Was a Captive in Korea.* New York: W. W. Norton, 1953.

——— *I Should Have Died.* Don Mills, Ontario: Longman Canada, 1976.

Kenyon, Albert. *Valiant Dust: Graphic Stories from the Life of Herbert A. Lord.* London: Salvationist Publishing, 1966.

Kinne, Derek G. *The Wooden Boxes.* London: Muller, 1955.

Lankford, Dennis. *I Defy! The Story of Lieutenant Dennis Lankford.* London: Wingate, 1954.

Strachan, Tony, ed. *In the Clutch of Circumstance: Experiences of Canadian Prisoners of War.* Victoria: Cappis Press, 1985.

KOREAN WAR POW NOVELS

Condon, Richard. *The Manchurian Candidate.* New York: New American Library, 1959.

Frazier, Raymond, with Keller Cox. *Buck: A Tennessee Boy in Korea.* Paris, TN.: Chogie Publishers, 1982.

Peters, Ralph. *The Perfect Soldier.* New York: Pocket Books, 1995.

Pollini, Francis. *Night.* New York: Bantam, 1960.

Stuart, Alex. *Gay Cavalier.* Toronto: Harlequin, 1974.

Thorin, Duane. *A Ride to Panmunjom.* Chicago: Henry Regnery, 1956.

PERIODICALS

"Almost All Released Prisoners Come Home Happily: A Few Renounce U.S. for Communism." *Life,* 7 September 1953.

Anderson, Maj. Clarence L., et al., "Medical Experiences in Communist POW Camps in Korea." *Journal of the American Medical Association* (11 September 1954).

"Back from the Death Camps: POWs Rediscover Freedom." *Newsweek*, 17 December 1951.

Ball, Harry, "Prisoner of War Negotiations: The Korean Experience and Lesson." *Naval War College Review*, September 1968.

Berquist, L., "Turncoat Comes Home." *Look*, 25 June 1957.

Biderman, Albert D., "Dangers of Negative Patriotism." *Harvard Business Review*, November–December 1962.

"Big Lie; How the Reds Got Germ Confessions." *Life*, 9 November 1953.

Bird, Roy, "Not Any Battlefield Heroics, but Sustained Bravery of Another Sort." *Military History*, December 1993.

Blair Mike, "Reds Slaughtered American Prisoners." *Spotlight*, 8 December 1950.

Boswell, Bryan, "The Pentagon POW Scandal." *The Weekend Australian*, 9–10 December 1989.

Bower, Bruce, "Emotional Trauma Haunts Korean POWs." *Science News*, February 1991.

"Brain-Washed Korean POWs." *Scholastic*, 12 May 1954.

Brean, Herbert, "Prisoners of War the Reds Say Do Not Want to Come Home to America." *Life*, 19 October 1953.

Brinkley, William, "Almost All Released Prisoners Come Home Happily." *Life*, 7 September 1953.

——— "Valley Forge GIs Tell of Their Brainwashing Ordeal." *Life*, 25 May 1953.

"Case Histories of Those 21: What Their Lives Show." *Newsweek*, 18 January 1954.

"Chance for Our Men." *Newsweek*, 3 January 1955.

"Code for Our POWs." *America*, 3 September 1955.

"Cowardice in Korea." *Time*, 2 November 1953.

Cuthbertson, Ralph, "The Korean War: A Former POW's Story." *AXPOW Bulletin*, March 1993.

Douglas, P. H., "Korean Prisoners of War Issues." *Vital Speeches*, July 1953.

Eisenhower, D. D., "What the President Said about the Prisoners of the Reds." *U.S. News and World Report*, 10 December 1954.

Essensten, Sidney, "Memories of Life as a POW 35 Years Later." *The Graybeards*, July/August, 1997.

Fleming, Dan B. and Burton I. Kaufman, "The Forgotten War: Korea." *The Education Digest*, December 1990.

"For Prisoners Who Broke, Kindness or Punishment? Letters to Defense Secretary Wilson Russel." *U.S. News and World Report*, 16 October 1953.

"Forced Confession." *Time*, 27 December 1954.

"Forgotten War: Remembering Korea 40 Years Later." *Airman*, June 1990.

"GI's Outshine Eggheads in Resisting Reds." *Saturday Evening Post*, 31 October 1953.

"GI's Prisonmates Accuse." *Life*, 11 October 1954.

Grey, Jeffrey, "Commonwealth Prisoners of War and British Policy During the Korean War." *RUSI Journal*, Spring 1988.

Harrison, Thomas D. with Bill Stapleton, "Why Did Some GI's Turn Communist?" *Collier's*, 27 November 1953.

Hill, G., "Brainwashing: Time for a Policy." *Atlantic*, April 1955.

"Homeward: Pro-Red Americans." *Newsweek*, 11 January 1954.

"How Reds Tortured U.S. Prisoners." *U.S. News and World Report*, 2 September 1955.

"How the Reds Treat Prisoners of War, and How the U.N. Cares for Communist POWs." *Newsweek*, 17 December 1951.

Howard, James T., "Beast in a Cage." *Newsweek*, 1 March 1954.

Hubbell, Jon G., "The Long Way Home." *Readers Digest*, April 1952.

"Inside Story Why Prisoners Balk at Coming Home." *U.S. News and World Report*, 25 December 1953.

"Is It a Crime to Crack Up?" *U.S. News and World Report*, 26 February 1954.

Kalischer, P. and D. F. MacGree, "Some of Us Didn't Crack." *Colliers*, 22 January 1954, 5 and 19 February 1954.

Kinkead. E., "Have We Let Our Sons Down?" *McCalls*, January 1959.

——— "Reporter at Large; American Prisoners in Korea." *New Yorker*, 26 October 1957.

"Korean Prisoner Issue." *Scholastic*, 9 January 1952.

"Korean Puzzle: Americans Who Stay." *U.S. News and World Report*, 9 October 1953.

Lavine, H., "Twenty-One GIs Who Chose Tyranny: Why They Left US for Communism." *Commentary*, July 1954.

Lawrence, D., "Americans for Sale." *U.S. News and World Report*, 24 December 1954.

——— "Communist Barbarism." *U.S. News and World Report*, 23 November 1951.

Lowenberg, M., "Progressive POW Corporal Smith's Story." *The Nation*, 30 January 1954.

Lyons, William, "Prisoners of War and the Code of Conduct." *Naval War College Review*, December 1967.

Manes, Donald L., "Barbed Wire Command." *Military Review*, 1963.

Martin, H. H., "They Tried to Make Our Marines Love Stalin." *Saturday Evening Post*, 25 August 1951.

Mayer, William E., "Moral Imperative." *Vital Speeches*, 15 February 1963.

——— "Why Did Many GI Captives Cave In?" *U.S. News and World Report*, 24 February 1956.

"Men Without a Country." *Newsweek*, 1 February 1954.

"Moral Mandate for All Americans." *Life*, 29 August 1955.

Murray, J. C., "The Prisoner Issue." *Marine Corps Gazette*, August 1955.

"One Won't Return." *Time*, 26 October 1953.

"POW Types Who Gave In." *Science Digest*, December 1955.

"Prisoner Killings Shock World." *Christian Century*, 31 December 1952.

"Prisoners Describe Realities of War." *Christian Century*, 12 August 1953.

"Prisoners of War." *Commonweal*, 21 March 1952.

"Prisoners Who Broke." *U.S. News and World Report*, 21 August 1953.

"Prisoners: Perversion of Loyalties." *Commonweal*, 16 October 1953.

"Pro-Communist Twenty-Three." *America*, 10 October 1953.

"POWs Who the Reds Say Do Not Want to Come Home to America." *Life*, 19 October 1953.

"Real Story of Returned GIs Back from Korea." *U.S. News and World Report*, 29 May 1953.

"Reception for Turncoats." *Newsweek*, 18 July 1955.

"Roots of Courage: Code of Conduct for All American Service Men." *Colliers*, 30 September 1955.

"Rules for Brainwashing." *The Nation*, 10 October 1953.

Ryan, Eileen, "Called to Korea Never to Return." *Baltimore Sun*, 11 June 2000.

Sharpe, Robert L., "God Saved My Life in Korea." *Saturday Evening Post*, 13 January 1951.

"The Sorriest Bunch; Pro-Red Americans." *Newsweek*, 8 February 1954.

Stapleton, B. and T. D. Harrison, "Why Did Some GIs Turn Communist?" *Colliers*, 27 November 1953.

Stern, Karl, "The Prisoners." *Commonweal*, 16 October 1953.

"Story of GI Turncoats; Interviews." *U.S. News and World Report*, 28 June 1957.

"Tough Prisoners." *Time*, 21 September 1953.

"Train Pilots to Resist Brain-Washing." *Science Digest*, January 1955.

"Turncoats Return." *Newsweek*, 29 September 1958.

"Twenty-Three Americans." *Time*, 5 October 1953.

"Twenty-Two Americans Choose to Remain in Communist Hands." *Commonweal*, 1 January 1954.

"Twenty-Two GIs Who Went Communist." *Scholastic*, 6 January 1954.

Ulman, W. A., "GIs Who Fell for the Reds." *Saturday Evening Post*, 6 March 1954.

Ursano, Robert and James Rundell, "The Prisoner of War." *Military Medicine*, April 1990.

Victoria, Sister Mary, "I Was a Prisoner of the Chinese Reds." *Collier's*, 9 May 1953.

"Washed Brains of POWs: Can They Be Rewashed?" *Newsweek*, 4 May 1953.

"What About Reds Among Freed U.S. Prisoners?" *Newsweek*, 17 August 1953.

"What to Do About Brainwashing?" *U.S. News and World Report*, 8 July 1955.

"Where Are Korea's Missing?" *U.S. News and World Report*, 7 December 1951.

"Why GIs Folded." *Newsweek*, 26 January 1959.

"Why POWs Collaborate." *Science*, 11 May 1957.

Wilson, R., "How U.S. Prisoners Broke under Red Brain-Washing." *Look*, 2 June 1953.

"Without Honor." *Newsweek*, 13 July 1953.

Wubben, H. H., "American Prisoners of War in Korea: A Second Look at the 'Something New in History' Theme." *American Quarterly*, Spring 1970.

"You're Guilty! But Don't Ask Why." *New Republic*, 13 February 1956.

U.S. GOVERNMENT PUBLICATIONS AND ARCHIVAL HOLDINGS

Korean War Escape Debriefs. Record Group 319, Entry 85, Item 950, 774. National Archives.

U.S. Air Force, Record Group 340. National Archives.

U.S. Department of the Army. *Communist Interrogation, Indoctrination and Exploitation of Prisoners of War.* Washington, D.C.: GPO, 1956.

———— *Court-Martial Transcripts.* Washington, D.C. Approximately 40 volumes on the investigations and proceedings of the fourteen Army and one Marine tried for collaboration and cooperation with the enemy.

U.S. Department of Defense. *POW: The Fight Continues After the Battle. The Report of the Secretary of Defense's Advisory Committee on Prisoners of War.* Washington, D.C.: GPO, 1955.

U.S. Military Personnel Who Died from Hostile Action (Including Missing and Captured Declared Dead) in the Korean War, 1950–1957. Washington., D.C.: National Archives and Records Administration, 1985.

U.S. Navy. "Report on Navy and Marine Corps Prisoners of War." *Statistics of Navy Medicine*, 11 March 1955, 3–5.

U.S. Senate. Committee on Government Operations. *Communist Interrogation, Indoctrination and Exploitation of American Military and Civilian Prisoners*, Senate Report No. 2832. 84th Congress, 2nd Session. 31 December 1956. Washington, D.C.: GOP, 1957.

U.S. Senate. Committee on Government Operations. *Korean War Atrocities*. Senate Report No. 848. 83rd Congress, 2nd Session. 11 January 1954. Washington, D.C.: GPO, 1954.

HOLLYWOOD FEATURE FILMS

The Bamboo Prison (Columbia Pictures, 1954)
Battle Flame (Allied Artists, 1959)
Five Gates to Hell (TCF, 1959)
The Manchurian Candidate (United Artists, 1962)
One Minute to Zero (RKO, 1952)
Prisoner of War (MGM, 1954)
The Rack (MGM, 1956)
Sergeant Ryker (Universal, 1967)
Time Limit (United Artists, 1957)
The Young and the Brave (MGM, 1963)

FILM AND VIDEO DOCUMENTARIES

Bloody Korea: The Real Story (Dane Hansen Productions, 1996).
Escape from a Living Hell (History Channel, 2000).
Korea: The Forgotten War (Fox Hills Video, 1987)
Korea: The Unknown War (Thames Television, 1988)
Korea: The Untold Story (Pyramid Films, 1988)
Korea: Tribute to the Forgotten Heroes (TSM Production, 1993)
P.O.W.: Americans in Enemy Hands (Arnold Shaprio Productions, 1987)
The Korean War (PBS Documentary, n.d.)
The Ultimate Weapon: The Minds of Free Men (early 1960s)
The Unknown War (BBC, 1990)

INDEX

Middleton, Bill, 41
Middleton, Harry, 19
Millar, Ward, 273n61
Mining Camp, 107, 108, 116, 277n1
momism, 3, 8, 269n7
Montgomery, Forrest, 218
Moore, James, 87
moral decay of Americans suggested, 5–11, 16–
    17, 19, 161, 164, 174, 227
Morgan, Jerry, 143–44, 151, 163, 192, 219, 254
    biographical sketch of, 264
Moskin, J. Robert, 205

Nam Il, 43
napalm, 169
Nardello, Ralph, 188
Nehrbas, Sergeant, 40, 41
Nelson M. Walker (ship), 219
Newsweek, 10, 203
night blindness, 157–58
nightmares, xv, 232–34, 239, 249, 253, 261
Noel, Frank, 215
noncombatants. *See* civilians
North Korea
    interrogation centers of, 121
    POWs killed on battlefield by, 50, 52–53
    POWs transferred to China by, 88, 122
    South Korean uniforms worn by soldiers of,
        52
    U.N. indoctrination of POWs of, 280n4

Olson, William, 185, 280n10
Operation Big Switch, 144, 214–18, 282n4
Operation Little Switch, 37, 214
Owen, Norman, 66

Pak, Colonel, 40
Pak's Palace, 121, 182–83, 187, 278n22
P'anmunjöm peace talks, 142, 157, 161, 213–
    14
    repatriation issue at, 214–15
Pasley, Virginia, 281n8
Pate, Arlie, 204
Pate, Lloyd W., 199–201, 281nn2, 3
    biographical sketch of, 264
peace talks. *See* P'anmunjön peace talks
Peaceful Valley, 187, 270n18
Peking Foreign Press, 209
pellagra, 154, 226
Perruche, Georges, 73
Pike's Peak, 278n22
pneumonia, 82–83, 104, 119, 140, 153, 223
Poirot, Don, xi, 117–18, 126–29, 134–35, 157–
    58, 182
    biographical sketch of, 265
    memoir by, 265
Polk, David, 111

Pough, Al, 175
POW: Americans in Enemy Hands, The
    (documentary), 240, 261
POW survival techniques, 112–12, 152–53
POWs
    collaboration by, 4–10, 17, 40–42, 46–47,
        86, 177–93, 219, 220, 226, 250–51, 254,
        270n18, 273n1, 282n4. *See also*
        Progressives; Reactionaries
    confessions by, 37, 138, 201
    defections by. *See* defectors
    diet of, 16, 82–83, 85–86, 109–12, 116, 117,
        121–27
    draftee, 272n50
    escapes by. *See* escapes
    films about. *See* films
    final release of. *See* Operation Big Switch
    games played by, 142, 143
    guard-baiting by, 132–35
    later deep-seated resentment felt by, 227
    mortality of, 2–3
    museum on, 240
    number of, 2
    painful interviews with, xiv-xv
    propaganda pictures of, 215
    punishment of, 135–38, 175, 201
    shipboard interrogations of returning, 37,
        218–21
    World War II, xiv, 2–3, 5, 6, 17, 30, 119,
        124
    See also ex-POWs
Prisoner of War (film), 2, 14
Progressives, 1, 131, 195–202, 221
Protocol Physical, 246, 248
PTSD (Post Traumatic Stress Disorder), 31,
    225–27, 232–33, 248, 258, 265
punishment, 135–38, 175, 201
Pusan, 99, 212
Pyöktong, 112, 114, 115, 121
P'yöngyang, 41, 50, 54–61, 88, 98, 100, 101,
    103, 121

Quayle, Dan, 250
Quinlan, Thomas, 66, 73, 82

Radio P'yöngyang, 41
Rafferty, Max, 19
Rats, the, 29, 195–200, 222
Reactionaries (resisters), 10–12, 18, 192, 195–
    202, 258, 261, 264, 266
Reactionary! (Pate), 264
Reader's Digest, 89, 263
Reagan, Ronald, 2
Rees, David, 18
Reid, Troy L., 225
religion, 142–46, 216–17, 229–30, 241, 257